SW[illegible]CTION

ONE OF THE GANG
BURIED TREASURE
KEEPING SECRETS
STRETCHING THE TRUTH

Written by
Jamie Suzanne

Created by
FRANCINE PASCAL

BANTAM BOOKS

TORONTO • NEW YORK • LONDON • SYDNEY • AUCKLAND

SWEET VALLEY TWINS COLLECTION

A Bantam Book

Sweet Valley High and Sweet Valley Twins are trademarks of Francine Pascal

Conceived by Francine Pascal

Produced by Cloverdale Press, Inc.

Cover art by James Mathewuse

ISBN 0-553-40011-8

Bantam Books are published by Bantam Books, Inc. Its trademark, consisting of the words "Bantam Books" and the portrayal of a rooster, is Registered in U.S. Patent and Trademark Office and in other countries. Marca Registrada. Bantam Books, Inc., 666 Fifth Avenue, New York, New York 10103.

Printed and bound in Great Britain by
Cox & Wyman Ltd., Reading

SWEET VALLEY TWINS

One of the Gang

Written by
Jamie Suzanne

Created by
FRANCINE PASCAL

A BANTAM BOOK®
TORONTO • NEW YORK • LONDON • SYDNEY • AUCKLAND

One

"Liz, can you come over here for a sec?" Jessica Wakefield asked her twin sister. "I'm stuck on this stupid math problem!"

It was Monday afternoon, and Jessica was doing her homework at the table in the Wakefields' Spanish-styled kitchen. California sunlight streamed through the windows. The twins' older brother, Steven, was working on his homework too—and driving Jessica and Elizabeth crazy at the same time! Steven was fourteen—two years older than the twins—and could be close to impossible at times. Just that day, out of the blue, he'd informed them that he had ESP—extrasensory perception—and had already "foreseen" everything they said or did.

"I knew you'd have problems with your

homework, Jess," Steven said now, looking smug. "My ESP is at work again."

Elizabeth, who was spooning the last bit of chocolate-chip batter onto a cookie sheet, couldn't help grinning. "I'm not sure you'd need ESP to guess Jessica was going to have trouble with math," she pointed out.

"What are you talking about?" Jessica said to her brother. "You're really getting weird, Steven. Do you know that?"

"I'm not weird," Steven objected. "I'm special, that's all. I happen to have ESP. In fact, I had my very first vision of the future this morning."

Jessica glared at him. "The only thing extra about you is that you're extra obnoxious," she said.

Elizabeth laughed. "Can you really see into the future?"

Jessica groaned. "Of course he can't," she wailed. "Liz, don't encourage him!"

Elizabeth slid the cookie sheet into the oven. "I'll help you in a minute," she told her twin. "Let me clean up over here first."

Jessica's blue-green eyes flashed with impatience. Sometimes she couldn't understand her twin's behavior at all. Imagine actually cleaning up after baking cookies! Jessica always left the dirty dishes in a pile for someone else to take care of. But, as the twins' mother often remarked, Jessica and Elizabeth weren't one bit identical when it came to personalities.

As far as looks went, it was virtually impossible to tell them apart, from their long blond hair and blue-green eyes to the dimple each girl showed when she smiled. But Elizabeth, who was four minutes older, often thought of herself as the "big sister." Conscientious in everything she did, she really *liked* working hard at school. Elizabeth was very active on *The Sweet Valley Sixers,* the sixth-grade newspaper. Jessica, on the other hand, wouldn't have wasted a second on something as boring as the school paper. She was much too busy with the Boosters, a cheerleading squad to which she belonged, and the Unicorns, a special group of girls whom Elizabeth and her best friend Amy Sutton considered snobs. Jessica loved the Unicorns. Lately she had been trying to think of new ways to impress Janet Howell, the eighth-grade president of the club.

"You don't believe I have ESP," Steven said, looking as if his feelings were hurt. "I don't think that's fair, Jessica. I didn't tell you, but I happen to have predicted that you'd be appointed chairman of the Mini Olympics committee."

Jessica tossed back her hair. "Well, *anyone* could have guessed I was going to be chosen. I'm perfect for the job, aren't I?"

"It must have been your modesty that made Mr. Butler decide to put you in charge," Steven said with a playful smile.

Elizabeth came over to join them at the table. "I think you'll do a great job, Jess," she said.

"You'll probably put together the best Mini Olympics the lower school has ever seen!"

The Mini Olympics were an annual tradition in Sweet Valley. Each year the sixth graders organized the day-long festival for the younger grades. The fifth and sixth graders also joined in the competitions, which included every kind of sport and relay event imaginable. Mr. Butler, the physical education teacher at the lower school, was the faculty advisor for this year's Mini Olympics. As student chairman, Jessica would be working closely with Mr. Butler to decide which events should be kept in from the previous years and which new events should be added. Jessica knew she could do a great job, and she had a feeling Janet Howell would be really impressed. Jessica wanted more than anything to be praised by the members of the Unicorn Club—and she was sure this would do it!

"My ESP tells me I'm going to be late for basketball practice if I don't get out of here," Steven said suddenly, slamming his history book shut and jumping up from the table. "See you two later!" He gave Jessica a serious look. "I'm getting that weird feeling again, Jess. I think you should make sure to stay inside today. Otherwise . . ." He let his voice trail off ominously.

"He's giving me the creeps," Jessica said when Steven had bounded out of the room. "How can we get him to stop this ESP nonsense? I can't stand it!"

Elizabeth looked thoughtful. "I know what

you mean. I think we may have to think of some way to get him to stop. He's getting to be a real pain."

"Who's getting to be a pain?" Mrs. Wakefield asked, opening the screen door and coming into the kitchen with her arms full of groceries. "Any chance one of you can grab the last bag from the car?"

"I'll get it, Mom," Elizabeth said.

"It's Steven," Jessica grumbled. "Mom, you should hear him going on and on about having ESP! It's not even funny. And he doesn't stop when we ask him to cut it out."

"He'll get sick of it soon," Mrs. Wakefield said lightly, setting the bags down on the table. With her blond hair and bright blue eyes, Mrs. Wakefield looked like a grown-up version of the twins. She worked part-time for an interior design firm in town.

"But we don't want to wait for him to get sick of it," Elizabeth protested, coming back inside with the bag of groceries. "Can't you talk to him about it, Mom?"

"Well . . ." Mrs. Wakefield's eyes twinkled. "I can try. But if I know your brother, he's not going to stop until he gets good and sick of it." She smiled at the twins. "I'm surprised you two haven't already put your heads together and thought of some way to make him stop. You're usually good at that sort of thing."

Jessica's eyes shone. "You're right, Mom!"

She looked long and hard at Elizabeth. "I don't know why we haven't struck back sooner. We've just got to figure out some way to make him hate ESP as much as we do!"

Elizabeth giggled. No doubt about it—things were always exciting when Jessica Wakefield decided it was time to take action!

Elizabeth still had almost an hour before her mother needed her help with dinner, and she decided to ride her bicycle to the library to see if they'd gotten in any new mysteries. She and her best friend, Amy Sutton, both loved to read. They would take turns getting books out from the library, and trade them back and forth.

Mrs. Donaldson, the librarian, gave Elizabeth a knowing smile when she came in.

"We just got the latest Amanda Howard mystery in," she said with a twinkle in her eyes. "Something told me you might be interested in it, so I tucked it away under my desk."

Elizabeth's face lit up. She thanked the librarian before moving away to look at the "new books" shelf in the young readers room. To her surprise, she saw Pamela Jacobson, one of her classmates, sitting in an armchair by the window.

"Hi, Pamela!" Elizabeth said with a friendly smile. "I didn't know you liked coming to the library!"

Pamela was a small, pretty girl with soft brown wavy hair which came down to her shoulders. She had a slightly pale complexion and blue-gray eyes. She looked up with a shy smile from the book she was reading.

"Oh, I come here all the time." she said. "Do you come here often?"

"Yes, but we must come at different times," Elizabeth said as she pulled up a chair. Elizabeth didn't know Pamela very well. Pamela had entered Sweet Valley Middle School in the sixth grade, and Elizabeth still thought of her as a "new girl."

"I love to read," Pamela added. "This book is great. Have you ever heard of Amanda Howard?"

Elizabeth burst out laughing. "She's one of my favorite authors," she confided.

Soon the two girls were discussing their favorite titles. Talk of books led to talk of *The Sweet Valley Sixers* school paper, which Pamela said she would like to write for.

"Our next issue is going to be a special one. We're covering the Mini Olympics Day," Elizabeth told her. "Maybe you can write a feature story about that. Mr. Bowman said it would be good to get more people involved in it." Mr. Bowman, their English teacher, helped Elizabeth organize the paper. He was a nice man, and Elizabeth liked him, though she had to agree with Amy that he was the worst-dressed teacher at the middle school. Sometimes he even wore striped shirts with plaid pants!

Pamela looked pleased. "I'd like to," she said.

"Are you excited about the Mini Olympics?" Elizabeth asked her. "Did they have something like that at your old school?"

Pamela blushed. "I can't really do anything athletic," she said, looking down. "I've got a heart condition. The school I used to go to was for special kids. We didn't have anything at all like the Mini Olympics."

Elizabeth felt like kicking herself. She hadn't known that Pamela's old school was for disabled children, but she should have remembered that Pamela wasn't allowed to participate in gym class.

"It's OK," Pamela said quickly, seeing how uncomfortable Elizabeth was. "Believe me, Elizabeth, I like it when people forget I'm different!" She looked shy. "It's much worse when people remember and make a big fuss. The truth is, I'm fine as long as I don't overdo anything. I mean, I can't run, and I'm not allowed to exert myself very much. But as long as I follow everything my doctor tells me to do, I'm perfectly fine!"

Elizabeth looked at her with admiration. "You have such a good way of looking at it. You seem to want to do everything you can for yourself."

"That's why I left Ridgedale," Pamela told her. "Because everyone there was 'special,' I started to think of myself that way too." She frowned. "Some of my teachers thought I was making a mistake when I said I wanted to try a regular school. They thought I wouldn't be able to keep up—that I'd feel left out."

Again Elizabeth felt terrible for having brought up the Mini Olympics. It seemed just the sort of event that was bound to make Pamela feel excluded.

Pamela appeared to read her mind. "Every once in a while there's bound to be something I can't do," she said softly. "But I don't mind. I just want the chance to show everyone that I'm OK—that I'm just a normal girl after all." Her eyes shone. "The last thing I want is to get special treatment of any sort!"

Elizabeth nodded in understanding. But she couldn't help feeling that the Mini Olympics Day was unfair. It was meant to be a day everyone could be part of. And that meant Pamela Jacobson should be included too.

Two

"I'm really glad Mr. Butler chose you to be in charge of the Mini Olympics," Janet Howell told Jessica the next day.

The girls were all changing into their striped gym shorts in the locker room. A small group of Unicorns had clustered around Jessica and Lila Fowler, including Betsy Gordon, Tamara Chase, and Kimberly Haver—seventh graders whom Jessica particularly wanted to impress. Lila Fowler, a tall, slender girl with auburn hair and a pretty face, was also a Unicorn. She was the only daughter of one of the wealthier men in Sweet Valley. Whatever she'd ever wanted was hers for the asking. Lila had been selected assistant chairman of the Mini Olympics. But from the expression on her face when Janet spoke, it was apparent she wasn't pleased about Jessica having been put in charge ahead of her.

"What sort of events are you planning to add this year?" Lila asked casually.

Jessica had been giving this matter a great deal of thought. She wanted to make the Olympics more competitive. Usually the classes were divided into four equal teams—the Red team, the Blue team, the White team, and the Black team. Points were awarded to each team throughout the day, and at the end of the Mini Olympics one team was declared the victor. "I think we need to have individual trophies this year," Jessica declared. "And we should have more field events, more jumping activities, and a triathlon of some sort."

"That's a great idea," Janet said, her eyes shining. "I'm really proud that the Unicorns have two members working on the committee," she added.

Lila groaned. "Jessica, you just want to add more events that you happen to be good at," she complained. "Everyone knows what a good jumper you are. Shouldn't you be a little fairer to the rest of us?"

Jessica glared at her. "The whole point is to make it a contest," she pointed out. "If it's too easy, where's the challenge?"

Lila didn't look as if this answer satisfied her. "You know, *I* have some really good ideas," she began.

"What's keeping you guys? Ms. Langberg

wants us to start up a volleyball game," Ellen Riteman said, strolling over to the group assembled in front of the lockers. Ms. Langberg was their gym teacher. Ellen was another Unicorn.

Jessica, however, hadn't even noticed Ellen's arrival. She was far too annoyed with Lila. *Why does she always try to steal the spotlight away from me?* thought Jessica. *Isn't it bad enough that she gets a huge allowance and that her father buys her anything she wants if she so much as asks?* Jessica's face was burning. She had to show the others that Lila couldn't get away with criticizing her this way.

"Lila, I think it would be a lot easier for us both if you were behind me," she pointed out.

Lila's eyes flashed. "Behind you! I guess that means just shutting up and letting you do whatever you feel like!"

Ellen put her hand on Lila's arm. "What's going on here?" she asked, disturbed. Ellen liked Lila *and* Jessica, and clearly wanted to end the argument.

"You two shouldn't be arguing," Janet said. "The whole point is that it's wonderful to have *two* Unicorns on the committee." Her face looked dreamy for a moment. "Do you suppose you could have a Purple team this year?"

Everyone laughed. Purple was the Unicorn's favorite color. They used it wherever and whenever they could, and each of the members tried to wear at least one piece of purple clothing each day.

Like the name of their club, it was supposed to signify how special and beautiful they were.

"Janet is right," Tamara chimed in. "You two should be working together. The important thing is to make sure the Unicorns get all the glory, no matter what. Remember?"

Jessica didn't say anything. She couldn't help thinking that she and Lila were fighting about more than just the Mini Olympics. Lila was too spoiled to let Jessica take charge without making things difficult for her, Jessica decided.

But Lila hadn't counted on one thing, Jessica thought with determination: She wasn't going to budge an inch. She had very definite plans about the Mini Olympics, and she fully intended to see them carried out.

Pamela Jacobson took a deep breath as she walked from the locker room into the chilly gymnasium. This was the hour of the day she dreaded most. She bet none of the other girls even thought twice about taking gym class—it must seem like nothing to them!

But for Pamela it was an ordeal.

For as long as she could remember, Pamela had been a special case. It started the minute her parents learned she had been born with a rare heart condition. Pamela was the youngest one in her family, and the only girl. Her two brothers, Sam and Denny, were both perfectly normal. The doctors had explained that Pamela would always have to be careful. She underwent an operation before she was two years old, and another when she was seven. Those operations had saved her life, but they couldn't make her one hundred percent better. Her heart was always going to be weak, and though her doctor believed she would be able to live a full, long life, she still had to live under a shadow. She couldn't do many of the things her friends could do. No running. No strenuous activities. She had to take medication, and above all—and this was the very worst part—she had to put up with her parents' concern.

Pamela's father was a doctor himself, and Pamela sometimes thought that made everything even worse. Dr. Jacobson was the most overprotective father in the world. He was the one who had insisted Pamela go to Ridgedale, the private school twenty miles from Sweet Valley for special-needs students. He treated Pamela as if she were an invalid, even though he knew she wanted to be treated just like her brothers. Dr. Jacobson had been upset when she begged to leave Ridgedale. Only after months of pleading would he listen to her at all—and that was mostly because her mother was on her side.

In the end Dr. Jacobson had backed down. But he had only agreed to let Pamela leave Ridgedale with the understanding that at the slightest sign of fatigue, depression, or any other danger signal, Pamela would have to return to Ridgedale.

It made her cringe just thinking about it. Not that Ridgedale was a bad place. She had made a lot of friends there, and she cried the day she left. It was just that Pamela wanted a chance for a normal life. She wanted to prove—to her father *and* to herself—that she could do it.

But she was finding it wasn't that easy. Little things that no one else even thought twice about were difficult for her. At Ridgedale there were ramps instead of stairs, so that children in wheelchairs could manage on their own. Pamela got tired easily, and even a short flight of stairs had to be taken slowly. Sweet Valley Middle School was almost twice as large as Ridgedale, and that meant the distance between classes was longer—and the time to get from one to the next much shorter. Pamela found herself arriving late to every single class. If she hurried, she'd risk tiring herself—and injuring her heart.

But these problems could be handled. Her teachers understood her condition, and no one objected when she arrived late. The hardest part by far was that Pamela felt left out. Most of the activities she longed to join involved exercise—like the Booster Squad or the gymnastics club. And then there were the Mini Olympics coming up. It hurt Pamela to think of having to sit on the sidelines. At least at Ridgedale she didn't stick out. *Everyone* there had some sort of handicap. But here . . . here there was only Pamela.

She took a deep breath as she decided to go

sit in the bleachers. A fierce volleyball game had already started up. Somehow the Unicorns had all managed to get on the same team. Pamela looked on wistfully. She wondered what it would feel like to be a Unicorn. The girls in the club were all so pretty and confident. She couldn't help feeling a twinge of bitterness as she thought about the name they had chosen for themselves and the reasoning behind it. "We're called Unicorns because unicorns are special, and so are we." She had heard Janet Howell explain it that way to Ken Matthews. Pamela shook her head. She could tell them all a thing or two about being "special." For instance, that being special in a crowd was a lot easier than being special alone.

Tamara Chase suddenly caught sight of Pamela sitting on the sidelines. "Pam, come play with us!" she urged.

Pamela's face turned red. "I can't," she said.

"But we need a ninth person," Tamara pressed her.

Pamela shook her head. "No—really. I'm not allowed to."

Tamara frowned. She didn't say anything, but her message came through to Pamela loud and clear. She could feel tears welling up in her eyes. *I'm such a weakling,* she thought, feeling completely disgusted with herself. The tears spilled over, and Pamela got to her feet. She stumbled blindly to the door of the gymnasium. Why had she chosen to sit in on gym class today? If only she had gone to study hall instead. Maybe her father had been right after all—maybe it had been a mistake to believe she could fit in. She wasn't normal at all. She'd been foolish to believe she could make it through the year.

"Poor Pamela," Elizabeth murmured to Amy. They were in the cafeteria, looking over at the small brunette, who was eating lunch by herself. Elizabeth and Amy were talking about what had happened in gym class that morning. They really sympathized with Pamela. Elizabeth couldn't imagine what it must be like, feeling so shut out from ordinary activities. Turning to Amy, she said, "Let's go over to see her. Maybe I can talk to her again about the newspaper."

Amy nodded enthusiastically, and the two girls hurried across the cafeteria, their trays in hand. Pamela's eyes brightened when she saw them, but Elizabeth could see she had been crying.

"Volleyball," Elizabeth said after a minute, "is probably the world's stupidest game."

"Yeah," Amy added. "I can't stand it. I hate it when Ms. Langberg makes us play."

Pamela wiped a tear from her cheek. "You guys are just trying to cheer me up," she murmured.

Elizabeth giggled. "Who, *us*? Amy, did you just hear what she accused us of doing?"

Amy pretended to cover her ears with her

hands, and in spite of herself Pamela began to smile a little.

"I know it's silly to get so upset," she said softly. "The thing is, I feel like . . . I don't know, like such a wimp! I hate not being able to do what everyone else does."

"It must be really hard," Elizabeth said softly, sitting down beside her. "I think you've got a lot of guts, Pam. You promise you'll let us know if there's ever anything we can do to help you?"

Pamela sighed heavily. "I'm afraid no one can help me with the thing I want," she said. "I want to prove to my father that I can make it here, that I don't need to be in a special school." She looked miserable. "He's already been saying that I look more tired than I did last year, when I was at Ridgedale. And he's upset because I'm left out of so many activities." She bit her lip. "I think he's been trying to convince my mom to have me transferred back to Ridgedale." Pamela shook her head. "And I just want to convince him that I can do it! But I don't know how."

Elizabeth and Amy exchanged glances. The thought of Pamela being sent back to Ridgedale upset them both. Elizabeth decided then and there to talk to Jessica about taking Pamela's case into consideration in planning the Mini Olympics.

"Don't worry, Pam. We'll help you find some way to stay," she said quickly. Elizabeth knew her promise was rash. But she also knew she had to do something to help!

Three

"OK, Liz—now remember the plan," Jessica whispered to her sister. The twins were out in the backyard, by the Wakefields' swimming pool, enjoying the late afternoon sunlight and waiting for their brother to get home from basketball practice so they could try out their scheme.

"I still don't think it's going to work," Elizabeth objected.

Jessica's blue-green eyes were indignant. "Trust me, Lizzie! As soon as we make Steven feel he really *does* have ESP, he's going to be really scared. The only reason he's been going on and on about it is because he thinks it's all a joke."

Elizabeth had planned to talk to her sister about Pamela Jacobson and the Mini Olympics the minute she got home, but she had found Jessica so excited about her plan to get back at Steven that she couldn't get a word in edgewise.

"So remember—make sure that whatever Steven predicts is going to happen really *does* happen," Jessica advised her. "And be sure to egg him on. Ask him all about his 'visions,' and let's pretend to get really scared." She grinned. "As soon as we start to take him seriously, he's going to flip! He'll be sorry he ever said a word about ESP!"

"I bet you guys are glad I'm here," Steven declared a moment later, opening the screen door and coming out to join them. He had a bag of cookies in one hand and a carton of milk in the other, and Elizabeth made a face.

"How you can eat all that junk is beyond me," she muttered.

Steven stared. "I had a premonition today," he announced. "My ESP is getting stronger all the time, you guys. This morning"—he popped a cookie in his mouth—"I had the most amazing feeling that one of you was in trouble." He chewed the cookie solemnly. "It was about ten-thirty," he added.

Jessica poked Elizabeth, her eyes widening with mock horror. "Ten-thirty? Are you serious?" she gasped.

"Yeah," Steven said, surprised by the strength of her reaction. So far no one had paid any attention to any of his "omens." "Why?" he asked. "Was I right? Did something happen to one of you?"

Jessica paused dramatically. "Steven, I didn't believe you up until now, but you really *must* have ESP!" She shuddered. "I was in gym class at ten-thirty, and I just missed getting hit in the head with a volleyball. Ms. Langberg said I could have been hurt really badly."

Steven's eyes widened. "Wow," he said. "That really happened at ten-thirty?"

Jessica nodded energetically. "Cross my heart," she fibbed.

Elizabeth knew the nudge her twin was giving her meant it was her turn. "What about me? Have you had any weird feelings about me lately?" she asked.

Steven thought for a minute. "Well, yeah. I guess I did. This afternoon, during basketball practice, I had this sudden feeling that you . . . uh, that you had just found some money." He looked closely at her. "But I guess ESP isn't right one hundred percent of the time, is it?"

Elizabeth winked at Jessica. "I can't believe it," she said to her brother, feigning astonishment. "You must have overheard Amy Sutton telling someone about the five-dollar bill I found on the way home!"

Steven blinked, looking confused. "How could I have possibly run into Amy? I was at basketball practice, and then I just came straight home."

Elizabeth gave Jessica a look of mock concern. "We thought he was making it all up," she said.

Jessica nodded seriously. "Steve, we owe you an apology. This is incredible—you really do have ESP!"

Steven looked a little alarmed. "Liz, you really found a five dollar bill this afternoon?" he demanded.

Elizabeth nodded solemnly.

Steven looked slightly pale. "Listen, I've got to make a phone call," he said abruptly, getting up from the deck chair and hurrying across the patio toward the back door.

Jessica and Elizabeth exchanged triumphant grins.

"See, I told you," Jessica said happily. "He never really expected we'd start taking him seriously. Now that he thinks he really has ESP, he's scared to death!"

Elizabeth looked thoughtful. Now that her brother was gone, she wanted to turn the conversation to Pamela.

"Jessica, I've been wanting to ask you something about the Mini Olympics," she said. "I know you've been putting a lot of time and effort into the whole thing, and I'm really impressed with some of your ideas. But there's one thing that's been bugging me."

"What's that?" Jessica asked, only half listening as she thumbed through her notebook, looking over the plans she and Mr. Butler had drawn up so far.

"Well, I had a talk with Pamela Jacobson at

lunch," Elizabeth began. "It really made me do some serious thinking. Do you know she isn't allowed to participate in any of the regular gym activities?"

"Mmmm," Jessica said, flipping through pages with a frown. "Yeah, she had to sit out our volleyball game this morning. I don't really see why she came to gym at all today. What's the point? If she's too sick to play, she shouldn't bother coming."

"That's the whole point—she isn't *sick*," Elizabeth said, defending her. "She's got a heart condition, and that's different. It's never going to go away."

Jessica looked up, her eyes slightly narrowed. "Liz, what does Pam Jacobson have to do with the Mini Olympics? I don't mean to be rude, but I just sort of assumed she wouldn't even show up. What would be the point?"

"There wouldn't be any point—not the way things have been run in the past. Not the way you're planning to run them again this year," Elizabeth said slowly. "The truth is, Jessica, it seems kind of unfair. Why shouldn't someone like Pamela be able to join in?"

Jessica frowned. "She could help decorate posters or something," she mused. "Is she any good at typing? We've got a bunch of flyers we want to send out to parents."

"That wasn't what I meant, Jess," Elizabeth said firmly. "I don't think Pamela wants to *work* for this. I think she'd like the chance to compete—to actually get involved, like everyone else."

"OK," Jessica said. "But I don't think she's going to have much of a shot. Most of the events we've got planned are pretty hard. She's going to have to get in much better shape if she wants to win anything."

Elizabeth looked horrified. "Jessica, she *can't* compete in difficult events! She could really hurt herself!"

Jessica put her notebook down with a frown. "Isn't that what I said in the first place? Come on, Liz. You're not making any sense."

"What I was thinking," Elizabeth said, sitting up straighter, "was making some changes in the events this year. Why not include some races or relays that don't require much strength or speed? What about adding a talent contest in the afternoon, or having a tent with puzzles and games in it? That way some of the smaller kids in the lower school would participate too."

Jessica sighed. "That sounds like a nice idea and everything, Liz, but Mr. Butler and I already put tons of work into the arrangements. You wouldn't believe how much time it's taken. Besides, what's the point of going to all the trouble to rearrange everything when I like it the way it is?"

"It doesn't seem to me like it would take that much work," Elizabeth said. "And I think it would really be worth the extra trouble. Jess, think what it must feel like for Pamela. Here she is, trying to prove she can make it in a normal school, and what does she find—that she isn't allowed to take part in half the things the rest of us do!" She looked intently at her twin. "Try to picture something you do every day that you never think twice about—like climbing the stairs or something."

"Yeah," Jessica said. "I'm picturing it."

"Well, now think about what it would be like if you had to make a really big effort to do it—just to climb the stairs!" Elizabeth exclaimed, upset.

"Listen, I feel sorry for Pamela too," Jessica assured her sister. "But I don't see any way to solve her problem. Who knows," she added, picking up her notebook again. "Maybe it was a mistake for her to try coming to a regular school. Maybe she should have stayed where she was."

"I can't believe you can even say something like that!" Elizabeth cried. "Jessica Wakefield, take that back!"

Jessica looked up at her with surprise. "OK, OK—I take it back," she said quickly. She wasn't used to seeing her sister so upset, and she decided she had better keep things calm. She promised to think over what Elizabeth had suggested.

"I'll talk to Mr. Butler about it," she said. "But I really think it might be too late, Liz."

"As long as you try," said Elizabeth. "That's all I'm asking, Jessica." Her eyes shone. "You're a great sister, you know that? I owe you a favor in return—whatever you want. OK?"

Jessica's face brightened. "Good," she said,

setting her notebook down again for good. "Because I *do* have a favor to ask of you." She leaned forward confidentially. "It has to do with Steven. I've got the perfect plan to finish off what we started this afternoon. With a little luck we should have him so frightened he won't even be able to look at his own shadow without getting the creeps."

Elizabeth sighed. "What have you got in mind this time?" she asked. Knowing Jessica, it could be anything. Elizabeth hoped she hadn't spoken too soon when she'd promised to help her!

"You know, Steven," Jessica said that night at dinner, buttering a piece of bread, "I looked up ESP at the library the other day, and according to the book I found, people who have it sometimes see visions—usually at night."

Steven put down his glass of milk, frowning at her. "Really, I haven't seen anything at night," he said.

"Steven, you've barely eaten a thing!" Mrs. Wakefield exclaimed, looking concerned. Steven's enormous appetite was a big joke in the Wakefield household, and any change was usually a sign that something was seriously wrong.

"I'm just not very hungry," Steven said.

Jessica gave Elizabeth a meaningful look. Their plan seemed to be working. "Maybe you're being affected by the supernatural vibrations," she suggested hopefully. "Maybe that's what's spoiling your appetite."

"Sounds to me like too many chocolate chip cookies after school," Mrs. Wakefield said with a smile.

"Maybe," Jessica said, taking a bite of her hamburger, "you'll see a spirit one of these nights when you're sleeping, Steven. Did you ever think of that?"

Steven was beginning to get angry. "I *don't* see things, Jessica," he muttered. He got up from the table, threw down his napkin, and stormed out of the room.

"What on earth—" Mrs. Wakefield began.

"He's just a little touchy today," Jessica said sweetly. "Liz and I think his ESP is beginning to get to him."

Mr. Wakefield gave Mrs. Wakefield a concerned glance. "I hope he's all right," he said. "You don't think he really *believes* any of this nonsense he's been feeding the girls about ESP, do you?"

Jessica and Elizabeth exchanged glances. Steven might not have believed it to begin with, but with their help, he was obviously starting to get worried.

And after what they had planned for that night, he was never going to consider ESP a joking matter again!

Four

"I still think this is a bad idea," Elizabeth said in a low voice. She and Jessica were out in the garage, using flashlights to find their way in the dark. It was past midnight, and they were trying their hardest not to make any noise. If Mr. or Mrs. Wakefield found out they weren't in bed, they'd get in very bad trouble. Not to mention the fact that they were about to do something really rotten to poor Steven. Elizabeth felt terrible about it. She wished she hadn't promised Jessica a favor.

"Shhh," Jessica said. She almost tripped over a piece of garden hose, and her face went white as she grabbed Elizabeth by the arm. "Darn. It's so hard trying to do this in the dark!"

"Let's forget it," Elizabeth begged her. "Can't we just keep doing what we've been doing?

Steven's already getting spooked. He'll cut out this ESP stuff any day now."

But Jessica had already managed to get the ladder off its hooks on the garage wall. "No way," she whispered back. "We've got to teach him a lesson. Help me with this thing, Lizzie. It weighs a ton."

The twins had to struggle with the ladder before they got it safely out of the garage. It was heavier than they'd expected, and so it was no easy chore to carry it over to the side of the house where Steven's bedroom was located. Jessica took the ladder from her sister and opened it up against the side of the house. "That's perfect," she whispered. "Now, stay right here while I go back for my ghost costume."

Elizabeth shook her head and frowned, but before she could say a word, Jessica was running back to the garage in the dark, her flashlight making a bright bouncing mark as she ran. It was chilly out, and Elizabeth shivered.

It seemed ages before Jessica came back, holding a white sheet in her hand. It was left over from a Halloween party. "Remember—pass it up to me once I'm up at the top," Jessica whispered as she started to climb the ladder.

"I really think we should go back inside," Elizabeth said again, this time more firmly. "Jess, what if we really scare him? He could get hysterical or something!"

"You promised to help out," Jessica reminded her. "Don't worry," she added. "He may be scared for a second, but then he'll probably just laugh. And he'll *definitely* get the idea. Then we won't have to hear any more about ESP!"

Elizabeth laughed. "I guess he does deserve it," she admitted. "Remember the time he scared you in that ridiculous Creature from the Black Lagoon costume of his?"

On Halloween night Steven had tormented Jessica by sneaking into her room in the dark and giving her the shock of her life. The more Elizabeth thought about it, the more she had to admit that Steven deserved a taste of his own medicine.

"I remember," Jessica said grimly. "He"ll be sorry for that—and for this ESP nonsense!" Soon she had climbed up to the top. The ladder was wobbling quite a bit, and Elizabeth began to feel nervous.

"Careful!" she warned, steadying the ladder with both hands.

Jessica reached down. "Give me the costume," she instructed.

Elizabeth passed it up to her, watching anxiously as Jessica balanced on the top of the ladder, holding onto the window ledge as she draped the sheet over herself. There were two holes cut in the sheet for the eyes, and Elizabeth thought Jessica really did look scary. It was strange how different everything looked out here in the pitch dark. She watched as Jessica inched closer to the window and tapped at the glass.

"I don't think he can hear me," Jessica said a minute later. "I'm going to try pressing my face against the glass."

Meanwhile Steven was sitting up straight in his bed, his heart pounding. What was that sound—that scratching at the window? He thought about what Jessica had said that night at dinner. Was it really true that people with ESP had visions? His face went pale. He'd never really believed he had ESP. He only told his sisters that to have some fun. Now he wished he'd never brought it up.

Taking a deep breath, he threw off the covers and padded over to the window. The shade was pulled down. He felt a terrible chill when he heard it again—a faint but definite knocking on the glass. The next moment he snapped up the shade and screamed as loud as he could when he saw—he didn't know what it was—something white and terrible pressing against the window. It was just inches from his own face!

"Jessica!" Elizabeth cried. She didn't know what had happened, but when the shade snapped up, Jessica started, and her left foot slid off the top rung of the ladder. The next instant she was clawing desperately at the sill, but it was too late for her to regain her balance. With a bloodcurdling scream she crashed down, pulling the ladder over with her. "Jessica," Elizabeth cried again, trying to pull the sheet off of her. "Jess, are you OK?"

Lights were being turned on all over the upstairs as Steven's and Jessica's cries woke Mr. and Mrs. Wakefield. By now Steven had yanked open his window and stuck his head outside. "What's going on down there?" he demanded, his color returning to normal as he realized that what he had seen wasn't a vision at all.

"Steven, get Mom and Dad—quick!" Elizabeth cried. "Jessica's hurt!"

"Jessica—" Steven choked out. "Why, that little . . ." His anger settled down as the meaning of Elizabeth's words finally struck him. "Is she OK? I'll be right down!" he cried.

"Don't tell them," Jessica moaned, trying to pull herself up. "Liz, they're going to *kill* us!"

"Are you all right?" Elizabeth demanded, leaning over her with concern. "Gosh, Jess—I thought you'd killed yourself!"

"So did I," Jessica grumbled. "Liz, try and help me up. I think I hurt my ankle."

Elizabeth gave Jessica her arm, but Jessica couldn't pull herself to her feet. "Something's really wrong, Liz," she groaned, leaning over and clutching her ankle. "I think I broke it!"

Elizabeth peered unhappily down at her sister's leg. "You must have caught it in the rung when you fell," she said sorrowfully.

"Jessica! Are you all right?" Steven hollered,

racing toward them around the side of the house. Mr. and Mrs. Wakefield weren't far behind.

"What on earth is going on here?" Mr. Wakefield said angrily. The ladder was lying on the grass, and Jessica—her face stained with tears—was sitting shivering beside it, the sheet still wound partially around her.

"The ladder fell," Jessica whispered.

"Jessica's hurt," Elizabeth said quickly, shining the flashlight toward Jessica's leg. "Look—her ankle's starting to swell up!"

"She's not really hurt that bad," Steven said, looking disgusted. "Jessica, what do you think you were doing? I thought you were"—he swallowed—"a *burglar* or something."

Jessica looked up fearfully at her parents' stormy expressions. "We were just trying to scare him a little," she whispered. "We were pretending I was a spirit." She gulped. "We were sick of him acting like he had ESP."

Mr. Wakefield knelt down on the grass, expertly gripping Jessica's ankle. "Tell me when it hurts," he said, putting a slight pressure on the bone.

"Ouch!" Jessica cried.

"I think," Mr. Wakefield said, getting up with a frown, "that you and I had better make a trip over to the Emergency Room, Jessica. We'll talk tomorrow morning about what you two girls were up to and why. For now, I think we had better get a doctor's opinion about that ankle."

Jessica looked pale as her father picked her up in his arms. She knew she and Elizabeth were in trouble. But she was even more upset about her ankle. It hurt so badly it took all she had not to cry.

She couldn't believe her bad luck. She just had to hope against hope that it wasn't broken!

"Well," Dr. Lawrence said, coming out to the waiting room of the hospital, where Jessica and her father had been waiting for half an hour. "We've got the X-rays. You're lucky, Jessica. It's just a bad sprain."

Jessica let out a long sigh of relief. "That's great," she said. "I've got so much to do in the next few weeks! I don't know what I would've done if it was broken."

"Well," the doctor said, frowning down at the X-rays, "I hate to disappoint you, but you're going to find day-to-day activities a little difficult for the next couple of weeks anyway."

"What do you mean?" asked Jessica.

"Well, you've got quite a nasty sprain," Dr. Lawrence told her. "Most people don't realize it, but a bad sprain can be more painful than a break—and take almost as long to heal. You're not going to be able to put any weight on your left ankle for at least three weeks."

Jessica's eyes widened. "How am I going to get around? You mean I can't even walk on it?"

"That's right." Dr. Lawrence smiled. A look of horror washed over Jessica's face. "I wouldn't be so upset. You'll be able to use crutches, so you won't be confined to your bed or anything that drastic." He wrote something down on a piece of paper and handed it to Mr. Wakefield. "I'm prescribing this for pain," he said. "She should keep these to a minimum—one or two every four hours, as needed, for the first few days." He turned back to Jessica. "You'll have to keep the Ace bandage wrapped tightly around your ankle all the time, except when you're taking a bath. When you're sitting down, I want you to keep your leg elevated. And under no circumstances put any weight on it at all!"

Jessica bit her lip. "But I'm in charge of the Mini Olympics," she said sorrowfully, "and I'm cheering with the Boosters at the game on Monday, and—"

"No, you're not," Mr. Wakefield said. "First thing tomorrow morning I'll go out and get you a pair of crutches so you can get to school." He shook the doctor's hand. "Thank you very much for all your help," he said. "I think this young lady learned a lesson tonight. Haven't you, Jessica?"

"I guess so," Jessica mumbled. She looked down at her ankle with hatred. How in the world could she have been so clumsy? This was all she needed. She had more going on in the next few weeks than she could ever remember, and she wasn't even going to be able to walk normally!

Even worse, she knew that she was about to face her parents' anger—not to mention Steven's.

She had a feeling Elizabeth wasn't going to be too happy with her either.

All in all the little scheme she had cooked up to scare her brother had really backfired! She didn't know which was worse—the prospect of getting yelled at by her parents, or the terrible throbbing in her ankle.

She couldn't even get up from the chair by herself. Her father had to carry her out to the car like she was some kind of invalid!

"I'm not going to go through a whole lot of nonsense about what you and Elizabeth tried to do to Steven tonight," Mr. Wakefield said when they were alone. He put the key in the ignition and frowned. "I think you've learned your lesson. And if you haven't yet, I think you will." He started the car's engine. "I sprained my ankle when I was about your age, and I seem to remember that by the time it was better, I had made up my mind never to goof around again. Anyway, the sprain was punishment enough. And I think it will be for you too."

Jessica felt a little bit better. She thought her father was being extremely soft on her. True, her ankle was throbbing. But it was only a sprain. How bad could it be? So she'd have to use crutches for a few weeks. That couldn't be *that* bad.

No, she had definitely gotten off lightly. She couldn't wait to get home and brag about it to Elizabeth.

Five

"Jessica! What happened to you!" Caroline Pearce shrieked, making her way through the crowd surrounding Jessica in homeroom. Mrs. Wyler, their teacher, was trying to remind the class about the chocolate bars they were selling to raise money for the class trip at the end of the year. But no one was paying attention. They were too interested in Jessica's injury.

"You poor thing," Caroline gushed. Caroline, a redheaded girl with a sprinkling of freckles across the bridge of her nose, was a real gossip, and lived two doors away from the Wakefields. She loved knowing exactly what was going on with everyone, and Jessica could tell she was upset she hadn't been the first to hear about her ankle.

"It's no big deal," she said airily. "Just a sprained ankle."

But the truth was, it had been a hard morning. Everything that Jessica usually did took at least twice as long. Getting downstairs for breakfast was an ordeal, let alone managing to carry her books while she used her crutches. Still, it wasn't so bad. In a way it was even kind of fun. For one thing, she had never gotten so much attention. Everyone came up to her in the hall, wanting to know what had happened. Bruce Patman had carried her books for her from her locker to her homeroom—and he usually didn't even say hello! Bruce was a seventh grader—a really cute, dark-haired boy whose family was the wealthiest in Sweet Valley.

Only one thing was making her unhappy, and that was Steven. He couldn't believe she and Elizabeth weren't being grounded after what they'd done. He didn't believe his father's explanation that Jessica's injury would be punishment enough for her. As far as Steven was concerned, nothing was punishment enough! So he was refusing to talk to her. He had somehow come to the conclusion that Jessica was really to blame, not Elizabeth—so he was still talking to Elizabeth. It wasn't fair.

But Jessica was determined to put Steven out of her mind. She didn't want to dwell on the mishaps of the night before either. She was just going to bask in all the attention she was getting.

Lila came hurrying into homeroom. "Jessica! I heard you sprained your ankle," she said, sounding sympathetic. "I just couldn't believe it! But it seems to be true," she added, looking down at Jessica's Ace bandage. She made little clucking noises, shaking her auburn head. "I guess you won't be able to be chairman of the Mini Olympics anymore," she said after a minute.

Jessica's face burned. So that was why Lila was being so nice! "Why not?" she demanded. "It's only a little sprain, Lila. It's not really a big deal, and it certainly isn't going to affect my thinking!"

Lila looked taken aback. "Oh. Well, if you need any help . . ." she began.

But Jessica didn't even want to talk to Lila about it. Luckily, Mrs. Wyler interrupted the conversation by ringing a small bell on her desk. Homeroom really had to get under way—so Jessica, using her crutches, made her way over to her desk.

She noticed Pamela Jacobson giving her a sympathetic smile as she tried to arrange the crutches next to her desk. Finally she had to lean them against the window and hop back to her desk.

She didn't like what Pam's smile seemed to mean. After all, there wasn't anything really wrong with her—this was just a temporary thing. It wasn't as if she and Pamela had anything in common!

"Steven still isn't talking to me," Jessica said

glumly. She and Ellen Riteman were eating lunch together. It was Thursday afternoon, two days since Jessica's accident, and Jessica had to admit having a sprained ankle wasn't very much fun anymore. In the first place, people weren't paying as much attention to her as they had the day before. Now that everyone had tried her crutches and heard all about the accident, they seemed to have forgotten about it.

"You seem kind of down in the dumps," Ellen said.

"Well, having a sprained ankle today isn't half as much fun as it was yesterday," Jessica complained. "It's getting to be a real pain. Everything I do takes twice as long. I can't even get up or down stairs without it taking practically forever!"

"That's too bad," Ellen said sympathetically.

"I can't even ride my bike," Jessica said mournfully. "I can't do anything anymore!" She stuck her lower lip out. "And no one's even paying any attention to me. I don't think anyone even cares about my ankle—besides you, Ellen," she added hastily. She knew she was complaining, but she couldn't help it. Things suddenly seemed extremely gloomy.

Cheering with the Boosters, of course, was out. Jessica couldn't practice, so she sat on the sidelines and watched, feeling left out. They were supposed to be learning a new cheer that week, too, and she was sure she'd never get the hang of it by the time her ankle was better.

Then there were the Mini Olympics. Jessica had devoted so much time to planning them, and now she could barely make it to the meetings on time, let alone control them! It was infuriating. And Lila Fowler really seemed to be taking advantage of her predicament. She kept insisting that Jessica allow her to do more work, now that she was injured. If Mr. Butler had anything special he needed done, Lila begged him to let her do it—since, as she kept saying, it would take so much effort for poor Jessica on crutches. It was clear that Lila was trying to take over her job, and Jessica couldn't stand it.

"You don't seem very happy," Ellen said. "I guess it isn't much fun having to hobble around all the time."

"I'm not hobbling!" Jessica protested, putting down her sandwich. She'd lost her appetite. "I guess I'm getting a little tired of it," she admitted. "There are so many things I feel like doing, and it's no fun being left out."

"I know," Ellen said feelingly.

But Jessica wasn't sure she *did* know. Ellen had never been left out of anything! Until that week Jessica hadn't been either.

She didn't like it. Not one little bit.

"Today is it," Ms. Langberg said, after she had blown her whistle and gotten everyone's attention. "And I mean it! This is the final volleyball game, and I want you girls to give it all you've got."

Jessica sighed. She was sitting on the bleachers, watching the Unicorns giggling and patting each other on the back as they faced the net. She couldn't stand it. Here it was, Friday. Another long day dragging around on crutches. She'd do anything to be out there with Janet, Lila, and the others.

"Hi, Jessica," a familiar voice said. Pamela Jacobson had come over and was standing next to her. "Mind if I join you?" she asked timidly.

"No, go ahead," Jessica said with a sigh.

"Not much fun, is it?" Pamela said. She sat down, and the two girls watched the volleyball game in silence. "This is what I hate the most," Pamela said after a while. "I don't think there's anything in the world as bad as having to sit on the sidelines."

Jessica looked up at her thoughtfully. She hadn't known that Pamela wanted to be part of things so badly. "I guess you're right," she said.

"Of course," Pamela added, as if she were reading Jessica's mind, "it's probably worse for you. I mean, I've *always* been this way. It must be a lot harder if you're used to being in the middle of everything."

Jessica pretended to look at her fingernails. She didn't like to admit it, but it occurred to her—for the first time—that she had never really considered what it must feel like for Pamela. She shrugged. "I don't think so," she said. "I think it must be harder for you. I mean, I've only got to put up with this dumb ankle for the next couple of weeks."

Pamela thought this over. "Yeah," she said finally. "Maybe you're right."

The two sat together in silence for a while, watching the volleyball game. Jessica kept thinking how different it all looked from the sidelines. Everyone seemed to be having such a good time!

"Sometimes," Pamela said, "I think I should just give up and go back to Ridgedale."

Jessica forgot that she had said almost the same thing to Elizabeth just a few days earlier. She looked at Pamela with horror now. "Don't say that," she said. "I'm sure things will change around here—once everyone gets used to your condition. Things will get easier."

Pamela shook her head. "The thing that really gets to me is that at Ridgedale I was an outsider too—because I was so much better off than most of the kids! They resented me a little." She sighed. "I guess I hoped I'd finally feel like I belonged once I got to Sweet Valley."

Jessica didn't know what to say. She couldn't help feeling relieved that her own injury was temporary. Things seemed really rough for Pamela.

"Come on, Steven," Jessica begged, trying hard to keep up with him on her crutches. They were in front of the school, and Steven was definitely not interested in slowing down to listen to what she had to say.

"How many times do I have to say I'm sorry?" she cried.

Steven turned to glare at her. "Sorry isn't good enough this time," he snapped. "How would you like it if I tried to scare *you* to death?"

Jessica felt exhausted all of a sudden. The crutches were beginning to hurt her underneath her arms. She was also sick and tired of begging Steven to forgive her. "If you weren't such a big baby, you wouldn't have been scared. You wouldn't have screamed, and I never would have fallen off the ladder," she retorted.

Steven's face darkened with anger. "That just isn't true," he growled. "It was all your fault, and you know it!" He looked as if he were about to say something more, but instead he turned away and hurried off across the parking lot.

Taking a deep breath, Jessica tried to decide what to do for the next fifteen minutes before her meeting with Mr. Butler, Lila Fowler, and the rest of the Mini Olympics committee began. Then she remembered something.

Because of her ankle, it would probably take her fifteen whole minutes just to get to the gym and get herself ready for the meeting!

Six

The meeting wasn't going the way Jessica had planned at all. There were six people in the room: Mr. Butler, a woman named Ms. Ulrich from the PTA, Jessica, Lila, and the two fifth graders who were working with them on the Mini Olympics—Randy Osborne and Patty DuVal. Randy was a cute, dark-haired boy with a good sense of humor, and seemed to be devoting a lot of time and effort to his role organizing the four teams. Patty was in charge of publicity. Jessica considered her a really nice girl who had always listened to her in the past.

But this afternoon Jessica felt like she shouldn't have made the effort to show up. No one was listening to anything she said! At first she thought it was her imagination. She was trying to make a suggestion about the first event they had scheduled—the long jump. Jessica wanted it to be moved around so that they began with water races in the lower school pool. "It seems to make more sense to start off inside, and then move outside for the rest of the day," she said.

Lila cleared her throat. "Don't you remember, Jessica? We've already taken care of that. We're having three parts—first the pool and water events, then the sand pit for long jump and high jump, and then the field for races and relays." She gave Mr. Butler a smile so sweet that Jessica thought she was going to get sick. "Isn't that what we said, Mr. Butler?"

Mr. Butler nodded. "Yes, that's right," he said.

Jessica couldn't believe her ears. "When did you talk about it?" she asked, her voice a little unsteady. "I thought we had decided on Tuesday that—"

"Lila got in touch with me yesterday and said you two had decided this order would be better," Mr. Butler said, frowning. "Isn't that right, Lila? I was under the impression that you two had discussed it already."

Ms. Ulrich patted her hair and cleared her throat. "I'm sorry, but I have another meeting in less than half an hour. If we could just firm up these plans . . ."

"No problem, Ms. Ulrich," Mr. Butler said, frowning at Jessica. "We'll move through the rest of the events as quickly as we can."

Jessica stared at Lila. She couldn't believe it. What a sneak! Obviously Lila had been using Jessica's injury as a chance to move in on her role as chairman. Jessica decided it was time for immediate action.

"Can I just ask Patty how the publicity is going?" she asked. "We weren't sure on Tuesday whether or not to advertise the day at all, and I was wondering—"

"Oh, I took care of all that," Lila said airily. "I asked Daddy to ask some of the people at his advertising agency to run a full-page ad in the *Sweet Valley News*."

Jessica stared at her, her eyes wide with disbelief. She knew Mr. Fowler was rich and powerful, but she couldn't imagine that he'd buy his daughter a full-page newspaper ad! And she couldn't believe Lila was showing her up this way either.

"I thought I was supposed to decide that," she protested.

Mr. Butler frowned at his watch. "Jessica, Lila was just trying to be helpful. It's obvious that it's harder for you to get around now that you've hurt your ankle, and she was just trying to be a friend, that's all."

Jessica bit her lip, trying as hard as she could to control her temper. She couldn't stand the little smirk on Lila's face, though. She had to figure out a way to regain control of the Mini Olympics—no matter what!

The only question was how to do it!

"Boy, you sure don't look happy," Elizabeth said when she saw the look on her sister's face. "Is your ankle hurting a lot?"

Jessica glared at the Ace bandage wrapped firmly around her ankle. "It hurts, all right. But that's not what's bothering me."

"Is it Steven? I know he's been really mad, but he's bound to forgive you sooner or later." Elizabeth patted her twin on the shoulder. "I'll even talk to him if you want me to."

Jessica shook her head. "If Steve wants to give me the silent treatment, let him! That isn't what's bothering me either. It's Lila. She's stealing the whole Mini Olympics right out from under me!"

"What do you mean?" Elizabeth asked, surprised.

Jessica's lower lip trembled a little, the way it did when she was really upset. "It isn't fair! She's just using the fact that I'm hurt to try to take over the whole committee. She keeps coming up with all these suggestions, and if I object to any of them, it makes me look bad. I mean, here I am, injured. And Lila is perfectly ready and willing to do all sorts of things I can't do." Jessica's face turned red. "I just wish she weren't quite so ready to take over everything."

"Maybe she thinks she can do a better job running things than you can," said Elizabeth. "I mean, now that you can't compete in the actual events anymore yourself."

Jessica stared at her. "I'd forgotten about

that," she murmured. "I'm not going to be able to even *be* in the Mini Olympics!"

"Well, I'm sure Lila hasn't forgotten it," Elizabeth said, watching closely for her twin's reaction. "She probably just thinks that she'll have to take over eventually and she might as well do it now. After all," Elizabeth said matter-of-factly, "the Mini Olympics have been planned to exclude certain kinds of people. And I'm not just talking about someone like you or Pamela Jacobson."

"What do you mean?" Jessica demanded. "Who else is being excluded?"

"Well, what about some of the really little kids, and the smaller fifth graders?" Elizabeth asked. "In the past they've always been divided equally among the four teams. But wouldn't it be better if instead of seeing them as handicap points, they got to participate in events where they had a chance of winning?"

Jessica shrugged. "I don't know. Anyway, I still can't think of a single event where any one of them would stand a chance against someone like Jerry McAllister," Jessica said, naming one of the biggest boys in the sixth grade.

Elizabeth laughed. "You're just not using any imagination," she teased her sister. There was a silence for a minute before Elizabeth began pressing her point further. "Then," she said slowly, "there are the older kids who just aren't any good at sports. Think about Lois Waller, for instance."

Jessica made a face. "*You* think about Lois

Waller," she said. Lois, clumsy and overweight, was in the sixth grade. Jessica and the Unicorns loved to make fun of her. "Lois is just lazy," Jessica added. "She *needs* exercise, Lizzie! Are you suggesting we plan the Mini Olympics so that every single weakling has the same chance to win that some big strong athlete has?"

Elizabeth laughed. "That's exactly what I'm saying," she said. "Only you put it much better than I could have."

Jessica shook her head. "Only you would consider remaking the Mini Olympics so that Lois Waller and Pamela Jacobson could win blue ribbons, Liz. It's a nice idea and everything, only I just don't see how—"

"And," Elizabeth cut in, "of course *you'd* get all the credit for thinking of it, wouldn't you?"

Jessica stared. "What do you mean?" she demanded.

Elizabeth shrugged. "Just that it sounds like Lila Fowler is being her usual pushy self, that's all. And she probably doesn't realize how insensitive she's being either. If you gave Mr. Butler and Ms. Ulrich a new plan—one that would include *everyone* and make the Mini Olympics totally fair—Lila would end up looking like a rat."

Jessica's eyes shone. "She would, wouldn't she!" she cried. "She barged in without one tiny bit of sympathy for me. She hasn't even asked if I'm still planning to try to be in any of the events.

She's just assuming she can edge me out and be rid of me!"

Elizabeth nodded. "So," she finished casually, pretending not to know the exact effect her words were having on her sister, "a few casual remarks to Mr. Butler now would really solve two of your problems, wouldn't it? First, if you changed the Olympics, you'd be able to take part after all. And second, you'd get control over the whole day back again."

Jessica shook her head in admiration. "Did I ever tell you you're the smartest twin in the whole world?" she cried. "Lizzie, get me my crutches, OK?"

Elizabeth handed her the crutches. "Going somewhere?" she demanded, a curious smile on her face.

"I'm going to call Mr. Butler," Jessica declared. "Elizabeth Wakefield, you're a genius! I'm going to try and convince him that we need to start planning from scratch."

"Good," Elizabeth said sweetly, watching her sister struggle with her crutches as she made her way down the hall to the telephone. She couldn't believe how easy it had been to persuade her sister. She couldn't wait until Jessica was off the phone so she could call Pamela Jacobson and tell her the news.

Pamela's voice sounded funny when she

came to the phone—almost as if she'd been crying. "Oh, hi, Liz," she said, not sounding very excited.

"Are you OK? You don't sound like yourself," Elizabeth said.

"We've been having a big talk here," Pamela said in a low voice. "My dad came home early from the hospital. He thought I'd been going to clubs or over to friends' houses in the afternoons. I guess he's really upset that I'm not getting out more." She sighed. "In fact, he and my mom are downstairs now, talking about it. They don't sound very happy either."

Elizabeth felt terribly sorry for Pamela. "Listen, I called because I think Jessica is trying to do something about the Mini Olympics to change the events. If it works, everyone will be able to participate—including you!"

Pamela's voice sounded dull. "That sounds nice, Liz," she said flatly. "Listen, I have to get off the phone now, OK? My dad wants to talk to me."

"OK," Elizabeth said, concerned. A second later she heard a click as Pamela put the receiver back on the hook. She wished there was something more she could have done or said to give Pamela support. It didn't sound like Pamela was having a very easy time explaining things to her parents.

Elizabeth just hoped that the new plans for the Olympics didn't come too late to prove to Dr. Jacobson that Pamela had a real chance to fit in at

Sweet Valley Middle School. She couldn't bear to think that the Jacobsons were giving up so soon.

Elizabeth was sure that given the chance, Pamela could really prove herself.

All she needed was that chance. And Elizabeth was going to fight as hard as she could to see that she got it!

Seven

Pamela had been dreading this moment for ages. She had suspected for some time now that her father was losing patience with her attending Sweet Valley Middle School. He'd been so bitterly opposed to it from the start that the slightest hitch was all he needed to decide that she ought to go back to Ridgedale.

To her surprise, her brothers were sitting in the living room with her parents when she came home that afternoon. Sam, her oldest brother, was a sophomore at Sweet Valley High. He had curly dark hair and a friendly expression that drew people to him naturally. The look he gave Pamela when she entered the room told her he was on her side.

But Pamela knew Denny felt differently. Denny was in the eighth grade, and he had taken his father's side when the family began to discuss where Pamela would go to school. Denny joined every club there was and excelled in every sport. Pamela was ashamed of herself for feeling this way, but sometimes she suspected that he was a little embarrassed to have her in the middle school with him. She knew she wasn't the kind of sister he would have liked to have. He probably would have liked someone like Jessica Wakefield: Someone who was a Unicorn, and in the Boosters. Not a wimp like Pamela, who had to get an excuse to be late to every class because she walked so slowly!

"Pamela," said Dr. Jacobson. "We've been talking about the Mini Olympics your class is putting on for the lower school next Friday. Why didn't you mention it to us? If it hadn't been for Denny, we never would have known about it!"

Pamela blushed. "I . . . uh, I guess I was just waiting to tell you about it when it got a little closer," she said faintly.

Mrs. Jacobson's dark eyes looked concerned. "Honey, we're not trying to grill you. Your father was just afraid that you'd been excluded from it, that's all."

Pamela's eyes burned with tears. Bad as it was being left out of things, it was a million times worse having to tell her family every time it happened.

"The Olympics are really athletic," she said, swallowing hard over the lump in her throat. "I've been thinking about trying to get involved in other ways—like working on the special edition of the class newspaper."

Dr. Jacobson looked at her with a sad frown on his face. "Pamela, we don't want to put you on the spot. It's not your fault that you can't participate. We're only trying to learn more about what life has been like for you at the middle school so we can come to a rational decision about what's best for you."

Rational, Pamela thought miserably. Her father always used that word. Maybe it was because he was a doctor, and he thought the best approach was to find out what was wrong and then think of the most reasonable way to fix the problem. She knew deep down that it probably wasn't *rational* to want to stay at Sweet Valley Middle School so badly. At Ridgedale she got so much more attention. There were only eight or ten students in each class. At Ridgedale she didn't have to take any risks. She could finish middle school at Ridgedale and go on to Parker Academy, the high school for disabled students. That way she would never have to feel hurt and embarrassed about trying to do things that were too hard for her.

But that wasn't what Pamela wanted. She *wanted* to take a risk. She wanted to prove she could do something difficult, that for once she didn't need to have things cushioned and protected for her. Pamela had always longed to be treated the way Denny was treated. No one ever gave him a break. They expected things from him, and he lived up to expectations. He got good grades, he had lots of friends, he was good at games. *Denny* had won three blue ribbons at the Mini Olympics the year he was in the sixth grade!

"Your father is afraid you're isolated from people at school," Mrs. Jacobson said, putting her arm around Pamela. "He's afraid you haven't really been meeting very many people. But you're making friends, aren't you?"

"Yes," Pamela said. "I am."

"Why aren't they coming over to the house?" Dr. Jacobson asked. When Pamela's face fell, he added, "I'm really not trying to hurt you, honey. I just want to find out a little more about what your life has been like there. Can't you tell me?"

Pamela sighed. "I guess things are moving kind of slowly," she admitted. "But I'm shy too. It's not easy being in a new school. It never is!"

"Pamela," her father said softly, "how much time do you think you ought to give it? We want to be supportive of you. But we don't want to see you get hurt."

"We said a year!" Pamela cried, anguished. "You promised I could stay for all of sixth grade."

"But we didn't know what it was going to be like then—any of us," her father reminded her. "I'm just wondering whether you still want to stay all year or whether you'd like to consider going back to Ridgedale sooner. Maybe next month."

Pamela's lower lip began to tremble. "I want to stay," she whispered. Her mother hugged her, sympathetic tears welling up in her eyes.

Denny looked disgusted. "You're making a big mistake," he declared. He jumped up and ran out of the room.

"Denny's wrong," Pamela said miserably. "I think I've got a chance at school! It's just going to take a little time."

No one said anything, and after a minute Pamela couldn't bear the silence. She got up from the couch and went into the hallway and to her bedroom, which was on the first floor off the foyer.

She closed the door, tears streaming down her face. She had a lot of thinking to do. And she really needed to be alone.

Pamela was so unhappy she could barely concentrate on the Amanda Howard mystery she was reading in the big, comfortable chair in the reading room of the town library. Her eyes kept filling with tears, and the words looked blurry on the page.

"Amanda Howard!" Elizabeth Wakefield said in surprise. "Twice in a single week! You and I must have ESP."

Pamela made an effort to smile, but Elizabeth could tell at once something was seriously wrong.

"Are you OK?" she asked. She pulled a chair over to join Pamela.

Pamela swallowed. "I guess," she said dully. "I've been thinking so hard all day, and everything seems so confused. My father wants me to go back to Ridgedale next month," she concluded.

Elizabeth's heart sank. "You've got to talk him out of it," she said. "Pamela, I know you can make everything work out!"

Pamela shook her head. "I don't think so," she said. "Maybe my father's right. What's the point of trying to stay at Sweet Valley when things are only going to get harder and harder? I don't belong in a normal school, Elizabeth. I belong with people like me. I need special help and special attention." She shook her head, knowing that she was only saying the things her father always said. She sounded as if she had memorized his words.

"I don't believe that," Elizabeth declared. "You just need to keep trying, Pamela. Don't you think that it's important that people in so-called normal schools find out more about so-called special students?"

"What do you mean?" Pamela asked.

"I mean," Elizabeth said, "that the way things are run now at school, all sorts of people are excluded. Unless you're really pretty, or really good at sports, or really smart, no one notices you. And most people aren't any of those things. Think of all the kids you know at school who are bad at sports, and imagine how much they suffer through things like gym class or the Mini Olympics."

Pamela looked thoughtful. "I guess I hadn't really thought about that," she mused. "I know it's been hard for your sister since she sprained her ankle. Is that what you mean?"

Elizabeth shook her head. "Jessica's ankle will be better in a few weeks. I'm thinking more about people like Lois Waller, who are just naturally bad athletes. Or Jimmy Underwood." Jimmy was one of the smallest boys in the sixth grade, and though he was good at schoolwork, he was always chosen last for teams.

Pamela didn't look convinced. "It's one thing to be bad at sports; it's another to be handicapped. I can't even *try* at Sweet Valley Middle School. And I think my father's right. I don't think it's a very healthy place for me. I need to be with people who are like me."

Elizabeth got the feeling nothing she could say was going to change Pamela's mind. But she felt terrible about the decision Pamela had made. And she could hardly wait to get home and find Jessica. If Jessica was going to try and change the format of the Mini Olympics, she was going to have to hurry.

It seemed to be the only chance to change Pamela Jacobson's mind.

"OK, OK," Jessica said, holding the edge of the kitchen counter as she hopped over to the sink. "I can't wait till this stupid ankle gets better," she added, filling a glass with water and taking a sip. "Now tell me again. Pamela's having fits because of the Mini Olympics, so she's planning to drop out of school and go back to Ridgedale."

"Her father wants her to go back as soon as possible," Elizabeth said gloomily. "I feel terrible for her, Jessica. I think you should get her involved in the new Olympics committee."

Jessica looked thoughtful as she sipped the water. "That's not a bad idea," she murmured. "I could probably even make a stronger case if I brought Pamela in with me. That way Mr. Butler and Ms. Ulrich would feel really sorry for her. And they'd be way too embarrassed to say we shouldn't consider her feelings if she's standing right there!"

"You'd better be careful," Elizabeth warned. "Pamela's very sensitive."

"I know that," Jessica said. "Pamela and I have been spending a lot of time together, remember? We sit next to each other on the sidelines in gym."

"Well, I think it's a great idea," Elizabeth said. "When are you supposed to meet with the committee?"

"I called Mr. Butler and asked him if we could hold an emergency meeting tonight. The Mini Olympics are only a week away, and if we're going to change the plans, we've got to get going."

"Good," Elizabeth said. "And I'm going to talk to Mr. Bowman and see if he can help me to get Pamela to work on the special edition of *The*

Sweet Valley Sixers." She pulled her blond hair back from her face with both hands, the way she often did when she was thinking hard about something important. "I think if we can get Pamela involved in things, maybe she'll forget all about Ridgedale."

Jessica didn't comment. She didn't really care where Pamela Jacobson went to school. She just wanted to make sure that she got back control of the Mini Olympics . . . and that she made Lila Fowler realize once and for all who was really in charge!

Eight

Half an hour later Jessica was ringing the door bell of the Jacobsons' house. She hoped she'd be able to get Pamela to come to the meeting with her. It had been so difficult getting over there! There was nothing like a sprained ankle to make getting around a real pain in the neck, she thought ruefully.

At last a tall, dark-haired man whom Jessica assumed must be Pamela's father came to the door. "Hello," he said, looking surprised.

"My name is Jessica Wakefield," Jessica said politely. "Is Pamela home?"

"She's in her room. I'll go call her," Dr. Jacobson said. He looked at her ankle. "I'll bet that hurts," he added. He looked pleased that she had come by to visit.

Jessica nodded. Her eyes brightened as she

caught sight of Denny Jacobson in the front hall. "Hi, Denny," she said warmly, getting into the house with an effort. Denny was one of the cutest boys in the eighth grade, and Jessica, who loved to flirt, suddenly realized there might be advantages to spending more time with Pamela.

Denny smiled at her. "How'd you hurt your ankle?" he asked her.

Jessica didn't think he'd want to hear about the real story, so she decided to tell a white lie. "I fell trying to learn a new Boosters cheer," she said. She knew Denny loved the Boosters.

Unfortunately, Pamela came out just then, so her conversation with Denny was interrupted. "Hi, Jessica," she said, looking even more surprised to see her than Dr. Jacobson. She gave her father a little glance, as if to say, "See? People *do* come by to see me!"

"Pamela, I've come to talk to you about the Mini Olympics," Jessica said, not noticing the startled expression on Denny's face. "Can we sit down somewhere and talk? I really need your advice."

"Sure," Pamela said, wide-eyed. "I don't know what advice I can possibly give you, but I'd be happy to help in any way I can."

Soon Jessica was sitting on the flowered bedspread in Pamela's room. She looked around her, suppressing a sigh. Everything was so tidy—it was as bad as Elizabeth's bedroom! No posters of rock stars, no jumble of clothing on the floor—nothing to make it look comfortable and lived-in, like Jessica's own bedroom. Still, she hadn't come over to inspect the Jacobsons' house. She didn't have much time, and she'd have to go to work on Pamela right away.

"Has Elizabeth talked to you about the Olympics being unfair?" Jessica asked, getting right to the point.

"A little," Pamela said. "But I don't really see what can be done about it. Contests are always unfair. If they were *fair,* they wouldn't be fun."

Jessica frowned. "I don't know about that. Sure, we need to have competition. But doesn't it seem like the events should test different kinds of skills, instead of being all sports? The way Lila has things planned now, people like you—and me—are left out in the cold."

"I didn't know Lila was the one who wanted it that way," Pamela said, surprised.

Jessica looked at her sadly. "It's hard to believe, isn't it? She seems so nice and everything. Believe me, Pam, I've done everything I could to get the committee to be more open-minded." She lowered her voice confidentially. "Just between you and me, it's reaching the point where I think Lila and I are going to have some kind of showdown."

"Wow," Pamela said, her eyes wide.

"But I need your help," Jessica added. "First

of all, I don't know much about special kinds of races and stuff. I figure you guys must have had things like Special Olympics at Ridgedale, right?"

Pamela nodded. "Sure. We had wheelchair races and a whole bunch of contests that anyone could do. You know, things involving brainpower more than strength."

"That's exactly what I was thinking of!" Jessica cried. "We could even have a race where everyone had to use crutches," she added slyly. Jessica was sure by next Friday she'd be good enough on crutches to beat anyone in the sixth grade.

"But do you really think the committee wants to change the Mini Olympics?" Pamela asked. "I thought everyone was happy with things as they were."

"Oh, I guess some people were," Jessica said, ignoring the fact that before she'd sprained her ankle she had been more than happy with the events that had been planned. "But it doesn't matter if people are *happy* with the events, Pamela. People need to learn. They need to realize that not everyone can throw or run really fast or climb ropes." She was getting warmed up to this idea now, forgetting she had taken it from Elizabeth.

"You're really amazing, Jessica," Pamela said, looking excited. "If you can pull this off, and convince them to let you make some changes—"

"Of course I can pull it off!" Jessica declared. She gave Pamela a quick look. "I mean, *we* can pull it off," she amended. "Pamela, I think Mr. Butler and Ms. Ulrich will be much more likely to think about the changes I suggest if you come along with me to the meeting tonight. We have to make them see just how unfair they've been. Will you do it? Will you come with me?"

Pamela thought it over. "I don't see why not," she said. "It sounds like a really good idea, Jessica. If I can help, at least I'll have done *one* useful thing before I leave Sweet Valley Middle School."

Jessica got to her feet with an effort, reaching for her crutches. "Do you think your mom and dad could give us a ride to school? That's where we're supposed to meet the others."

Pamela nodded. "I'm sure one of them can," she said.

"Then let's go," Jessica cried. "I'm sure between the two of us we can convince them to do exactly what we want!"

And in the meantime we can make sure Lila Fowler comes out looking like a real creep, she thought happily. If that wasn't killing two birds with one stone, then what was?

"Well," Mr. Butler said, taking off his glasses and looking at Jessica and Pamela with a frown. "I have to admit you two are pretty convincing. Jessica, why didn't you bring any of this up earlier?"

"I was afraid to," Jessica said. She looked pointedly at Lila. "I was afraid some of the others wouldn't approve."

Lila's pretty face was pinched with anger. "I suppose you mean *me,*" she snapped.

"Lila, please," Ms. Ulrich said. "It seems to me that Jessica and Pamela have a very legitimate point of view. One that we really should consider carefully." She frowned at Lila. "I don't see what good it can do to argue about it."

"But the whole thing is planned," Lila wailed. "We've put so much time into everything, and it's only a week away!"

Jessica cleared her throat. "I used to feel just the way Lila does," she said, shaking her head. "I kept thinking that once we'd gotten the plans under way, it was too late to make any changes. Then I realized that I was just being lazy. I was doing what people always do when they really know—deep down—that things could be changed, but they don't want to go to the trouble of doing anything about it."

"Hear, hear!" Ms. Ulrich cried, striking the side of her chair with the rolled-up copy of the plans for the Mini Olympics.

Lila's face was positively stormy. "Before you sprained your ankle you weren't worried about people with 'special needs,'" she accused Jessica. "I think you just want to make sure *you* still get to be involved!"

"Lila," Mr. Butler said reprovingly, "you can't really mean that—"

"No, Mr. Butler," Jessica said generously, "Lila is partly right. Until I sprained my ankle I didn't realize what it's like trying to do simple things in a world made for people who don't need crutches or wheelchairs. Just one week of trying to get around like this has made me realize how unfair our whole world is." She shook her head, beginning to throw herself into the dramatics of the speech now. Soon she had given a lengthy description of the ways in which handicapped people were treated with prejudice by the rest of so-called normal people. Her performance was so stirring that even Mr. Butler began to look misty-eyed. Only Lila continued to glare at her.

"Well, Jessica, as far as I'm concerned, you have my permission to make any changes you think appropriate," Mr. Butler said. "What do you think, Ms. Ulrich?"

Ms. Ulrich was clasping her hands, beaming. "I think these two girls deserve special recognition," she declared. "Jessica Wakefield, I'm going to see that you get the PTA Civic Service Award! You are an amazing young woman, and you truly deserve a commendation."

Lila pouted, her lower lip sticking out, the whole time Pamela and Jessica arranged with Mr. Butler to meet the next day to begin rethinking the Mini Olympics. She waited until the adults had left the room before telling Jessica what she thought.

"You're a rotten creep," she said furiously. "You knew I was doing a great job getting things in shape! Why did you have to butt in?"

"Lila," Jessica said reprovingly, "you're making it sound like I have *selfish* reasons for wanting these changes. Remember what Ms. Ulrich said. It's the good of the whole school that Pamela and I are thinking of. Isn't that right, Pamela?"

"Right," Pamela said, glancing at the plans for the Mini Olympics with a frown. She wasn't very interested in the argument Lila and Jessica seemed to be having. She was much more interested in the replanning of the Mini Olympics.

In fact, she could hardly wait to begin.

"Steven," Jessica called from the kitchen. "I know you're giving me the silent treatment, but could you come out here and help me carry this? I can't carry a snack and use my crutches at the same time."

"I'm through with not talking to you, anyway," Steven said, coming into the kitchen and taking the bowl of popcorn from her. He popped several pieces into his mouth. "I've been having premonitions again," he added smugly. "Something tells me you've been up to trouble."

"I thought you were through with ESP," Jessica grumbled, following him into the family room.

"It's back. Can I help it?" Steven said.

Jessica decided the best thing to do was to ignore him. Instead of discussing his ESP, she told him about the meeting that evening and the changes she and Pamela were going to make in the Mini Olympics.

"My ESP tells me this has something to do with your ankle," Steven said dryly. "Like the fact that you want to make sure you've still got a shot at winning some events, right?"

Jessica gave him a cold look. "That isn't right at all," she told him. "For your information, Ms. Ulrich happens to think I should get the Civic Service Award from the PTA this year."

Steven groaned. "Civic service, my foot," he said sarcastically. "The only service you care about is Jessica Wakefield service. You couldn't be more selfish if you tried!"

"Be quiet," Jessica snapped. "You don't know anything about it."

Personally, she liked the thought of winning an award for caring so much about others. She thought it was an appropriate end to a long, hard task. And she couldn't wait to get started working on the Mini Olympics again and show Lila Fowler what *real* leadership was all about!

Nine

Jessica could scarcely believe it was four-thirty already. The day had flown by. It was Sunday, and she and Pamela had been hard at work down in the Jacobsons' basement since noon. Papers were strewn all around them, and next to Jessica was a stack of notebooks—records of previous Mini Olympics she had borrowed from Mr. Butler.

"It's really weird that no one ever objected to the way the events have been organized before," Jessica said, thumbing through the records from several years earlier. "You'd think—in all this time—someone else would have come up with some changes like this."

Pamela shook her head. "People don't like change," she said. "That's one reason it's so hard for those of us who just don't fit in. We've got an extra hard time of it—first, convincing people that we even exist. And second, making them want to do something about it."

"Well," Jessica said, "I think you and I are going to go down in Sweet Valley Middle School history, Pamela." She couldn't help thinking secretly that *she* would probably get all the credit. As it was, everyone at school thought she was a saint for helping Pamela. At first, when the news broke that Jessica had convinced Mr. Butler and Ms. Ulrich to let her reorganize the whole day, no one could believe it. But within hours it was all over school. Jessica had decided it was unfair not to have events *everyone* could take part in. The way she and Pamela were going to make it, even little kids—and bad athletes—were going to have a chance.

All through the following day people stopped Jessica in the hallways. Everyone wanted to know when she'd gotten the idea, how she'd ever found the courage to approach Mr. Butler about it, whether it was true she and Lila weren't getting along anymore, and if her sprained ankle had anything to do with the change in the Olympics. Jessica adopted a new humble pose. After all, she was soon to be a famous Good Citizen. She merely smiled graciously, tossed her hair, and admitted she had always thought sports events were unfair. It was just time to do something about it, that was all.

"You're such a natural leader, Jessica," Caroline Pearce said admiringly Friday morning in homeroom. "Maybe you should run for Student Council."

The elections were coming up, and Jessica couldn't help agreeing that Caroline might have a point. Granted, she had never been interested in student government. Elizabeth had been talking about running for treasurer, and Jessica had already told her that she couldn't imagine anything duller than sitting around for hours arguing about things with faculty representatives. Not when she could be having fun with the Boosters, or shopping at the mall! But now she saw things differently. It was fun being the center of attention. *Maybe it wouldn't be so bad running for office after all. Jessica Wakefield, first woman president of the United States,* she thought dreamily, riffling through the pages of the old records.

"I think you're doing a terrific job," Pamela said loyally. Her eyes looked a little moist. "Jessica, I'm so lucky to know you and your sister. School has been so much more fun these past few days!" And her father had noticed the improvement, too, she thought. He had already mentioned several times how glad he was that Jessica had been coming by so often.

Jessica felt alarmed. It was one thing standing up for her and rearranging the Olympics on her behalf—especially since Jessica got to reap most of the benefits. But she certainly didn't want Pamela getting the wrong idea. She seemed like a nice enough girl, but Jessica had always been *very* choosy about her friends. Not like Elizabeth, who seemed to be drawn to serious types like Amy Sutton. Jessica just hoped Pamela didn't start following her around all the time, expecting to be asked to be a Unicorn or something.

But Pamela didn't seem the type, and Jessica relaxed as they turned back to their work. She liked being over at the Jacobsons' house, especially when Denny was around. "Your brother is cute," she told Pamela as they began to put together the master list of new events. "Does he like anyone at school?"

Pamela shook her head. "He doesn't like girls. Especially not me," she confided.

Jessica thought that was too bad. She had been secretly hoping he would notice her, especially since she'd been coming around to the Jacobsons' house so much. Maybe he'd change his mind about girls when he got to know her better. "Janet Howell and Ellen Riteman are coming over to my house tonight," Jessica told Pamela. "I'm going to show them the plans we've made. Do you want to come?"

Pamela shook her head. "No, but thanks for asking me. I promised my father I'd stay in tonight. He thinks I'm overexerting myself."

"OK," Jessica said, gathering her things together. *Just as well,* she thought. This way she could be sure she got all the credit for the long hours she and Pamela had put in these past few days.

"I didn't know you were coming over too," Jessica said to Lila. She couldn't believe Lila could wear the kind of clothes she did. She looked straight out of *Seventeen* magazine in a suede skirt and boots.

"I'm *sorry,*" Lila said coldly, sweeping into the house.

"Let's go up to my room," Jessica said quickly, catching sight of her brother. She didn't want Steven to start having his "ESP" in front of her friends.

"See, we've completely reorganized everything," Jessica said proudly once her door was closed and they were all out of Steven's earshot. "We're still going to have four teams. But no one will be allowed to sign up for a specific event. Say you have someone like Winston Egbert on your team, who you know is a good runner. You can't sign him up for the three-legged race. The way it'll work is this: at the start of each event a representative from each of the teams will draw a slip of paper out of a hat. Each team member has a number. If your number is called, you're in that event. That way it's completely fair—everyone has an equal shot at the event."

"But if you're good at sports, won't you still have an advantage?" Janet demanded.

Jessica shook her head. "We've changed the events so only some of them require physical strength or speed. We're going to have a lot of events that just require brainpower. Puzzle solving, for example. In one event two people from each team will be tied up, and they'll have to untie themselves. We're going to have a bed-making competition—who can make a bed the fastest, including hospital corners. And an egg race. The water events are all going to be changed too. In one you have to use a kickboard to balance a bowl of water, and whoever knocks the least amount of water out wins."

Lila frowned. "It sounds ridiculous," she said. "Who ever heard of a bed-making contest in a Mini Olympics?"

"There are lots of things like that," Jessica said calmly. "Dr. Jacobson is getting us four wheelchairs from the hospital, and we're going to have wheelchair races." She grinned. "We're even going to have an event called Crutch Croquet. A croquet field will be set up, but the contestants have to use crutches—one to walk with, and one to hit the balls."

Lila groaned. "And I suppose you're just going to magically draw the right number so you'll get to be in that event, right?"

Jessica pretended to look hurt. "I don't understand you, Lila," she said. "I'm trying my hardest to change things so it'll be a fun day for everyone, and you're not being a very good sport."

"Good sport!" Lila looked furious. "How can I be a good sport when you're just changing everything so you can still participate?"

"That isn't true," Jessica said hotly. "I happen

to be thinking about Pamela—and other people like her."

"Come on, you two," Ellen said uneasily.

"You should have seen Jessica buttering up Mr. Butler and Ms. Ulrich," Lila complained. "It was sickening! I knew she was only thinking about herself the whole time, and here Ms. Ulrich practically wants to make her a saint. It was awful."

Jessica's eyes flashed. "Lila, you've been really rotten about this whole thing from the minute you were made the assistant chairman! You're not being one bit supportive. I think I've had a good idea, and I'd appreciate it if you'd stand behind me, instead of trying to make me look selfish all the time."

"I can't help it," Lila grumbled. "I want the Olympics to be just like they were last year—and the year before."

Jessica was about to snap back when she saw the expression on Janet's face and stopped. Janet was Lila's cousin, after all. It was hard to tell how they really felt about each other, but Jessica certainly didn't want to hurt her position with the Unicorns. Maybe she'd better not make her feelings so obvious.

Anyway, she knew she had the support of Mr. Butler and Ms. Ulrich. That was all that mattered. It was pretty obvious that Janet and Ellen both thought her ideas were great, and the PTA was going to give her a special commendation for good citizenship. As long as she didn't tell Lila off in front of Janet, it looked to Jessica as if she had emerged from this whole thing a clear victor.

And Lila would be sorry when she saw how well it all came off this Friday. Jessica was sure of that.

"Jessica?" Mrs. Wakefield said, coming into her bedroom. It was nine-thirty, and Jessica was just turning to her math homework. She was tired from the events of the day, but she knew she had to get this done or she'd be in trouble in school.

"What is it, Mom?"

"Your father and I have been talking," Mrs. Wakefield said. "We just wanted to let you know how proud we both are of you. I think what you've done this week takes real courage. It would have been a lot easier just to let things stand as they were. Instead you were willing to make waves. And I think what you've done will make a real difference—not just this year, but in the future too."

Jessica couldn't believe her ears. Her mother never talked to her this way!

"We've been saying as much to your brother and sister too," Mrs. Wakefield said with a smile. "We told both Steven and Elizabeth how proud we feel of you. And I'm sure they feel just the same too."

Jessica couldn't believe her ears. *Boy, Steven must've loved hearing how generous and caring I am!*

she thought. But she didn't have long to wait before she heard her brother and sister's reaction.

"I can't believe what a snow job you've done," Steven said a few minutes later, when Mrs. Wakefield had gone back downstairs. He and Elizabeth came into Jessica's room looking indignant. "You've sure fooled them! I told them that I'm having the strongest signal ever from my ESP—that the minute your ankle is better you're going to forget all about the handicapped. But they didn't believe me."

"Thanks, Steven," Jessica said dryly. "Nothing like a big brother's vote of confidence, that's what I always say." She gave Elizabeth an injured look. "You don't believe me, either, do you?"

Elizabeth didn't know what to say. She wished she believed that Jessica had suddenly turned so good-willed, but she couldn't help thinking there was a grain of truth in what her brother said.

Anyway, Jessica's ankle was getting stronger. She had a feeling they'd find out before too long what the true story behind Jessica's new outlook on things really was.

Ten

"Do you really think you're going to have time to write a story about the changes you and Jessica have made in the Mini Olympics?" Elizabeth asked Pamela. The two girls were sitting together in the library at school. Elizabeth had been explaining the way *The Sweet Valley Sixers* worked. Mr. Bowman would want a final draft of the story by Thursday afternoon so it would be ready for Friday's special edition of the paper.

Pamela looked thoughtful. "I've never written this kind of thing before, but I think I can do it. You know, Elizabeth, isn't it weird how one thing leads to another?"

"What do you mean?" Elizabeth asked curiously.

"Well, I thought about trying to write something for the paper before, but I guess I felt . . . I don't know. It was as if I didn't want to try, because I felt so hurt about being excluded from the things I really *did* want to do. Like the Boosters." Pamela smiled shyly at Elizabeth. "I don't think the kids at Sweet Valley Middle School are the only ones who need to learn about being handicapped, Elizabeth. I think *I* need to learn a little bit myself."

Elizabeth looked surprised. "But . . . what can you possibly have to learn?" she asked her.

Pamela looked as if she were trying to think of the best way to phrase what she wanted to say. "I don't think I've made things terribly easy since I started school here," she admitted. "It's easy enough to put all the blame on my father. And it's true that my dad has been against my attending a normal school from the start. But I think I made things harder too. I had such high expectations!"

"Like what?" Elizabeth demanded.

"Like . . . I don't know, like thinking people were going to come to *me*, asking me to join things, trying to make friends." She shrugged. "I guess I felt special when I came here and I expected people to treat me differently from everyone else. And that's silly. The truth is, I didn't try all that hard to get involved in the things where my handicap wouldn't matter. You tried to get me involved in the paper about half a dozen times," she reminded Elizabeth.

Elizabeth nodded. "That's true. I was beginning to think you just weren't interested."

Pamela shook her head. "But I am interested! I guess it's taken me a while to see that *I'm* the one who has to make sure I fit in here. You and Jessica have really helped me to see that, Elizabeth." She smiled. "Anyway, I'm thrilled to be able to write up what we've done. I don't know how good a job it's going to be, but I can certainly try my best!"

"That's great news," Elizabeth declared. "I don't know about you, Pam, but all this talk about the Mini Olympics is really getting me excited. I can hardly wait for Friday!"

"Me too," Pamela said happily. And from the way her eyes were shining, Elizabeth knew that she was telling the truth.

"What are we going to *do* about him?" Jessica demanded glumly, coming into her sister's room and slamming the door shut behind her. "Liz, I just don't think I can stand it anymore. Steven is driving me crazy!"

"Why? What's he doing now?" Elizabeth asked, looking up from the magazine she was reading.

"He claims he's got a psychic *hunch* about which team is going to win tomorrow. And he's threatening to make a lot of money out of it by setting up bets and charging people for his 'ESP' tips on how to place them."

"At least he's using his business sense," Elizabeth said cheerfully. "Oh, Jess, I wouldn't worry about it," she added, seeing how glum her sister looked. "I'm sure he'll get sick of all this psychic stuff before long."

"Yeah, well, I'm sure sick of it," Jessica muttered. "I don't think I can stand another minute of it, to tell you the truth."

"Is it my imagination," Elizabeth said, "or are you feeling a little bit . . . how should I put it . . . funny?"

Jessica sighed. "Liz, I can't tell you how hard it is, being a famous good citizen. Do you realize Ms. Ulrich actually wants me to go to a lunch with the PTA, to accept this dumb award?"

"Well, that doesn't sound so bad," Elizabeth said. "I would've thought you'd like all the attention—seeing as you're such a famous good citizen and all," she added.

Jessica set her crutches down and wriggled her ankle experimentally. "I think it's getting better," she announced. "It doesn't hurt so much anymore. I can't wait to get rid of these crutches!"

"I still don't see why you mind about the awards lunch," Elizabeth said, closing the magazine and giving Jessica her undivided attention. "You're glad about the way the Olympics have been changed, aren't you?"

"Well, I guess so," Jessica sighed. "I'm just sick of being *good*, that's all." She leaned forward confidentially. "What would you say if I told you the only reason I wanted to change it in the first place was because I couldn't stand being left out?"

Elizabeth pretended to think this over and react with utter horror. "I would never believe it," she declared. "Not in a million years. Not a supremely good citizen like you, Jessica Wakefield!"

Jessica frowned, getting back on her feet with an effort. "It's boring, being a good citizen," she announced, stabilizing herself on her crutches and making her way to the door. "I wouldn't be surprised if I got sick of it pretty soon after the Olympics end," she added.

Elizabeth hid a smile and turned back to her magazine. She wouldn't be surprised either. In fact, the only thing surprising Elizabeth right then was that Jessica had managed to remain a good citizen even for this long!

"Mom," Pamela said shyly, coming into her parents' bedroom. "Can I talk to you for a second?"

"Of course, sweetie," her mother said, looking up at her with a smile. "What's up? Are you excited about the big day tomorrow?"

Pamela nodded. "I really can't wait. It's so nice of Daddy to have gotten us the wheelchairs," she added. She toyed with a hair ribbon, wishing she knew how to say what she wanted to say.

"Are you worried about school?" her mother asked gently.

Pamela nodded, her eyes shining with tears. "I'm starting to like Sweet Valley Middle School," she confessed. "Mom, do you think Daddy might let me stay for the whole year? I really feel like things are starting to get better."

"Oh, Pamela!" her mother exclaimed, hurrying over to engulf her in a warm hug. "Honey, it's really *your* decision. You know your father and I only want what's best for you. If you decide to stay at the middle school, we'll support you one hundred percent."

"But what do you think the right decision is?" Pamela asked anxiously. "I don't want to make a stupid mistake."

Her mother frowned, shaking her head. "I'm not sure I can answer that, Pam. I think you're the only one who knows for sure. I know that it meant a lot to you to try a regular school for a while. And at the same time I've gotten the impression that you've been lonely sometimes. Do you ever miss Ridgedale?"

Pamela thought very hard. "Ridgedale was comfortable," she said at last. "I knew everyone. I knew all the rules. Everyone knew the things I wasn't supposed to do, and there weren't any risks. But . . . I don't know, it wasn't very challenging. I like having to try," she concluded helplessly.

Mrs. Jacobson hugged her again. "I admire you for that," she murmured. "You're a real fighter, honey. You always have been. The doctors say that's what saved your life the two times you had operations on your heart." She held Pamela away for a minute, inspecting her with misty eyes.

"Who knows? Maybe you're fighting for your life in a way this time too. And your father and I never knew it."

"Oh, Mom," Pamela said, throwing her arms around her and feeling tears flow down her cheeks. "I want to stay at Sweet Valley Middle School," she said at last. "I want to try my hardest and see if I can make it."

"Pamela, if anyone can, then you can," her mother told her, her own eyes wet. They were both quiet for a minute, obviously thinking the same thing. "There's still your father to talk to," Mrs. Jacobson said.

The two of them sighed at the thought.

"Maybe tomorrow will help convince him," Pamela said hopefully. "He's coming to the Mini Olympics, isn't he?"

Mrs. Jacobson nodded. "I hope you're right," she said at last. "I don't know why he's been so stubborn about your leaving Ridgedale!"

Pamela didn't know either. She just hoped her father really would leave the decision up to her. Especially now that she felt she knew—for the very first time—where she wanted to be.

Eleven

Jessica couldn't believe it was finally Friday—*the* day. Her worries about being a good citizen completely disappeared as she finished getting dressed, tying a purple ribbon around her ponytail so the Unicorns would know she was remembering them. She was getting a ride from Pamela's mother to the lower school, where the festival was being held. She had to admit Pamela had been a lot of help over the last week. Pamela had lots of good suggestions, and was really good at organizing things. Lila, of course, had been nothing but trouble ever since the Olympics had been changed. But then, Jessica expected as much.

By nine-thirty everyone had arrived at the lower school playground, where team assignments were being made. Mr. Butler read names off from the computer printout made the day before.

The classes had all been divided into four teams. Jessica and Pamela were both on the Blue team. Elizabeth was on the Black team; Ellen Riteman was on the White team; Lila, Janet, and Ken Matthews were all on the Red team. Amy Sutton shrieked with joy when she found out she was on the same team as Elizabeth. Finally the activities got under way. Mr. Butler was the head referee, and he announced the opening events.

The day was divided into three parts. First, there was a talent competition. Each team had to write a song and make up a short skit. These would be judged by Ms. Ulrich and other members of the PTA before lunch. Next, there would be an hour of Brainpower. Tents stocked with games were set up in the fields. There were puzzles, word games, spelling bees, a Password competition, and a junior version of Wheel of Fortune.

Then the final part of the competition would begin. This last phase would involve many of the events Pamela and Jessica had thought up—the wheelchair races, Crutch Croquet, the three-legged race, egg-balancing, pool events, among others.

Jessica was banking on being a contestant in Crutch Croquet. She thought she'd win hands down. Not wanting to leave it to chance, she had already convinced Mr. Butler to let *her* take care of drawing the numbers for her team. After all, she was the chairman. And if she just happened to choose her own number for Crutch Croquet, who would possibly object? Wasn't she a good citizen? No one would accuse a good citizen of rigging the drawing for Crutch Croquet!

The talent part of the Mini Olympics went extremely well. Parents had been invited to come for the whole day and were sitting on the bleachers surrounding the lower school baseball diamond, where each team would perform its skit and song. Jessica thought the Blue team had it all wrapped up. Their skit was called "The Butler Did It" and made fun of Mr. Butler's lower school volleyball coaching. And their song, "The Blue Team Blues," was really catchy. Pamela wrote the lyrics:

Haven't you heard the news?
We've got the Blue Team Blues.
You wake up in the morning and you're
feeling out of sorts; you don't like
dancing and you're tired of sports . . .
What are you going to do?
What are you going to choose?
You know what you've got,
You've got the Blue Team Blues.

None of the other teams came close. The Red team had a really silly skit, which Jessica suspected Lila had made up because it was mostly making fun of a bed-making contest and really didn't make any sense. Their song was silly too. It was called "Dread the Red" and sounded like a Booster cheer. The Black team was pretty good—

their skit definitely showed Elizabeth's touch, as it was all about news reporters trying to find out who was winning the Mini Olympics. Their song, "Black Magic," was cute, with a nice rhyme on "tragic" and "magic." The White team was the worst. Jessica felt embarrassed for them. A fifth grader did a stand-up comic routine instead of a skit, and their song was really a chant without any of the rhymes in the right places.

Jessica and Pamela were practically delirious when Mr. Butler announced that the Blue team had won first place in the talent competition. That gave them one hundred points. The Black team came in second, with ninety points; the Red team came in third, with eighty; and the poor White team trailed with seventy.

"I'll bet you're feeling pretty proud of yourself," Lila hissed to Jessica as they went in for lunch.

Jessica could barely hide a smile. She knew her team was going to win—she just knew it!

After lunch the competition really got serious. Jessica was heartbroken when the Red team won the Brainpower section. The Blues came in third, the Whites came in second, and the Blacks lost—making the score 170 for the Reds and Blues, and the Whites and Blacks tied with 160 points each. It was looking like a much closer race than anyone had expected. The third set of events was going to prove crucial.

Everyone was getting very excited. Parents were cheering loudly, and so were teachers. Jessica could hardly wait for Crutch Croquet. She just knew she could win first place for her team.

The first event of the ten scheduled races was the bed-making contest. To Jessica's joy, Lila was chosen as the entrant for the Red team. She was pitted against Patty DuVal from the White team, Caroline Pearce from the Blue team, and Elizabeth from the Black team. Four mattresses were set up under the flagpole. Each entrant was given a set of sheets, and when Mr. Butler called "Go!" each raced to make her bed. Jessica screamed "Go, Caroline!" so loudly that her throat hurt. Pamela was waving her arms with excitement. Caroline came in second, after Elizabeth. But Lila—and the Red team—had placed last! Jessica was secretly overjoyed. She knew she would never forget the blistering look Lila gave her as she tromped off the field, still holding her top sheet in her hands.

"I'm not surprised you won," Jessica said to her sister. "You get enough practice at home." Elizabeth always made her bed neatly, whereas for Jessica it was at best a once-a-week activity.

The next two races took place in the pool. The first was the kickboard-and-bowl-of-water race Jessica had described to Ellen and Janet. This time the Red team won. The Red and the Blue teams were really neck and neck. The Blue team, however, won the third event. This race was Pamela's idea.

Called the Water Walk, it required that each contestant get in the water and walk across the shallow end of the pool, balancing an egg on a spoon at the same time. Whoever got to the other end first, without dropping the egg, won.

The fourth event was called Untie Yourself. Two entrants from each team were chosen, tied together with twine, and timed as they tried to free themselves. The Red team managed a close win, though their members caused a great deal of laughter—one was tiny Sally Strong, a fifth grader, and the other was Aaron Dallas, one of the biggest sixth graders. The spectators seemed to especially enjoy this event.

Next came the three-legged race, the water-balloon throw, and Pineapple Bowling. Only two events were left: the wheelchair race and Crutch Croquet. Crutch Croquet was the next event, and to her delight Jessica drew her own number out of the hat. "Wow—isn't that weird," she said loudly. "I drew myself!"

"What a coincidence," Lila said in a scathing voice.

"You're just mad because we're beating you," Jessica said.

"You are not. We're ahead by two points," Lila snapped.

"Well, you won't be for long. I'm going to cream you," Jessica said, hurrying off on her crutches to the starting point for the race.

She had to admit she had a real advantage.

None of the other four contestants was used to crutches, whereas she was a real pro. She had raced around the course in less than ten minutes, knocking the croquet ball expertly with her crutch. She wondered if anyone could tell she'd been practicing. In any case, the Blue team won the croquet game easily. The second-place ribbon went to a member of the Red team named Kady Johnson. Lila looked fit to be tied.

"OK," Mr. Butler said, putting his hand up. "We've come to the very last event of the day. Let me just read the scores aloud so you all know where you stand. The Red team and the Blue team are tied for first place—they each have two hundred fifty points. In third place we have the Black team, with two hundred ten points. And in last place the White team, with two hundred points. Now, the final event is a very special event. Each contestant has to steer a wheelchair down the course, and whoever wins this one determines who wins the entire Mini Olympics. Are you all sure you understand?"

Everyone understood. Wild cheers accompanied the drawing of each name. The Red team went crazy when Ken Matthews was called. He was small, but a really good athlete; they were sure now they were going to win. The Black team drew Timmy Peterson, a skinny, sweet-faced lower schooler; the White team drew a fifth grader named Lisa Geiger; and the Blue team drew Pamela Jacobson. A hush seemed to fall across the whole field.

"Good luck," Jessica said solemnly to Pamela, shaking her hand.

"Aw, we've got it all wrapped up," Ken Matthews said in disgust. "It isn't fair—letting me take on two little kids and a . . ." He looked at Pamela, then away again.

"It's OK," Pamela said evenly. "I don't think it's unfair, Ken." She winked at Jessica. "In fact, I wouldn't get overconfident if I were you." She walked over to her wheelchair and sat down, giving Mr. Butler a big smile.

"And they're off!" Mr. Butler called a minute later. The crowd went into a screaming frenzy as they cheered on the four contestants.

Racing in a wheelchair proved to be much harder than anyone could have guessed. Pamela was ahead of Ken by about a foot; and Jessica was screaming "Go, Pam!" so loudly, she thought she'd never be able to talk normally again. Someone else was yelling louder than she was, though. It was Dr. Jacobson. He was cheering so loudly from the bleachers, the whole field seemed to reverberate.

Suddenly it looked as if Ken was closing in on Pamela. He was! He was closer . . . right up next to her . . . and then passing her. Jessica's heart pounded. Ken was inching past Pamela, inching past her . . . and then it happened! He caught his hand in the spokes, lost his momentum, and fell behind as his wheelchair veered to the right. The crowd went wild. Pamela crossed the finish line first. She had won the race *and* the Mini Olympics for the Blue team!

The frenzy that accompanied Mr. Butler's whistle was unbelievable. It was impossible to tell who was hugging whom. Everyone was jumping up and down and shouting, and Jessica thought her ribs would break as her teammates surrounded her.

She knew she had to give special thanks to Pamela, and she made her way through the crowd. Dr. Jacobson lifted Pamela up on his shoulders. He was beaming, and next to him, Denny was patting Pamela's leg over and over again, saying "Way to go. I knew you could do it all along!"

Jessica hoped she wasn't all sweaty from Crutch Croquet. Denny was *so* cute.

"Pamela, you were wonderful!" she said, smiling up at her.

Pamela's eyes were shining. "Wasn't it fun, Jessica? Thank you so much for letting me show I could do it. Daddy, tell Jessica what you just told me."

Dr. Jacobson grinned. "I guess I got a little bit of an education today too," he said to Jessica. "When I saw Pamela out there I realized I'd been trying too hard to protect her." He shook his head. Especially when it's obvious she can take perfectly good care of herself."

"Daddy says I can stay at Sweet Valley!" Pamela told Jessica, her smile glowing.

"That's great," Jessica said, shifting a little on her crutches. "I've got to go now," she added, catching sight of Ms. Ulrich talking to Mr. Butler.

She was sure they were talking about what a model citizen she was. And she supposed she would just have to go over and let them tell her what a great job she had done!

All in all, it had been a wonderful day. And Jessica knew it had meant a lot to Pamela too. The best thing, Jessica thought, was that everything had turned out just the way it was supposed to.

Namely, that Lila Fowler and her team had lost. And Jessica Wakefield had gotten all the glory!

Twelve

"Look!" Jessica exclaimed triumphantly, walking into the sunny kitchen and displaying her empty hands. "No crutches!"

Steven and Elizabeth were eating pancakes. It was Saturday morning, over a week since the Mini Olympics. Elizabeth's eyes widened. "I can't believe it," she said. "Doesn't it hurt to put weight on it?"

Jessica looked scornful. "Not much. It was only a little sprain," she added, opening the refrigerator and studying the contents.

"*Only* a little sprain?" Steven mimicked. "Here we've heard about nothing else for weeks. Didn't I tell you, Liz? The minute her ankle gets better she forgets all about being handicapped."

Jessica made a face, still inspecting the refrigerator's contents. "Don't be a baby, Steven. I don't need to be injured to be—what was it Ms. Ulrich said at the PTA lunch—'an unusually considerate young lady.'"

"You'd need a head injury to mistake Jessica Wakefield for a 'considerate young lady,'" Steven retorted.

"Jessica," Mrs. Wakefield said, returning to the kitchen, "are you going to take something out of there, or are you just cooling off the kitchen?"

Elizabeth giggled. She loved it when her mother teased Jessica.

Elizabeth couldn't help thinking that everything had turned out extremely well. Pamela Jacobson was like a new person since the Mini Olympics. Her story had been included in *The Sweet Valley Sixers,* and everyone agreed it was great—very moving and well written. Pamela was even talking about joining the newspaper staff.

She had definitely decided to stay at Sweet Valley Middle School, and after her heroic victory the week before, she had her father's complete support. It was apparent how much the day had meant to Pamela. She was really beginning to come out of her shell, and had even made suggestions in gym class for games that she could participate in. Now that Pamela was learning to speak up for herself and her needs, Elizabeth knew she would be fine.

"What are you guys doing today?" Jessica asked, bringing a box of cereal over to the table and pouring herself a generous bowl.

Steven closed his eyes, pretending to concentrate. "Wait!" he said. "I'm seeing something . . . it's faint now, but it's getting clearer and clearer . . . it's . . . it's—"

"I can't stand it," Jessica said, rolling her eyes. "Steven, do you have any idea how stupid you look right now?"

"I'm seeing what your day looks like," Steven told her. "Something tells me it's going to be unbelievably dull."

Jessica gave him a lofty look. The truth was, she was going to spend the day with Ellen Riteman. They were going to watch the new music video her older brother had just bought, and then meet Janet and Lila at the mall. Jessica and Lila were still a little cool to each other, but Jessica had been thinking it was almost time for a truce. After all, she could stand to be generous. *She* was the one who had come out of the Mini Olympics with all the glory!

"Your ESP isn't working any more," she told Steven, pouring milk over her cereal. "You couldn't be further from the truth!"

Elizabeth had to agree. That was one thing about her twin sister. Wherever she was going and whatever she had planned, one thing was certain—Jessica's day sure wasn't going to be dull!

"I don't think I like the girls Toy Car has been using in their videos," Ellen complained. She and

Jessica were in the living room of the Ritemans' spacious stucco home.

Jessica loved the Ritemans' house. It was older than most of the homes in Sweet Valley, and it had high ceilings, large fireplaces, interesting little nooks and crannies. And the Ritemans had a great living room with wooden floors, perfect for practicing dance steps.

"What are you going to buy at the mall this afternoon?" Ellen asked. "I wouldn't mind a pair of earrings like the lead singer in Toy Car has. They're really cool."

"Your mother would die," Jessica said with a smile. She was about to add something when they heard footsteps approaching from the foyer.

"Hey, Ellen," Ellen's little brother Mark said, his face streaked with tears. "I need your help."

"What is it?" Ellen said, not sounding overjoyed. Mark was nine years old, and it seemed like he had a new crisis every minute.

"It's Leon. Whiskers ate him," Mark said sorrowfully.

"Who," Jessica said in a low voice, "is Leon?"

"Leon is Mark's pet parakeet," Ellen said.

"*Was,*" Mark said. "I hate that dumb cat! I just left Leon for one second while I was looking for his birdseed, and Whiskers jumped right in the box and—"

"Try not to think about it," Ellen said, getting to her feet and patting him comfortingly on the shoulder. "What are you doing with that?" she added, peering into the cardboard box.

"I want to bury him," Mark told her. "Will you help me?"

Ellen rolled her eyes at Jessica. "Come on, Mark. You don't want to bury him. Let's just take the box outside and—"

Mark started to cry in earnest. "I want to bury him!" he cried.

"Oh, all right," Ellen said crossly. "Come on, Jessica. It looks like we're going to have to perform a funeral before we can go to the mall." She turned off the VCR, and she and Jessica trailed Mark out to the backyard.

For the next ten minutes they followed Mark around while he selected the perfect resting place for Leon's remains. Ellen, who had her father's gardening shovel in her hands, started to look annoyed. "This is really morbid, Mark," she said at last. "If we're going to do it, let's just do it. Jessica and I have to go someplace."

"OK," Mark said at last, stopping under a tree at the end of the yard. "Right here!"

Ellen came over and handed him the shovel. "You dig," she instructed.

"OK," Mark said. "But first I have to read the service."

"Oh, boy," Ellen said, throwing herself down on the grass. Jessica sat down too.

Mark read out loud from something he had

written on a piece of paper in his pocket. He described Leon in great detail—where Mark had bought him, how much he cost, what kind of food he liked. "It's too bad Leon died before he learned how to speak," Mark added, looking mournful.

Jessica and Ellen clapped respectfully. "Now why don't you start digging," Ellen instructed.

Mark started to dig. "I think I hit a root or something," he said a minute later. "The shovel is sticking."

"Just keep digging—it'll be OK," Ellen said, not really paying attention.

"Maybe it's a rock," Mark said. "The shovel is sticking against something. Listen—it's making a funny noise."

Jessica looked interested. She had heard Elizabeth describe something like this from one of the Amanda Howard mysteries she was always reading. "Let me try," she said, taking the shovel from Mark.

Sure enough, the shovel struck something hard. It sounded like metal. Jessica dug deeper, and after several minutes of exertion, she had cleared away enough dirt to see the edge of something made of gray metal.

"It's a box!" Mark cried, peering down into the hole.

Ellen and Jessica exchanged glances. "Back up, Mark," Ellen said. "Let me see it."

Soon she and Jessica had lifted the small

metal box from the hole and brushed the dirt off it. It wasn't very large, but it was heavy, and securely locked.

"Wow!" Mark said. "It's buried treasure!"

Jessica gave Ellen a significant look. "Mark," Ellen said, "I think we should bury Leon now. We'll worry about this later." She put the box down beside her.

Mark eyed it uneasily. "We can wait to bury Leon," he told her. "I want to open the box."

"Later," Ellen said, "Come on, Mark. We can't interrupt a *funeral*."

Jessica knew she and Ellen were thinking the same thing. They wanted to find out what was inside that box. And they wanted to make sure whatever it was, they kept it away from Mark.

Especially if it really *did* turn out to be buried treasure!

SWEET VALLEY TWINS

Buried Treasure

Written by
Jamie Suzanne

Created by
FRANCINE PASCAL

A BANTAM BOOK®
TORONTO • NEW YORK • LONDON • SYDNEY • AUCKLAND

To Page McBrier

One

Jessica Wakefield looked at the small, unopened metal box and shook her head in disbelief. The last place she ever thought she'd discover buried treasure was in Ellen Riteman's backyard.

It had been a cloudless Saturday afternoon in Sweet Valley. Jessica and Ellen were in the living room of Ellen's house watching a music video. Ellen's little brother Mark appeared in the doorway with tears in his eyes. Whiskers, the Ritemans' cat, had attacked Mark's pet parakeet Leon, and Mark wanted to have a funeral for the bird. He'd convinced Ellen and Jessica to help bury him.

After locating a spot in the backyard under a tree, Mark started to dig. A few minutes later, the shovel hit something.

"I think I hit a root," he said.

"Let me try," Jessica said. "It feels like metal." She then scooped away some more dirt.

Mark peered down at the hole. "It's a box!" he said.

Jessica got down on her hands and knees, and she and Ellen scraped away the rest of the dirt by hand. Very carefully, they lifted a small, rusty metal box out of the hole. It was sealed with a sturdy lock.

"Wow!" said Mark. "It's buried treasure!"

Jessica and Ellen exchanged glances. "Back up, Mark," said Ellen. "Let me see."

As the girls stood staring at the box, Jessica knew that she and Ellen were thinking the very same thing. The last thing they wanted to do was share the contents of the box with Mark. Still, Jessica couldn't help feeling excited. A real buried treasure! She was dying to find out what was inside.

"I want to open it," said Mark. "We can wait to bury Leon." He eagerly tugged at the lock.

"Later," said Ellen. "Come on, Mark. We can't interrupt a *funeral*." As she pulled Mark back, he stumbled over Jessica's foot.

Jessica let out a scream. "Ow! Watch it," she said. "That's my bad ankle." Several weeks earlier she'd injured her ankle. Although she had completely recovered, she still worried about hurting it again.

"Sorry," mumbled Mark.

Jessica knelt down and rubbed her foot. Maybe this was just the distraction she and Ellen needed to get rid of Mark. She caught Ellen's eye and then moaned dramatically. "Ohhhh," she cried. "I think you hurt it again."

Mark shifted his weight and stared at the ground. "I didn't do it on purpose," he said.

Jessica stretched out her arms. "Help me into the house," she groaned. "I need to put my foot up."

"But what about the buried treasure?" said Mark. "And Leon?"

"Don't you have any manners, Mark?" said

Ellen. "You practically crippled Jessica, and all you're worried about is that stupid box." She bent down and wrapped Jessica's left arm around her shoulder. Mark stood very still. "The least you can do is help me," Ellen snapped. Mark quickly wedged himself under Jessica's right arm.

Ellen and Mark escorted Jessica into the house and helped her onto the living room sofa. "Now what?" said Mark.

Jessica fluttered her eyelids. "I think I'm going to need my crutches," she said. "They're somewhere in my closet. At home."

"But I hardly touched you," Mark said.

Jessica sat up and rubbed her foot. "The doctor told me to be extremely careful."

Ellen nodded in agreement. "Mark, since *you* hurt Jessica's ankle, *you* should go get her crutches."

Mark glanced at the backyard. "But what about—"

"Mark!" said Ellen. "If Jessica has to go back to the doctor, you're going to be in really big trouble."

Mark narrowed his eyes suspiciously. "OK," he said. "But you'd better not open that treasure until I get back."

"Don't worry about it," said Ellen. She and Jessica watched Mark rush out the front door and disappear down the street.

Jessica immediately hopped up and ran toward the back door. "Hurry," she said. "We don't have much time."

Several blocks away at the Wakefield house, Jessica's identical twin sister, Elizabeth, was sitting in her bedroom with her best friend, Amy Sutton. Although it was hard to tell Jessica and Elizabeth apart, the two girls couldn't have been more different. Jessica lived for the moment and was interested in clothes, movie stars, and boys. Elizabeth, who was four minutes older, preferred books to music videos. She liked to spend her spare time working on *The Sweet Valley Sixers,* the sixth-grade newspaper she'd helped start.

Elizabeth glanced over at Amy, who was sitting cross-legged on the floor, bent over a large sheet of poster board. "How about this?" said Amy. "Your Money's in Good Hands with Elizabeth. Vote E. W. for Student Council Treasurer."

Elizabeth shook her head. "No," she said. "Too flat." The two thought quietly for a moment. "Wake Up with Wakefield?" Elizabeth suggested.

"What's that have to do with being student council treasurer?" inquired Amy.

Elizabeth shrugged. "I was trying to come up with something catchy," she said.

"Don't worry," said Amy. "Anything's better than Don't Despair with Peter."

Elizabeth laughed. Peter DeHaven was her competition for student council treasurer, and even Elizabeth, who was usually kind to everyone, had to admit that Peter was a little odd.

Amy jumped up and hiked her pantlegs way above her ankles. "Ms. Wyler, I think you made a mistake on my math grade," she whined. "I should have gotten a ninety-eight, not a ninety-seven." She moved her eyebrows up and down like Peter.

Elizabeth couldn't stop laughing. "Amy, that's not nice," she said. Just then the doorbell rang.

"You'd better watch it," said Elizabeth. "That's probably Peter right now." She and Amy ran downstairs and opened the front door. It was Mark, Ellen Riteman's little brother.

"What's wrong?" asked Elizabeth.

Mark was out of breath. "Jessica needs her crutches," he said. "I accidentally bumped her ankle. It wasn't my fault."

"Her bad ankle?" said Elizabeth. "Oh, no!"

"Is she in pain?" said Amy.

"I'm not sure," said Mark. "I think she'll be OK. I hardly even touched it."

Elizabeth relaxed a little. Jessica *did* have a tendency to be a bit overdramatic. Maybe she was just playing it safe by using her crutches.

Mark stared anxiously upstairs. "Can I get the crutches now?"

Elizabeth led Mark to Jessica's room. "Good luck finding them," she said, opening the door. Jessica's room was in its usual condition. Clothes were flung everywhere, and several dirty dishes and a crumpled cookie carton littered the floor.

"Wow," said Mark. "I thought *my* room was bad."

"Let's try the closet first," Elizabeth said. She dug around for several minutes. "What's this?" she said. She pulled out a large cardboard box and peered inside. "I don't believe it." The box was filled with chocolate bars. "She hasn't sold a single one," she said.

The chocolate bars had been distributed to everyone in the sixth grade nearly a month earlier. They were supposed to be selling them to earn money for a class trip to Disneyland.

"How's she going to sell all those chocolate bars by next week?" said Amy. It was her job to collect the money every week and give it to Ms. Wyler, their homeroom teacher, for safekeeping.

"Beats me," said Elizabeth. She began rummaging through the closet again. "Hmm," she said finally, "they're definitely not in here."

Mark looked around the room. "How about under the bed?" he said. He ran over, pulled up the bedspread, and pushed several pairs of mismatched socks aside. He popped his head back out and grinned. "I found them," he said. He dragged the crutches out and quickly hurried down the stairs. " 'Bye," he called.

Elizabeth looked anxiously down the stairs. "Mark?" she said. Mark stopped. "Would you tell Jessica to call me?" she asked. Mark nodded. Elizabeth turned to Amy. "I hope she's OK."

As soon as Mark had left the Ritemans', Jessica and Ellen carried the metal box up to Ellen's bedroom and locked the door. Now they were both bent over the rusty lock. "Hurry up," Jessica was saying. "He'll be back soon."

Ellen pursed her lips and continued to saw at the lock with the hacksaw she'd found in her father's toolbox. "It's almost . . ." She tugged on the lock. "There!" The lock fell to the floor.

"Shh," said Jessica. She cocked her head and listened for a moment. She wasn't sure if she'd heard someone. "Check the door," she whispered.

Ellen peered out into the hall. "All clear," she said. She closed the door and locked it again.

"Good," said Jessica. Very carefully she opened the lid. She blew away a layer of dust and dirt.

"I can't believe it!" whispered Ellen. On the top of the chest were a large pile of yellowed twenty-dollar bills, still in their wrappers. Underneath were two old photographs and some faded letters.

Jessica snatched the money off the top of the pile and began counting.

"How much?" said Ellen.

Jessica couldn't believe their luck. "Two hundred dollars," she said. She tossed the money in the air. "We're rich!" she cried. She and Ellen began giggling and hopping all over the bedroom.

"We're rich," screamed Ellen. "Rich, rich, rich." She danced around some more and then ran back over to the box. "Let's see what else there is," she said. "Maybe we can find out where the money came from."

Trembling with excitement, the two girls removed the photographs and the letters. The photos were of a man and a woman. The woman was quite beautiful. She had dark hair and dark eyes and was seated in a carved wooden chair. Covering her shoulders was a silky-looking flowered shawl. Her dress draped gracefully to the floor. The portrait of the man was completely different. He had on coveralls and stood stiffly beside a tractor. His large hands clutched a garden rake.

"Let's open the letters," said Ellen.

Jessica removed the first one. It was written in neat old-fashioned script. The date on it was March 13, 1928. "Dearest Jane," it began. "Yes, I do remember the first time we met. You were about eight years old, I was nine. Your father had brought you along to meet the new gardener, and I was outside our cottage, playing with some old bricks. Your father helped you out of the car and introduced us. I thought you were the most beautiful girl I'd ever met. I still do." Jessica and Ellen sighed.

"How romantic," said Ellen. "Love letters."

Jessica read on. "Dearest, I know that your father has opposed our marriage and is pressuring you to marry the 'more suitable' young man he has chosen. Please, Jane, I beg you to reconsider. What could be greater than our love?"

Jessica folded the letter. "Is that it?" said Ellen.

Jessica picked up the next letter. "Maybe this one has her answer." She quickly skimmed the contents. "Uh-oh. Not good. He tells Jane that if she loves him, she should have the courage to stand up to her father. He's proud to be the gardener's son."

"I think she should marry the man she loves," said Ellen. "Don't you?"

Jessica nodded and read through another letter. "Wow," she said. "Now he's begging her to elope with him. The two hundred dollars is money he'd saved so they could run away."

"This is like a movie or something," said Ellen with a sigh.

"I know," said Jessica. She read the last letter and frowned. "Listen to this," she said. "Dearest Jane, I wish only to spend the rest of my life with you. Meet me tonight at six o'clock under the grape arbor. I won't ask again, my dear Jane. No matter what happens, I will always love you. William."

Ellen stared at the letters. "Is that the last one?" she said.

Jessica nodded sadly. "Poor William. What do you think happened? Did she marry him or not?"

"I think if she'd married him, she would've spent the money," said Ellen.

"Maybe," said Jessica. "Or maybe she was rich enough not to need his money." They both sat quietly for a moment, still wrapped up in the story.

Jessica picked up the two hundred dollars. "What do you think we should do with the money?" she asked.

"If we tell everyone what we found, then we have to share the money with Mark," said Ellen.

"Right," said Jessica.

"Or," said Ellen, "Mom would want me to find out who lived in this house before us and see if it's their money."

Jessica and Ellen stared at the pile of bills. They each knew what the other was thinking. Jessica cleared her throat. "We *could* just tell Mark that all we found were some love letters," said Jessica.

"That's true," said Ellen. "He doesn't have to know about the money. We'll just divide it. A hundred dollars apiece."

Jessica quickly split it up. "Swear you won't say a word to anyone."

Ellen put her hand on her heart. "I swear." She stuffed her share into her back pocket and unlocked the bedroom door. "Come on," she said. "Help me take this box back to the yard before Mark sees us."

* * *

When Mark hurried into the Ritemans' living room, he was relieved to see Jessica sitting right where he'd left her. "Here are your crutches," he said, thrusting them into her hand. "Elizabeth says you should call her."

"Thanks," said Jessica. She delicately hoisted herself off the couch. "She's probably worried, right?"

Mark nodded, then quickly looked around the living room. "Where's Ellen?"

"Out in the yard," Jessica said. "She's trying to get that rusty old lock off the chest."

Mark ran out the back door. He saw Ellen look up and wave at him. "Perfect timing," she said. "I just broke the lock."

Jessica hobbled over. "Oh, good. Let's see what's inside."

The girls opened the chest and riffled through the contents. "Hmm," Ellen said. "Just some old letters and photographs."

Mark pushed his sister aside. "Let me see," he said. He peered inside the chest.

"I guess it wasn't buried treasure after all," said Jessica.

Mark looked at Jessica and then at Ellen. "Are you sure you guys didn't open this while I was gone?" he asked suspiciously.

"Of course not," said Ellen. "What do you think we are?" She swung her gaze over to the tiny cardboard box still sitting on the lawn. "What about Leon?" she said. "Are we going to bury him or not?"

"I guess so," Mark muttered. He sighed and picked up the shovel. Even though everything looked perfectly normal, something still didn't seem right to Mark. He suspected that somehow he'd been tricked.

Two

Elizabeth paced her bedroom floor nervously. What had happened to Jessica? Suppose she was on her way to the hospital or something? When she'd phoned Ellen Riteman's house, there had been no answer. Just then Elizabeth heard the front door slam.

"I'm home," called Jessica.

Elizabeth raced to the top of the stairs. "Jessica! Are you OK?"

Jessica looked up in surprise. "Of course. Why?" She suddenly remembered her ankle and that she'd forgotten to call Elizabeth. "Oh, Lizzie," she said, clapping her hand over her mouth. "I forgot, didn't I?"

"I've been so worried all afternoon," said Elizabeth.

Jessica threw down a pile of packages. "False alarm," she said apologetically. "I feel fine now."

"Thank goodness," said Elizabeth. She was so relieved that she sat down with a thud on the stairs.

Jessica stared at Elizabeth. "You really *were* worried, weren't you?" she said.

"Of course I was!" Elizabeth answered. "If I didn't hear from you in another five minutes, I was going to call Mom. Or maybe even the police. No one even knew where you were."

Jessica sat down beside Elizabeth and gave her a hug. "I'm really, really sorry, Lizzie," she said. "My ankle just felt so much better that Ellen and I decided to go to the mall."

Elizabeth smiled and shook her head. "So I noticed," she said, staring at the pile of packages. She playfully punched Jessica's arm. "I thought you didn't have any money."

"I don't," Jessica replied quickly. "These things belong to Ellen. I was just carrying them for her."

Elizabeth looked doubtfully at her sister. "I don't get it," she said. "Why did you bring them here?"

"You won't believe what happened today," Jessica said, changing the subject abruptly. She grabbed one of the bags and pulled out a brand-new Walkman. "I found this at the mall!"

"Jess!" exclaimed Elizabeth. "You actually *found* it? That's incredible." Several weeks earlier Jessica had carelessly left her own Walkman outside and it had been ruined in the rain. She'd been begging her parents for a new one ever since, but they weren't about to give her a second chance.

"It is incredible," Jessica said, shaking her head. "But it's true. It was sitting in this shopping bag on a bench outside Sweet Valley Fashions."

"You're so lucky," said Elizabeth. "It's exactly like the one you ruined too."

"I know," said Jessica. She stood up abruptly and began to gather the packages. "Thanks for worrying about me," she said. "I'm sorry I forgot."

"That's OK," Elizabeth replied with a grin. "I

should have known my goofy sister would forget completely about calling."

"The student council elections are just two weeks away. Who are you going to vote for as president?" Julie Porter asked Elizabeth in school on Monday. They were in their weekly cooking class, making mini-pizzas.

Elizabeth sprinkled flour on the dough and picked up a rolling pin. "That's easy," she said. "Olivia Davidson."

"Me too," said Julie.

Olivia was sure to win the election, Elizabeth thought. She didn't even know who Olivia was running against.

"Have you written your speech?" Julie asked.

"Not yet," said Elizabeth. "Amy's my campaign manager, so she wants to help with it."

"Aren't you nervous about giving a speech in front of the whole school?" said Julie. "I would be."

Elizabeth nodded. "I'm trying not to think about that part." She finished rolling out the dough. "Now what?"

Julie looked at the recipe. "We spread on the tomato sauce."

A commotion broke out on the other side of the room. "Gross!" someone shouted. The entire class rushed over to see what was going on. Peter DeHaven was staring sadly at his pizza. His partner, Charlie Cashman, pointed an accusing finger at him. "He's putting dead flies in there," he said.

"I am not!" shouted Peter.

Mrs. Gerhart, the cooking teacher, clucked her

tongue. "Shame on you both," she said. She clapped her hands loudly. "Everyone, please! Back to your cooking stations."

Elizabeth could hear a lot of snickering as she and Julie returned to their tomato sauce.

"I feel sorry for Peter," said Julie. "Everyone always picks on him."

"I know," said Elizabeth. She thought about how she and Amy had made fun of him the other day, and felt guilty. "He's not that bad, really," she added. "Just weird, that's all."

As soon as the bell rang, Elizabeth and Julie made their way down the hall to homeroom. Ms. Wyler's classroom was at the other end of Sweet Valley Middle School, and with only five minutes between classes, Elizabeth always felt as if she were rushing. She heard someone calling her name and turned. "Hi, Amy," she said.

"How's this?" said Amy. "Elizabeth Makes Cents. Get it? Cents, sense."

"That's cute," said Julie.

Amy beamed. "It came to me while I was doing my math homework."

"That makes *sense,*" said Elizabeth with a grin.

All three girls groaned. They walked into the classroom just as the bell rang.

Ms. Wyler waited for everyone's attention. "Before we begin, is there any candy money this week?" she said.

Elizabeth was surprised to see Jessica raise her hand. As usual, Jessica was sitting on the other side of the room with Lila Fowler and Ellen Riteman. All three girls belonged to the exclusive Unicorn Club.

The Unicorns knew they were popular, and always acted like they were special.

Jessica waved a five-dollar bill. "Here, Ms. Wyler," she said.

Elizabeth frowned. She hadn't remembered Jessica going out to sell candy since Saturday.

Now Ellen Riteman was waving a five-dollar bill. "Might as well turn mine in also," Ellen said.

Ms. Wyler looked really pleased. "Good work," she told the class. She handed the money to Amy. "Please make sure this goes into my locker sometime today," she said.

Ms. Wyler opened her math book. "Class, let's turn to page fifty-nine."

As Ms. Wyler droned on, Elizabeth absent-mindedly scribbled on her notebook. ELIZABETH MAKES CENTS, she wrote. She smiled and then filled in the letters with red Magic Marker. Amy had come up with a great idea, she thought. It would be a perfect campaign slogan.

After school Amy came over to the Wakefields' to help make posters. "We'll put them up tomorrow," she said. "Maybe we can even get Ken to help." Ken Matthews was Amy's "sort-of" boyfriend. Amy carefully sprinkled a little red glitter across Elizabeth's name. "This'll help your name stand out," she said.

Elizabeth hesitated. It seemed so flashy to her. "Are you sure?" she asked.

"How else are people going to notice it?" Amy asked.

"I guess," said Elizabeth. She looked at the

small clock on the dresser. "It's six o'clock already. Can you stay for dinner?"

"Sure," said Amy. "Let me call my mom."

Elizabeth ran downstairs to ask her mother's permission. As she burst through the door, she said, "What smells so good?"

"Frozen pizza," her mother replied. Mrs. Wakefield worked part-time as an interior designer, and didn't always have time to cook.

"Oh, no," said Elizabeth.

"What's the matter?" her mother asked. "I thought you liked pizza."

Jessica wandered in from the living room, wearing Elizabeth's favorite pair of sweatpants. "We made pizza in cooking class today!" she said.

The twins' older brother, Steven, stuck his head in the door. "And *we* had pizza for lunch," he added. Steven was a freshman at Sweet Valley High.

Mrs. Wakefield sighed. "Maybe we should go to the Dairi Burger." The Dairi Burger was the popular hamburger stand where the high-schoolers hung out. Sometimes the Unicorns held their meetings there.

"Can Amy come?" asked Elizabeth.

"Fine with me," said Mrs. Wakefield. "Your father won't be home until late."

Mr. Wakefield was a successful lawyer in Sweet Valley. Sometimes his busy practice kept him at his office until late in the evening.

Ten minutes later Mrs. Wakefield pulled into the Dairi Burger with Elizabeth, Amy, Jessica, and Steven. Outside, a group of teenagers were sitting on a car hood, talking.

Steven immediately noticed several people he knew, and realized he didn't want to be seen with his mother. "I'll go in and order, Mom," he said. "We can eat in the car."

"I thought we'd eat inside," said Mrs. Wakefield. She opened the door and got out of the car.

Jessica could tell what Steven was thinking. "That's OK, Mom," she said. "Steven and I can go and bring the stuff back to the car."

Mrs. Wakefield headed for the door. "Don't be silly," she said, and walked purposefully into the Dairi Burger.

Jessica looked at Steven and shrugged. No point in making a big deal about it now.

Soon they were all sitting in a booth near the front. Steven ordered two Dairi-Deluxe burgers and two orders of fries. He finished everything in less than five minutes. "Charity?" he asked, reaching for Elizabeth's fries.

Elizabeth slapped his arm. "I'm not finished yet," she said.

He turned to Jessica, who put her hand protectively over her fries. "Don't be such a pig, Steven," she said.

"Steven," said Mrs. Wakefield, "if you chewed more slowly, you'd fill yourself up a little better."

Steven noisily slurped the last of his milk shake. "OK, OK," he said. "I'll try."

A group of people entered the restaurant. "Look," whispered Amy. "It's Peter DeHaven."

Elizabeth stared at Peter. There was definitely something a little strange about him. Maybe it was his clothes. Most of the time he wore the same pair of brown pants with a matching belt and sturdy oxford shoes. Tonight, though, there was something different about him.

Amy giggled. "Look at his pants."

Elizabeth leaned forward. Instead of the usual pants and belt, Peter had on a new pair of brightly colored surfer shorts. He looked pretty silly in them, especially since he still had on his brown socks and brown shoes. Most embarrassing of all, though, was the price tag that dangled from his back pocket.

Jessica looked at Elizabeth and Amy and rolled her eyes. Steven snorted into his milk shake container and tried not to laugh. Jessica began to snicker loudly.

Peter looked over at her and realized that all eyes were on him. He shifted his weight uncomfortably and stared glumly at the floor. One of the high school boys walked slowly past. As soon as he reached Peter, he tugged sharply on the price tag and then kept walking. Peter spun around angrily. "Hey!" he shouted. His hand groped across his back pocket and felt the tag. His face flushed crimson.

This was too much for Steven. He began to laugh so loudly that now people turned to stare at him.

Peter looked at Steven, horrified. Then, without another word, he ran outside.

"Real nice, Steven," Elizabeth said.

Steven made a face. "I couldn't help it," he said.

Jessica was still laughing. "Wait'll they hear about this at school."

"Poor Peter," said Amy.

Jessica and Steven howled. Mrs. Wakefield looked at them with disapproval.

Elizabeth shook her head. "You know, he's

really not that bad," she said. "If he'd do something with his hair and get someone to help him with his clothes, he'd almost be cute."

Jessica giggled. "A Peter DeHaven makeover," she said.

Steven moved Elizabeth's french fries closer to him. "Why should you care?" he said. "Do you have a crush on him?"

Elizabeth wrinkled her nose. "Gross." She snatched her plate of french fries back. "It was only a comment, Steven," she said. "Don't get the wrong idea."

"Jessica, will you hurry up?" Elizabeth called. "We're going to be late." It was the next morning, and Elizabeth stood at the bottom of the stairs and waited. If she hadn't needed Jessica's help carrying her campaign posters, she would have left already.

Jessica appeared at the head of the stairs. "How does this look?" she asked. Jessica was wearing a pair of pink stretch pants with a baggy, purple sweatshirt. Purple was the Unicorns' favorite color.

"Good," said Elizabeth. "Where'd you get the sweatshirt?"

"I traded with Lila," Jessica said. "You know that sweatshirt with the lion on it that I never wear?"

"That's *my* sweatshirt!" said Elizabeth. "I got it from Aunt Shirley for Christmas last year, remember?"

"But you never wear it," said Jessica. "You don't even like it. You said it's too bright."

"But that doesn't mean I said you could give it away," said Elizabeth.

"I'm sorry, Lizzie. I didn't think you'd care. Want me to get it back?"

Elizabeth laughed. "You're too much," she said. "I'm probably the only girl in Sweet Valley whose sister trades away her clothes."

"I'll talk to Lila this afternoon," said Jessica.

Elizabeth shook her head. "OK, but now let's just go," she cried.

Later, as Elizabeth hurried down the hall, she noticed that several people had already put their campaign posters up. Olivia Davidson's were beautiful. Olivia was an excellent artist, and she'd obviously done all the work herself.

Elizabeth spotted Peter DeHaven hanging a poster near the cafeteria. She decided to take a quick peek. "Hi, Peter," she said.

Peter jumped when he heard his name. "Oh, hi, Elizabeth," he said, turning around. He pointed to his poster. "What do you think?"

Elizabeth stared at his poster. *It looks boring,* she thought. It looked as though he'd scribbled his campaign motto on with pencil. She was glad Amy had talked her into using a little glitter. "Uh, it's nice," she said. She stared uncomfortably at the floor. "Peter! You got new shoes!"

Peter looked at his feet. "Yup."

Elizabeth had never seen him in a pair of sneakers. They looked a little strange with his brown socks. What if he asked her what she thought of *them*? "Gotta go," she blurted.

Elizabeth bolted down the hall toward English class. She made it to her seat just as the bell rang.

* * *

By lunchtime everyone in the sixth grade was talking about Peter's new sneakers. At the exclusive Unicorns' table Lila Fowler said, "Do you believe it? And with brown socks too. Barf-o."

"Peter's such a nerd," said Ellen. All the Unicorns laughed.

Jessica couldn't wait to tell everyone what had happened at the Dairi Burger. After the Unicorns heard the story, they all shrieked with laughter. "Jessica, that's hysterical," said Janet Howell. "I wish I'd been there." Janet was the eighth-grade president of the Unicorns, and her approval really mattered to Jessica.

"Thanks," Jessica replied modestly.

Janet clapped her hand over her mouth. "I just had the greatest idea," she said. "Listen." The Unicorns huddled close together. As Janet whispered, the others nodded in agreement. Janet finished whispering and straightened back up. "So we'll do it tomorrow, OK?" she said. The Unicorns nodded in unison. "OK," they chorused.

Jessica grinned and smiled to herself. This was the meanest trick they'd played in a long time. She couldn't wait.

Three

Ms. Wyler looked around the class and frowned. "Amy, may I speak to you for a minute?" she said. As Amy got up from her chair, she leaned over and whispered to Elizabeth, "Ken says he'll help us with the posters after school."

"Great," said Elizabeth.

Ms. Wyler waited until Amy was beside her desk. "Amy," she said quietly, "did you remember to add yesterday's candy money to the amount in my locker?"

Amy clapped her hand over her mouth. "Sorry, Ms. Wyler," she said. "It's still in my desk. I'll get it."

Ms. Wyler put her hand on Amy's arm. "No, wait," she said. She lowered her voice. "I'm afraid the money for the class trip has disappeared."

Amy gasped. "But it was there last week," she said. "I took the key from your desk and put the money into the cigar box in your locker myself."

Ms. Wyler looked distressed. "And when I went to get something from my locker this morning, the cigar box was missing. I don't know what we're going to do. I've looked everywhere."

Amy felt terrible. She was supposed to be in

charge of that money, and now it was gone. What were people going to think?

Ms. Wyler got the class's attention. "I have some very bad news," she said. "It appears that someone has taken our candy money."

Everyone began talking at once. "You mean somebody stole it?" shouted Charlie Cashman.

"I'm afraid so," said Ms. Wyler. "The last time Amy or I remember seeing that cigar box was last week."

Amy stood uncomfortably next to Ms. Wyler's desk.

"But what about our trip to Disneyland?" asked Julie.

Ms. Wyler sighed. "Unless the money is returned, there won't be a trip to Disneyland."

The class reacted angrily. "I sold a lot of candy bars for that trip," said Ken Matthews. Other people in the class nodded in agreement.

"We've been planning for months," said Pamela Jacobson.

"Yeah!" said Jerry McAllister. "What sort of creep would take our money?"

Ms. Wyler shook her head. "I'm really sorry about this," she said. "I thought the money would be safe in my locker." Everyone continued to grumble.

Elizabeth shot a sidelong glance at Jessica. She looked as upset as the rest of the class.

As soon as the bell rang, Elizabeth saw Jessica and Ellen Riteman huddle together and start whispering. Elizabeth wondered what the big secret was. When Elizabeth walked over to her, Jessica quickly straightened up. "What do you want?"

"Nothing," said Elizabeth. She stood there with

her arms wrapped around her books, not sure what to say next. "Isn't it awful about the class money?"

Lila Fowler came over. "Ooooh, Ellen," she said, "where'd you get those earrings? They're the same ones the lead singer in Toy Car has, right?"

Ellen pulled her hair away from her ears to reveal an elegant pair of gold-and-silver dangles. She looked at Jessica. "Uh, my aunt gave them to me," she said.

Lila shrieked. "You're so lucky. They're gorgeous. I saw a pair like them at the mall. They cost a fortune."

Ellen looked at Jessica again and smiled. "Georgio Fabio designed them," she said.

"Let's go, Ellen," said Jessica sharply.

Elizabeth watched as the two girls left the classroom and hurried down the hall. They were being so secretive all of a sudden. What were they up to? A horrible thought occurred to Elizabeth. It was a little strange that Ellen and Jessica had both shown up with expensive new things around the same time that the class money had disappeared. First Jessica's Walkman and now Ellen's earrings . . . Elizabeth shuddered at the thought. But she knew it was impossible. Jessica did some crazy things, but she would never steal. Elizabeth dismissed the thought from her mind.

"Earth to Elizabeth, earth to Elizabeth," said Amy, cupping her hands like a megaphone.

Elizabeth snapped back to reality. "Sorry," she said. "I was thinking about something."

"Time to put up posters," said Amy.

Ken was standing next to Amy. "I heard you needed someone tall," he said. He and Amy laughed. Ken was one of the shortest boys in the sixth grade.

Elizabeth followed Ken and Amy to the cafeteria entrance. "OK," said Amy. "I think this'd be a good place to put a poster."

Elizabeth nodded. While she and Amy held the poster in place, Ken taped it to the wall. "That's so rotten about the candy money," he said.

"I know," Elizabeth replied. Ken deserved to be angry, she thought. He'd probably sold more candy bars than anyone in the class.

Ken turned to Amy. "When's the last time you saw the money?"

"Last Tuesday," said Amy.

Ken tore off a piece of tape. "So sometime between last Tuesday and this Tuesday the money disappeared, right?" he said.

"Last Tuesday and today," said Amy. "I hadn't added yesterday's money yet."

"Why not?" said Ken.

Amy narrowed her eyes. "Because I forgot, Ken," she said. "Do you mind?"

Ken finished putting up the last piece of tape. "I just can't believe that a big cigar box like that could disappear," he mused. "First of all, it was inside Ms. Wyler's locker, inside the faculty room. No one's even allowed in there unless they have permission."

Amy fidgeted uncomfortably. What was Ken trying to say?

Elizabeth cut in. "But everyone knows that Ms. Wyler keeps her locker key in her desk," she said. "Anybody could have taken it and gone into the faculty room when no one was watching."

"I guess," said Ken.

Amy grabbed the stack of posters. "C'mon," she said. "We've got a lot more to do." She stomped into the cafeteria.

"What's wrong?" said Ken, catching up to her.

"Nothing," said Amy. "Just forget it."

Outside the Ritemans' house Mark was riding his bike in a large circle and thinking. Something strange was going on. It had been several days since he, Ellen, and Jessica had found the metal box, but the girls still hadn't told anyone. And when Mark started to tell his parents about it during dinner, Ellen had kicked him under the table. Later she said he shouldn't say anything because she and Jessica didn't want to return the letters to their original owner. He couldn't understand it. What was the big deal about a bunch of letters?

Mark stared down the street. Ellen wouldn't be home from school for another fifteen minutes. Maybe now was his chance. He parked his bike and ran inside. Seconds later he was sitting on Ellen's closet floor, examining the chest.

Inside, everything looked the same. He picked up the packet of letters, took out the first one, and started to read. Yuck. This was the one that Jessica and Ellen had gotten all mushy over.

He stuck the letter back in its envelope and opened the next one. It was hard to decipher the handwriting, but he managed to get through it. By the fourth letter Mark started to feel discouraged. Who cared about this mushy stuff anyway? "Dearest Jane," the letter began, "I've saved this money so that we might begin a life together. I know $200 may not seem like a fortune to you, but it's enough to get started."

Mark stopped. What two hundred dollars? He hadn't remembered this letter. Could this be what Jessica and Ellen were hiding? The front door slammed.

"Anybody home?" called Ellen.

Mark squeezed himself into the back of the closet. If Ellen caught him in there, he'd be dead. He could hear her running up the stairs.

"I guess nobody's here" she said. She walked into her room and slammed the door.

"Guess not," said someone else.

Mark strained his ears. It was Jessica!

"How much were those earrings?" said Jessica.

"Fifty-five dollars," said Ellen. "Thanks for reminding me. I can't let Mom see them or she'll ask where I got them."

Mark heard the dresser drawer open and close. "There!" said Ellen. "She'll never find them."

"Do you think we should have told Mark about the money?" said Jessica.

"Why should we?" said Ellen. "He's just a little kid."

Mark stiffened. He hated to be called a little kid.

"But he's pretty good about keeping secrets," said Jessica.

"He is not!" said Ellen. "Remember when I told him that I liked Travis Taylor and he swore not to tell anyone?"

"Oh, yeah," said Jessica. "You're right. Besides, we'd have to share the money with him."

Inside the closet, Mark shifted quietly. So there *had* been something more than love letters. He knew it!

"I'm going to change," Ellen said.

Mark panicked. He squeezed himself as far back as he could and held his breath. The closet door opened.

"What should I wear?" said Ellen. She rattled a few hangers.

"How about your white-and-purple sweatshirt?" said Jessica.

Mark stared at Ellen's knees.

"Nah," said Ellen. "I don't like it anymore." She pulled something else off a hanger. "Where are my tennis shoes?" she said suddenly.

Mark felt Ellen's hand grope across the closet floor. She grabbed his sneaker and stopped. Mark's heart started to pound.

"What's this?" cried Ellen. She thrust back the hangers and revealed Mark.

"Oh, hi, Ellen," he said.

Ellen grabbed his shirt and pulled him out of the closet. "You little brat," she screamed. "You were spying on us, weren't you?"

Mark squirmed uncomfortably. "Let go of me," he said.

Ellen noticed the open treasure chest. "What have you been doing in here?" she said.

"You're ripping my shirt," said Mark. "Leave me alone."

Jessica gasped. "He must've heard what we were talking about."

Ellen tightened her grip. "What did you hear?"

Mark was getting angry. "Nothing," he said. "Just leave me alone."

"Not till you tell us what you heard," she said.

Mark howled. He'd had enough. "Everything!" he yelled, wriggling free of his sister's grip. "And if you don't give me my share of the money, I'm telling Mom."

Ellen stopped. "You wouldn't dare," she said slowly.

Mark didn't move. "Wanna bet?"

Ellen looked at Jessica. "Mark Riteman," she said, "if you say one word, you're going to regret it for the rest of your life."

Mark clenched his fists. "Then give me my money," he said.

Ellen tried to grab Mark's shirt again. "Help," he screamed. He ran down the hall to his room, slammed the door shut and locked it.

Ellen chased him, then pounded her fists on the door. "Open up!" she shouted.

"Never," said Mark. "Not in a million years. Give me my money or I'm telling Mom."

Ellen stopped pounding. "You'll be sorry," she said. "Just wait." She stormed back to her room and slammed the door. "Don't worry, Jessica," she said breathlessly. "I have a plan."

Elizabeth walked slowly up the street. With Ken's help, putting up the posters had taken no time at all. She was home from school much earlier than she'd expected. Suddenly she remembered her campaign speech. Maybe this would be a good time to work on it, even though Amy wasn't around.

Speeches were scheduled for next week, and she still had no idea what she was going to say.

Elizabeth walked in the front door. "Anybody home?" she called.

There was no answer.

She took a can of soda from the refrigerator and then sat down at her desk. She turned on her typewriter and inserted a clean sheet of paper. "My name is Elizabeth Wakefield, and I'm running for student council treasurer," she typed. "I think you should vote for me . . ." She glanced at Jessica's room and frowned. Had Jessica remembered to get back her sweatshirt? She finished the sentence. ". . . because I'll do a good job." Elizabeth made a face. "Yuck," she said. "Too stuck-up." She backed up the typewriter carriage and put *x*'s over what she'd just typed. She stared at Jessica's room again. Maybe she'd better go look for the sweatshirt.

She stood up, walked into Jessica's room, and opened her closet door. On the floor were the shopping bags Jessica had carried home the other day. Several brand-new pairs of knee socks and a pale orange-and-purple sweatshirt hung out of one of the bags. Why hadn't Ellen come to pick them up? Elizabeth pushed the clothes aside and was surprised to discover Jessica's box of candy bars on the floor of the closet. Hadn't Jessica given Ms. Wyler five dollars? Why was the box still full? Elizabeth picked up the shopping bags again. She gasped. Inside one of the bags was a receipt for a Walkman.

Suddenly Elizabeth felt sick. Jessica hadn't found the Walkman at all. Where had Jessica gotten the money? With an anxious sigh she flopped down on Jessica's bed. *Stay calm,* she told herself. Jessica wasn't the type of person who would steal. There had to be a good explanation for all this.

Elizabeth took a deep breath and tried to think clearly. There must be an easy solution. Maybe she didn't hear it correctly. She'd simply ask Jessica again where she'd gotten the Walkman. She was sure Jessica would tell her the truth. Elizabeth stared down at a pile of clothes next to the bed. She retrieved her sweatshirt from the bottom of the heap. Elizabeth tried to smile as she headed back to her room. By tonight this whole thing would be all straightened out, she told herself.

Four

Mark leaned his ear against the door and listened. Ellen had finally stopped pounding. Down the hall there was some whispering and then silence. What were Jessica and Ellen up to?

Mark stared at his clock. How long would he have to wait before he could exit his room safely?

"See you later, Ellen," he heard Jessica say. The front door slammed shut. He wished his mother would hurry up and come home.

At last Mark heard a car pull into the driveway. "Hi, kids," called Mrs. Riteman.

Mark slowly opened his door. The coast was clear. He raced down the stairs. "Mom," he yelled. "Me and Ellen and Jessica found buried treasure in the backyard. Ellen and Jessica said there was nothing in it but there was two hundred dollars and they took it." He took a deep breath.

Mrs. Riteman blinked. "What?" she said.

Mark pointed upstairs. "Ellen stole two hundred dollars," he repeated. "Go ask her."

Mrs. Riteman put down her bag and marched upstairs.

Ellen was lying on her bed, reading the latest issue of *Today's Stars*.

"Young lady," said Mrs. Riteman, "what's this I hear about some stolen money?"

Ellen sat up and put down her magazine. "What stolen money?" she said innocently.

Mrs. Riteman looked at Mark.

Mark ran to Ellen's closet. "I'll show you, Mom," he said. He pulled back Ellen's clothes. There was nothing on the floor except a few pairs of shoes. Mark frantically dug through Ellen's things, trying to find the metal box.

Ellen lifted one eyebrow and yawned. "Mark," she said, "*what* are you talking about?"

Mark remembered the earrings. "She's hiding some earrings in her dresser," he said. He pulled open the top drawer and started pulling out Ellen's socks and underwear.

"Do you mind?" said Ellen.

"Mom," Mark wailed. "No fair. Ellen found two hundred dollars, and now she's pretending she didn't."

Mrs. Riteman looked at Ellen and frowned. "Did you find some money and not tell anyone?" she said.

Ellen's eyes opened wide. "No, Mom," she said. "I swear. I don't even know what Mark is talking about."

Mark slammed his fist down on Ellen's dresser. "You are a liar," he said. "Liar, liar, liar."

Ellen calmly picked up her magazine. "Mom," she whispered, "I think Mark's been eating too much sugar. It's causing him to hallucinate."

Mark clenched his fists. "Ha, ha. Very funny," he said. "Just you wait. I'm going to find that treasure box and prove it."

Ellen lay back on her pillow and opened her magazine. "Whatever you say, Mark," she said.

Elizabeth rubbed her eyes and leaned over her typewriter. "So I hope you all vote for me for student council treasurer," she typed. "Thank you." She pulled the speech out of her typewriter and read it once more. It was OK, but nothing special. Tomorrow she'd show it to Amy.

Elizabeth heard the front door slam and then saw Jessica hurry by carrying a box of some kind. She waited several minutes and knocked on Jessica's door.

"Come in," Jessica shouted. She was listening to her Walkman and trying on the clothes Elizabeth had seen in the shopping bags earlier. "Do you think these shoes go with these socks?" she asked Elizabeth.

Elizabeth stared at the clothes. "Aren't those Ellen's?" she said.

Jessica looked surprised. "She told me I could borrow them anytime," she answered quickly.

Elizabeth wasn't sure how to begin. "How do you like your new Walkman?" she finally blurted.

"Fine," said Jessica. She turned abruptly. "What about these shoes instead?" she said.

Elizabeth sighed. Jessica wasn't making this easy. "Jess," she said, "are you going to tell me where you really got that Walkman?"

Jessica swallowed. "I *did* tell you," she said. "I found it on a bench at the mall."

"Are you absolutely, positively sure?" said Elizabeth.

"Of course," said Jessica. "Why?"

"How come you turned in five dollars for candy money and you still haven't sold any of your candy bars?" Elizabeth demanded.

Jessica bit her lower lip. "Uh, because Ellen and I were working together," she said. "We sold all of Ellen's candy bars first, and then we were going to sell mine."

Elizabeth stared at her sister.

"Really," said Jessica. She looked away.

Elizabeth couldn't tell whether Jessica was lying or not. She seemed to have a pretty good excuse about the candy bars, but still . . . "Jess," said Elizabeth, "I found a receipt for the Walkman in one of those shopping bags."

"I know," said Jessica, not missing a beat. "I found the *whole* package on the bench. Someone else bought the Walkman."

"If you're making any of this up, there's still time to return the money," said Elizabeth.

"What money?" said Jessica, looking confused.

Elizabeth began to wonder if she'd made a mistake. She looked at Jessica's Walkman.

"I told you," said Jessica firmly. "I found the Walkman at the mall. On a bench outside Casey's Place." She did a pirouette in the mirror. "I think these shoes look better," she said. She turned up the volume on her Walkman and began to dance. "I love this song," she shouted.

Elizabeth frowned. "Where did you say you found the Walkman?" she said.

Jessica pulled off her headphones and stopped dancing. "Uh, Casey's?"

Elizabeth shook her head. "Oh, Jess! Last time you said Sweet Valley Fashions."

Jessica grimaced. "I did?" She looked wildly around the room. "Oh, well, maybe that was it," she said. "I can't remember." She stuck her headphones on and started dancing again.

Elizabeth sighed. Why wasn't she telling the truth? Even if she hadn't taken the class money, she still couldn't explain the Walkman. And what about the way she and Ellen were so secretive? And Ellen's new earrings! Elizabeth walked back to her room and sat down on her bed. She had never been more disappointed in her twin in all their twelve years.

The next morning the Unicorns were huddled in a little group outside the cafeteria, whispering and giggling. Jessica hurried over to join them. "It's about time," said Janet.

"I overslept," said Jessica. "Sorry."

Janet lowered her voice. "OK, everyone," she said. "Follow me to the girls' bathroom."

The Unicorns looked like a small flock of purple birds as they tiptoed into the bathroom. Five minutes later they emerged wearing white sneakers with brown socks.

Bruce Patman, the cutest boy in the seventh grade, was the first to notice. "Look," he said. "Peter DeHaven clones."

"It's the new fad," said Janet with a straight face. "What do you think?"

"I think it's ugly," said Bruce. He started to laugh.

Janet stuck her nose in the air. "You obviously have no taste, Bruce Patman," she said. She strode up the hall, with the rest of the Unicorns giggling and trailing behind her.

At the other end of the hall Amy was taping up one of Elizabeth's posters which had fallen down. She saw the Unicorns walking toward her wearing smug expressions and brown socks. "That's not very nice," she said.

Janet stopped. "What do you mean?" she replied.

Amy's eyes narrowed. "It's not nice to make fun of people," she said.

Janet turned to the other Unicorns. "We're not making fun of anyone, are we?" she said. "We're starting a new trend." The Unicorns nodded in agreement.

Amy didn't answer.

Janet paused. "I hear your class isn't going to Disneyland," she said. "Someone stole the money."

Amy glared at Janet. "That's right," she said.

"Weren't you in charge of the money?" said Janet.

Amy swallowed. "Yes."

Janet nodded. "Hmm." She started up the hall again, the rest of the Unicorns trailing behind her. "Bye-bye, Amy."

Amy watched the Unicorns file past. She felt a tight little knot in her stomach. How dare Janet imply that she took the money! She glanced around the hall. Several people were standing in little groups, whispering. Amy was sure they were talking about her.

Just then Ken walked over. "Hi, Amy," he said.

"Hi," Amy mumbled.

"I was wondering," said Ken. "Do you think maybe you could have accidentally taken the cigar box out of Ms. Wyler's locker and left it on the floor or something?"

Amy stared at Ken.

"What's the matter?" he said.

Amy felt tears start to well up in her eyes. "Nothing," she blurted. She ran into the bathroom and locked herself into a stall. She couldn't believe that anyone would actually think she'd taken the class money.

Elizabeth was sitting in Mr. Bowman's room with Julie Porter, when Caroline Pearce burst through the door. Caroline had the biggest mouth in Sweet Valley and wrote the gossip column for *The Sweet Valley Sixers*.

"Did you see what the Unicorns are wearing?" she said. "Brown socks and white sneakers." She giggled.

Julie looked at Elizabeth. "Good thing Mr. Bowman doesn't wear sneakers," she said. Mr. Bowman was Elizabeth's English teacher. His taste in clothing wasn't so good either.

"Did Peter see the Unicorns?" asked Elizabeth.

Caroline nodded. "He pretended not to notice," she said. "But I could tell his feelings were hurt."

A typical Unicorn prank, thought Elizabeth. The tricks they played was one reason she never liked the Unicorns.

Mr. Bowman strolled over. "How's the election issue coming?" he asked.

"Good," said Elizabeth. "We decided to print the speeches and pass out the paper the day before the election."

"Great idea," said Mr. Bowman. "Keep up the good work." The class bell rang, and Elizabeth slipped into her seat. "OK, class," said Mr. Bowman. "Let's get out a clean sheet of paper and do a little free association."

Everyone except Elizabeth groaned. This was one of Mr. Bowman's favorite exercises. Everyone was supposed to take a blank sheet of paper and write whatever came to mind.

Elizabeth smiled. She was probably the only person in the class who enjoyed doing the free association exercise. She started to write furiously. To her surprise, the first thing she wrote was "Is Jessica a thief?" She stared at her paper uncomfortably. She realized that she needed to talk to someone about this huge problem, but who? She wrote a few more sentences. "Dear Abby. I am a twelve-year-old girl. I have a twin sister who I think stole some money, but every time I try to bring it up, she changes the subject. What should I do? I don't want to accuse her unless I'm really positive. Signed, Confused." Elizabeth sighed.

"OK, class," said Mr. Bowman. "Time's up."

Elizabeth crumpled her sheet into a little ball. She felt a tiny bit better now.

Elizabeth had promised to show Amy her speech that day during lunch. The two girls found an empty table in the corner of the cafeteria and sat down. Amy seemed quieter than usual. "Anything wrong?" asked Elizabeth.

Amy poked at her Sloppy Joe. "I never know how to eat these things," she said. She tried to take a bite, but the filling oozed out onto her plate. "See what I mean?" she said. She threw the sandwich down in disgust.

"Amy, what's really the matter?" said Elizabeth.

Amy stared unhappily at her sandwich. "Everyone thinks I stole the money," she blurted. "Even Ken." Her eyes began to fill with tears again.

Elizabeth put her arm around Amy's shoulder. "Amy!" she said. "Don't say that. It's not true!" She glanced uncomfortably across the room. Jessica and Ellen were whispering again. Elizabeth watched Ellen's earrings bob up and down. She took a deep breath. "Amy," she said, "if someone you knew was really broke, and then suddenly that person and her friend showed up with some brand-new things and no explanation, what would you think?"

Amy wiped her eyes. "I'd wonder where they got the money," she said.

Elizabeth hurried on. "And what would you do if you asked them about it and they ignored you?"

"I'd think they were hiding something," said Amy. She stared across the room and saw Jessica and Ellen huddled together. Suddenly it hit her. She knew exactly who Elizabeth was talking about.

Elizabeth watched Amy's face grow angry. She realized she may have made a horrible mistake. What if Jessica and Ellen were innocent? "Amy, I'm not really sure—" she began.

But it was too late. Amy jumped up.

Elizabeth panicked. "Where are you going?" she said.

Amy silently walked past the Unicorns' table. She could feel her cheeks burning. She stalked over to the next table and put her tray down beside Caroline Pearce's. "You'll never believe what I just found out," she said.

Caroline leaned over. "Tell me," she said.

Five

Jessica sat on the steps outside the front entrance to the school. Everyone was heading home, but Jessica had promised Ellen she would wait for her. Jessica reached into her book bag and pulled out her Walkman. As she listened to a Johnny Buck song, she swayed to the beat of the music and tapped her foot.

She noticed Charlie Cashman and Jerry McAllister walk slowly by. Charlie whispered something to Jerry and then they both stared at her. Jessica looked down at her outfit. Was there something wrong?

Sophia Rizzo and Nora Mercandy hurried past. When they saw Jessica, they both gave her dirty looks.

Jessica squirmed uncomfortably. Why was everyone looking at her? She was relieved when she saw Ellen's cheerful wave. She jumped up and pulled off her headphones. "It took you long enough," she said.

Ellen handed Jessica her earrings. "Here," she said. "Take these before I forget."

Jessica stuck the earrings into her book bag.

She'd been keeping them at her house with the metal box. "Do you notice anything funny about me?" Jessica asked.

Ellen stared at her. "No. Why?"

"Because everyone's looking at me," said Jessica. She glanced up and noticed two seventh-grade boys pointing.

Ellen glared at the boys. "Why don't you take a picture?" she shouted. "It lasts longer." The boys moved away abruptly. Ellen turned to Jessica. "Want to go to the mall?" she said. "This school is giving me the creeps."

The two girls slowly headed downtown to the Valley Mall. It was another perfectly cloudless California afternoon so they decided to walk. In the distance the girls could see the Pacific Ocean shimmering brightly.

"How much money do you have left?" Ellen asked as they strolled along.

"Not too much," Jessica replied. "The Walkman, class trip money, knee socks, and sweatshirt almost cleaned me out. I think I'm going to try and save the rest."

"Me too," said Ellen. They walked together in silence. "Mark is really mad at me," Ellen finally said. "You may have to keep the chest and earrings at your house forever."

Jessica sighed. "Maybe we should have told him," she said.

"It's too late now," said Ellen. She avoided Jessica's gaze.

"I was thinking," said Jessica. "What happens if the owner of the chest comes to get it? What do we say?"

"I don't know," said Ellen. She stared ahead at the mall. "No one will claim it," she said at last. "It's been so long."

That night Jessica had a lot of trouble sleeping. She dreamed that the girl in the picture had come back to get the chest. In the dream the girl was an old woman now. "You stole my money," the woman said, glaring at Jessica.

"No!" cried Jessica. She tried to run away, but the old woman grabbed her arm and held on with her long, bony fingers. "Help!" screamed Jessica. She awoke with a start and stared at her arm. What if something like that were to really happen?

Jessica got out of bed, tiptoed down to the kitchen, and poured herself a glass of orange juice. As she sat quietly in the eerie darkness, she had another terrible thought: What if the woman were buried in Ellen's backyard next to the chest! That would make them both grave robbers! They could be arrested and thrown into jail. Jessica gulped down the rest of her juice and hurried back to bed. She slid as far as she could under the covers. Outside, a tree branch tapped steadily against the side of the house. Jessica pulled her pillow over her ears and squeezed her eyes shut. It took her a long time to fall asleep.

By the next day practically everyone in Sweet Valley Middle School was talking about Jessica and Ellen. "I heard," whispered Brooke Dennis to Nora Mercandy, "that Ellen didn't really get those earrings from her aunt. They were one of a kind, and Caroline Pearce said the jeweler sold them to a young girl. For cash."

Nora nodded knowingly. "And what about Jessica's new Walkman? Do you really believe she found it?"

Brooke shook her head. "Poor Elizabeth," she said. "She must feel so embarrassed."

"If I were her, I'd say something, wouldn't you?" added Nora.

Brooke nodded. "Shh. Here she comes."

Elizabeth walked stiffly past. She felt terrible. Thanks to Caroline's big mouth the whole school was talking about Jessica and Ellen. Elizabeth knew that if she hadn't said anything to Amy, this never would have happened. She saw Peter DeHaven slide by and disappear into the boys' bathroom. Today he was wearing his white sneakers with thick cotton socks, the kind that everyone wore.

Elizabeth hurried on to history class. When she took her seat next to Amy, her friend didn't even look up.

After class Amy bolted for the door. "Amy, wait," Elizabeth called.

Amy stopped and turned around. "What do you want?" she said.

Elizabeth could feel her face turning red. "I have to talk to you," she said.

"I'm busy," said Amy.

Elizabeth ran after her. "I don't appreciate the fact that you're spreading rumors about certain people," she said.

Amy's face was set in a hard line. "They're not rumors," she replied.

Elizabeth grimaced. "We don't know that for sure," she said. "And besides, I told you something in confidence and you blabbed it to Caroline Pearce. You may as well have printed it in the newspaper."

Amy shrugged. "So?"

"So I thought I could trust you," said Elizabeth.

"Stop trying to defend your sister," Amy said loudly. "She's a thief and you know it."

Elizabeth's cheeks burned. Several people walking by slowed down to listen. "You can't prove it," she said helplessly. She ran over to her locker and threw it open. She rummaged through her things, pretending to look for something.

"Are you OK?" said someone behind her. It was Ken.

Elizabeth turned her head so Ken wouldn't see the tears in her eyes. It was all too much for her to take. She felt ashamed of Jessica and betrayed by Amy.

"Where's your next class?" asked Ken.

"English," mumbled Elizabeth.

Ken reached over and took Elizabeth's books. "Come on," he said. "I'll walk you there."

Elizabeth wiped her eyes. "Thanks," she said. She and Ken started down the hall. Out of the corner of her eye she could see Amy glaring at them both.

But Elizabeth ignored Amy. Right now she was just glad to have a friend.

At the other end of the building Jessica and Ellen sat hunched over their stools in art class. The teacher, Mr. Sweeney, had just asked everyone to pair up for a new project. Ellen leaned over and whispered in Jessica's ear, "Is everyone still treating you like you have leprosy?"

Jessica nodded glumly.

"Lila hasn't talked to me all day," Ellen said. "I don't get it." She glanced nervously around the room. "Yesterday Caroline asked me about the earrings. She wanted to know if they were the same pair she'd seen at the mall."

"This morning Brooke said she couldn't believe I found a Walkman," Jessica added.

Mr. Sweeney cleared his throat. "Students, please pay attention," he said. "This means you, Ms. Riteman."

Ellen stopped whispering and sat back.

"Now that we've done some drawing of faces we've seen in magazines, we're going to try drawing our partners.

Everyone groaned.

"Students, please," said Mr. Sweeney. "This is merely an exercise in observation. Please don't worry if your portrait isn't accurate. It took masters like Rembrandt years to perfect this craft."

Jessica quickly drew a long, thin face with beady eyes and short black hair. She added horns to the head and two long fangs to the mouth. Underneath it she wrote "Portrait of Mr. Sweeney by Jessica Rembrandt." She slid the picture over to Ellen.

Ellen began to giggle uncontrollably.

"Ms. Riteman," said Mr. Sweeney, "what's so amusing?"

"Nothing, Mr. Sweeney," choked Ellen. Her eyes began to water.

With her back to the teacher, Jessica looked cross-eyed at Ellen and stuck out her tongue. "No laughing," she whispered.

Ellen snorted out loud.

Mr. Sweeney put down his piece of chalk.

"Let's see what's got you two so entertained," he said.

Before Mr. Sweeney could reach their table, Ellen grabbed the piece of paper and stuffed it under her sweater.

"Ellen!" exclaimed Jessica. Several people started laughing.

Mr. Sweeney held out his hand. "Hand it over," he said. The class snickered. Soberly, Ellen removed the drawing. Mr. Sweeney spread it on the table and studied it for several seconds. Then he crumpled it up and threw it into the wastebasket. "In the future, Ms. Wakefield," he said, "please try to spend more time listening and less time amusing Ms. Riteman."

No one in the class said a word. Jessica stared at the table. She didn't dare look at Ellen.

Mr. Sweeney clapped his hands together. "Now then," he said briskly, "where were we?"

Later that afternoon Amy was on her way to booster practice when Ken stopped her in the hall. "Hi, Amy," he said.

"Hi," said Amy without stopping.

Ken followed her down the hall. "Is something the matter?" he asked.

Amy knew she shouldn't let it bother her, but it did. "Why did you walk Elizabeth to class?" she blurted.

Ken looked at Amy in surprise. "Because she was upset," he said. "She's your best friend, and I don't think you treated her very nicely."

Amy turned angrily. "Since when is that your business, Ken?" she said.

"It *is* my business," he replied.

Amy stared at Ken. Why was he defending Elizabeth? A horrible thought occurred to her. What if Ken was doing this because he liked Elizabeth! Now Amy's face turned red. Without another word she rushed off to the gym.

All during booster club practice Amy thought about her conversation with Ken. On the other side of the gym she could hear the basketball team practicing. Everything was starting to make sense now—the way Ken had been so nice to Elizabeth when they were putting up posters the other day, the way he smiled at Elizabeth when they were together. Amy heard Janet, the booster captain, calling her name.

"What's with you today?" said Janet. "You've been late starting every single cheer."

Amy looked down the long line. "Sorry," she said. She tried to concentrate.

At the other end of the squad Jessica and Ellen were dragging their pompoms through the next routine. Amy gritted her teeth and did a forward flip. "Go Sweet Valley," she shouted, right on cue. She peeked over at Ken. If only she could get him to like her again. She felt herself getting angrier and angrier with Elizabeth. There must be something she could do, she thought. Maybe if there were some way to make Ken jealous . . .

After practice Amy hurried to Mr. Bowman's room. Elizabeth and Julie were still there, working on the paper. "Listen, Elizabeth," said Amy coldly. "I've decided I can't be your campaign manager anymore. I don't think the student council treasurer should have a thief for a sister."

Elizabeth looked shocked. "But—"

"I'm sorry," Amy interrupted. She turned on her heel and walked out the door.

In the library Amy found Peter hunched over a stack of albums in the record corner. He was wearing a pair of oversized earphones and intently reading one of the jacket covers. Amy pulled up a chair and sat down beside him. Peter looked up abruptly. "Hi, there." Amy grinned. "What are you listening to?"

Peter pulled off the earphones. "Johnny Buck," he replied.

"Johnny Buck?" said Amy.

Peter gave a serious nod. "I collect his albums. I've got them all." He stuck the earphones back on and began mouthing the lyrics. He knew the song by heart. His timing was perfect.

"That's not bad, Peter," said Amy.

He smiled and tapped his foot.

Amy looked down at his sneakers. "Nice shoes," she said. "They look much better with white socks too."

"Thanks," said Peter. He banged his ballpoint pen against the library cart and kept time with the record.

Amy pushed her chair closer. "Uh, Peter," she said. "Could I interrupt you for a minute?"

Peter lifted up the record needle.

Amy took a deep breath. "I was wondering," she said. "Have you ever thought about having a campaign manager?"

Six

Elizabeth sat quietly by herself on the "thinking seat," a low branch of the large pine tree in the Wakefields' backyard. She just couldn't understand what had happened that afternoon with Amy. Why was Amy being so hateful toward her? *She* hadn't stolen the money. She didn't even know about it. And why was Amy so eager to spread rumors about Jessica and Ellen?

Elizabeth leaned back and stared up through the branches overhead. For her the thinking seat was the most peaceful spot in Sweet Valley. Whenever Elizabeth felt unhappy or confused, she would come here and try to sort out her feelings.

Elizabeth thought about the class money. That morning she'd seen Jessica take Ellen's earrings off her dresser and put them in her book bag. Why would Jessica be keeping the earrings unless she and Ellen didn't want Mrs. Riteman to find them?

Elizabeth rested her head against the tree and closed her eyes. She wished she could just erase the past few days and start over again.

Elizabeth heard the back door slam and felt

someone shake the tree branch. "Lizzie!" cried Jessica. "You won't believe what happened today in art class."

Elizabeth opened her eyes and peered up at Jessica's grinning face.

"Mr. Sweeney wanted us to draw portraits of our partners, and I had Ellen, only I drew this picture of Mr. Sweeney with fangs instead and Sweeney caught us. Then Ellen put the picture under her sweater but she wasn't quick enough." She began to laugh hysterically.

Elizabeth smiled faintly.

Jessica stopped laughing and looked closely at Elizabeth's face. "Have you been crying?" she asked.

Elizabeth didn't say anything.

Jessica crawled into the tree and sat down next to Elizabeth. "What's the matter, Lizzie?" she asked.

Elizabeth burst into tears. "Amy quit as my campaign manager," she said.

Jessica shrugged. "Is that all?" she said. "Gee, Lizzie. You had me worried there for a minute. I thought something was really wrong." She brushed her hands and started to climb back out. "Maybe Julie will help you out."

Elizabeth's anger started to rise. "You don't seem to understand, Jessica," she said evenly. "No one is going to vote for me anymore."

"Why not?" said Jessica. "They sure aren't voting for Peter." She laughed nervously. Something in Elizabeth's tone made her hesitate.

Elizabeth clenched her jaw. She'd had enough. "No one thinks the student council treasurer should have a thief for a sister," she said through gritted teeth.

Jessica's eyes opened wide. "You don't mean *me*?" she said incredulously.

"You're the only sister I have!" Elizabeth snapped.

"But what did I do?" said Jessica.

Elizabeth sighed. "You and Ellen stole the class money, didn't you?" she said. "Admit it, Jess."

"We *what*?" Jessica screamed. At that moment she realized why everyone had been staring at her and ignoring her. Jessica threw her hand across her heart. "Elizabeth, I swear I didn't take that money."

Elizabeth turned away.

"Elizabeth!" wailed Jessica. "How could you think I'd do something like that? Your own sister? Your own flesh and blood?"

Elizabeth stared stonily at her sister. "Then where did Ellen get those earrings?" she said. "And what about the Walkman? I know you're lying about finding it at the mall, Jessica. Don't deny it."

Jessica swallowed. "I'm not," she said. "And I promise I didn't take the class money."

"Give me a break," said Elizabeth. "Everyone in the class knows you're guilty, and I'm sick and tired of taking the blame for defending you. Why don't you just admit it?"

Jessica burst into tears. "You're wrong," she said, fleeing into the house.

Elizabeth wiped her eyes and stared after her sister. She heard the door slam. *It's true,* she thought sadly. *If Jessica had been innocent, she would have defended herself. But she couldn't.* Elizabeth closed her eyes and leaned back again. This was worse than any nightmare she had ever dreamed.

"Mom," said Jessica, "would you please ask Elizabeth to pass the butter?"

Mrs. Wakefield looked at her two daughters. Jessica and Elizabeth hadn't been talking to each other all afternoon.

"Elizabeth said you're a liar, too," Steven interrupted gleefully.

"I did not!" said Elizabeth.

"Steven," said Mr. Wakefield, "let's not aggravate the situation further." He cleared his throat. "Too bad you two aren't speaking," he said loudly. His eyes flashed mischievously. "I've got a secret to share with you both."

Jessica sat still. A secret! She stole a glance at Elizabeth. Elizabeth turned away. Jessica's curiosity was bursting. "What is it?" she said.

Mr. Wakefield shook his head. "I'm waiting for the right moment to tell you," he said.

Jessica's face fell. "Oh," she said, trying not to sound too disappointed.

Mrs. Wakefield started to clear the table. "I wish you two would tell me why you're not speaking to each other."

Elizabeth pursed her lips and turned her head. As long as Jessica wasn't talking, neither was she.

Steven rocked back in his chair. "I kind of like the quiet for a change," he said. "No jabbering. Nice and peaceful." He leaned across Jessica and helped himself to the rest of the green beans.

Jessica folded her arms and stared at Steven.

"Ha, ha," she said. "That's so funny I forgot to laugh." She shifted around in her seat and avoided looking at either one of her parents or Elizabeth. Things were starting to look bad for her. Maybe she and Ellen would have to change their story.

"May I be excused?" Elizabeth said. "I've got a lot of homework."

"Certainly," said Mrs. Wakefield.

Elizabeth carefully walked around the far end of the table so she wouldn't have to pass Jessica. Jessica picked up her half-eaten dinner and headed for the kitchen sink.

"Are you sure you're finished, Jessica?" asked Mrs. Wakefield.

"I'm not hungry tonight," Jessica replied.

The next morning Jessica waited anxiously outside the school building for Ellen. She'd had to walk to school by herself, since Elizabeth had sneaked out earlier. She saw Mary Robinson and Betsy Gordon, two seventh-grade Unicorns, heading in her direction. "Hi, you guys," she said, waving.

Mary and Betsy gave her cold stares and kept walking.

Jessica's heart sank. It was true! Everyone in the whole school thought she and Ellen had taken the money. Ellen came trudging through the parking lot, wearing a long face. Jessica ran over.

"I can't believe this," Ellen said. "You'd think I was contagious."

"I know," said Jessica. "It's awful." She reached into her book bag. "Want your earrings?" she asked.

"No, thanks," said Ellen. "I don't feel like wearing them today."

* * *

When Elizabeth had walked into Mr. Bowman's room that morning, no one was there yet—not even Mr. Bowman. Elizabeth put down her things and started to do some work on the election issue.

"Well, well," she heard Mr. Bowman say as he entered the room. "An early bird."

Elizabeth looked up and smiled. Mr. Bowman was wearing his loud plaid jacket again. Amy always said it made him look like a clown. Just thinking about Amy made Elizabeth wince.

"What are you doing here so early?" Mr. Bowman asked.

"I'm putting together all of the student council speeches," Elizabeth said. "I've gotten every one except for Peter's."

Mr. Bowman peered over Elizabeth's shoulder. "Very good." He picked up a piece of paper. "Yours?" he said.

"It's not too great," Elizabeth said.

"Mind if I read it?" said Mr. Bowman.

"OK," said Elizabeth. She pretended to fiddle around with the ditto masters while she waited for Mr. Bowman to finish.

"Sounds pretty good," he said, handing the speech back to her. "You might want to add a bit about why you think you're qualified for the job."

"But doesn't that sound stuck-up?" said Elizabeth.

"Not really," said Mr. Bowman. "It gives people confidence to know that they're voting for a qualified person."

Elizabeth nodded. Julie and Sophia burst

through the door. "Howdy, Mr. B," said Julie. She turned to Elizabeth. "Did you see Peter's new campaign posters?"

Elizabeth shook her head.

Julie grabbed her arm. "Come with me," she said. She pulled Elizabeth into the hall. Next to Elizabeth's poster another poster, twice as large, had been taped up. ROCKIN' PETER, it said in neon-orange letters. HE'S YOUR MAN. A generous amount of glitter had been sprinkled across the top.

Elizabeth looked at Julie and Sophia. "Rockin' Peter? Who thought that up?"

Julie pointed to the other end of the corridor. "Amy's working for Peter now."

Elizabeth stared down the hall. She could see Amy standing next to a cute boy in blue jeans. She did a double-take. It was Peter.

"Amy gave him a makeover," said Julie. "Can you believe it?"

Elizabeth's jaw dropped. The brown belt and brown pants were gone. In their place Peter had on some new jeans and a rumpled blue T-shirt that had a picture of the ocean on it. MAUI, it said in big black letters.

"He's kind of cute, don't you think?" said Julie.

"I guess so," said Elizabeth.

Peter and Amy started up the hall. There was a new bounce in Peter's walk, as if the clothes had somehow boosted his confidence. "Vote for Peter," Amy said as she handed out little handmade stickers with his name on them.

Elizabeth watched silently. Several other people had stopped to stare as well.

"Hey, Pete," shouted Charlie Cashman. "What happened to your clothes?"

Peter grinned good-naturedly. "I gave them to my sister," he shot back.

Charlie howled. "Not bad, DeHaven," he said.

Peter smiled.

"Are you going to vote for Peter?" interrupted Amy. She handed Charlie a sticker.

Charlie put the sticker on his shirt. "Sure. Why not?" he said. He grinned at Peter. "What did you say you're running for?"

That day in math class Jessica and Ellen sat by themselves in a far corner of the classroom, trying to look inconspicuous. "I'm sick of everyone giving us dirty looks," whispered Ellen.

Jessica peered gloomily around the room. "Me too," she said. "I wish we'd never found that buried treasure."

Ms. Wyler entered briskly. "Good day, class," she said. She opened her textbook. "Let's start today by going over our homework."

Class seemed to drag on forever. Jessica found it hard to pay attention. Finally the bell rang. As everyone got up to leave, Ms. Wyler said, "I'd like to see Jessica and Ellen at my desk, please."

The room suddenly became quiet as everyone turned to them.

Jessica gulped. She slowly collected her books and walked up to Ms. Wyler's desk. Ellen followed. No one else in the class moved.

Ms. Wyler waved her arm. "The rest of you can go," she said. She shuffled through her papers and acted as if nothing were the matter. "Go on, class," she said.

As soon as the last person left the room, Ms. Wyler walked over and shut the door. She returned to her desk and sat down. "I've heard something about you two and the class money," she said.

"It wasn't us, Ms. Wyler," Ellen burst in. "I swear on a stack of bibles."

Ms. Wyler frowned. "Then you know what I'm talking about?" she said.

Jessica's heart sank. Ms. Wyler must think they were guilty, she thought. "Ellen's right," Jessica said in her most convincing voice. "We would never take the class money. Never."

Ellen vigorously nodded her agreement.

Ms. Wyler flipped through a pile of papers. "I understand you both made some new purchases recently," she said. "A Walkman, a pair of earrings . . ."

Jessica looked at Ellen. "I *found* that Walkman at the mall," said Jessica. "On a bench near . . . Sweet Valley Fashions."

"And my aunt gave me the earrings," Ellen quickly added. "My Aunt Jackie. In Michigan. She's my dad's sister." Jessica gave her a nudge to shut up.

Ms. Wyler nodded. "I see," she said.

"Ms. Wyler, please," begged Jessica. "We're innocent. Really."

Ms Wyler looked at the girls. "As long as you tell me that you're innocent, I have no choice but to believe you," she said. "But if I find out otherwise, you'll have many, many people to answer to. Do you understand?"

"Don't worry, Ms. Wyler," said Ellen. She

shoved Jessica toward the door. "We're telling the truth."

Jessica and Ellen closed the door behind them, and Ellen leaned against the wall. "Great," she said. "She didn't believe one word. I'll bet she'll even call our parents. What do we do now?"

Seven

Later that same afternoon Elizabeth was about to go home when she noticed the campaign poster that she and Amy had hung earlier in the week. Someone had taken a black Magic Marker, crossed out the words ELIZABETH MAKES CENTS, and changed them to read JESSICA TAKES CENTS.

"Not very nice," observed Ken behind her.

Elizabeth turned around. "I'm beginning to feel like it's my fault about Jessica."

"Why?" said Ken. "I don't know anyone who's mad at you."

Elizabeth shook her head unhappily. "Amy is," she said. "She quit as my campaign manager."

Just then Amy and Peter walked out of the library. When Amy saw Ken and Elizabeth together, she began talking animatedly to Peter.

"Who's that with Amy?" said Ken.

"Peter DeHaven," said Elizabeth. "Amy's his new campaign manager. I guess she's trying to change his image."

Ken didn't say anything. He just kept staring at them.

"Are you OK?" Elizabeth asked.

Ken shrugged. "Sure," he said. He looked at Elizabeth. "When are the student council speeches?"

"The day after tomorrow," she said. She thought about her speech and how she was going to have to stand up in front of the whole school.

Ken continued to stand near Elizabeth. He kept glancing over at Amy, who was laughing hysterically at something Peter said.

"What position is Peter running for?" he asked abruptly.

"Treasurer," Elizabeth replied. "Against me."

Ken shuffled his right foot back and forth against the floor. "Oh."

Elizabeth took her ruined poster off the wall. "Guess there's no point in leaving this up," she said.

"Guess not," said Ken.

The next evening Jessica was lying on her bed, listening to her Walkman and singing along with Johnny Buck. "No one's been lonely as lonely as me," she crooned. "Why I'm alone is life's great mystery." She sighed and stared at the ceiling. *Johnny's right*, she thought. She'd never felt so abandoned. Even the Unicorns were avoiding her. She wondered if this was the way things were going to be for the rest of her life.

Mrs. Wakefield stuck her head in the door. "How's that homework coming?" she asked.

"OK, I guess," Jessica answered. She flipped open her math book and stared at the assignment. The truth was, she hadn't even started it. There'd been so much going on the past few days that she'd found it impossible to concentrate.

Jessica could hear Elizabeth practicing her student council speech in the next room. "Hello, my name is Elizabeth Wakefield, and I'm running for treasurer," she was saying. Jessica buried her head in her pillow. She wished she could ask Elizabeth for help with her homework, but she didn't dare.

Jessica heard Elizabeth get up from her desk and walk downstairs. A brilliant idea occurred to her. What if she just borrowed Elizabeth's homework without telling her? She could copy it and return it in the morning before Elizabeth ever noticed it missing.

Pleased with her plan, Jessica tiptoed through the bathroom that connected her room with Elizabeth's. The coast was clear. She dashed into her sister's room, snatched the notebook off her desk, and replaced it with her own, which was identical to Elizabeth's. Seconds later she was back in her room, copying the assignment. She didn't even blink when Elizabeth returned to her room. There was no way that Elizabeth would ever find out, she thought.

The next morning Elizabeth was up early. Student council speeches were scheduled for first period, and Elizabeth was already dreading them. She picked up her speech, read it over several more times, then stuck it inside her notebook for safekeeping.

Downstairs in the kitchen Elizabeth fixed herself a piece of toast and a glass of orange juice. She'd worn her favorite sweater, the pale blue one which showed off her blue-green eyes.

"Don't you look pretty," she heard her father say.

Elizabeth smiled. He was usually gone by the

time she made it downstairs. "Student council speeches are today," she said.

"Ah," said her father. "Good luck."

Upstairs Jessica was still tossing and turning in bed. She'd had another restless night and dreamed for hours about the girl in the picture. Her buzzing alarm clock woke her abruptly. Jessica sat up and rubbed her eyes. She could hear Elizabeth downstairs in the kitchen. "Uh-oh," she said suddenly. "Lizzie's notebook!" She reached under her bed, grabbed the notebook, and hurried through the bathroom. It only took a second to switch the notebooks, and by the time Elizabeth made it back upstairs, Jessica was already safe in her room.

Elizabeth threw her things into her book bag and hurried off. "'Bye, everyone," she called. "Wish me luck!"

"Good luck," Mrs. Wakefield answered cheerfully.

Jessica smiled to herself and pulled on her sweater. Good thing she'd remembered the notebook. She was in enough trouble already.

Elizabeth sat on a folding chair on the side of the auditorium stage and watched the classes file in grade by grade. Her hands nervously clutched her notebook. On the other end of the stage she could see Amy giving Peter some last minute instructions. Today he had on another new T-shirt. This one was bright orange and said DAVEY'S SURF SHOP on it. His looks had certainly improved, Elizabeth thought, studying him more closely. She could even detect the faint beginnings of a tan.

Olivia Davidson, the presidential candidate,

leaned over to whisper in Elizabeth's ear. "Peter must be taking cute pills."

Elizabeth had mixed feelings about what was happening. On the one hand, it was good that Peter's image was improving. But still, she wished it wasn't at her expense.

The school principal, Mr. Clark, strode onto the stage. He picked up the microphone and tapped it a few times. "Testing, testing," he said. The microphone shrieked loudly. "OK, boys and girls," he said. "If I may have your attention, please."

Elizabeth looked out at the audience and suddenly felt sick to her stomach. She'd never spoken to this many people in her life. She clasped her hands together to prevent them from shaking, and then her knees weakened instead. She tugged on her skirt and took a few deep breaths.

"Nervous?" said Olivia.

Elizabeth nodded.

"Me too," said Olivia. "Don't worry, you'll do fine. Once you start talking, you forget about it."

Elizabeth smiled gracefully. She noticed that Olivia had neatly typed out her speech on index cards. Elizabeth opened her notebook to take out her speech. She frowned and flipped through the pages. And then she panicked. *I put my speech in my notebook this morning. Where is it?*

Mr. Clark was speaking to the audience. "We'll start the speeches by hearing from the presidential candidate."

Elizabeth searched through her notebook a second time. Where was her speech? She began to get desperate. It *has* to be here, she thought. She reached behind her chair and rummaged through her book bag. It wasn't there either.

Olivia got up and walked to the podium. The audience became quiet. Elizabeth saw all those staring faces. Her mind was a blur. What was she going to do? What was she going to say? There was no time to write it down again. She'd just have to remember what she could.

She heard Mr. Clark announce the next candidate and then the next. Finally she heard him say Peter's name. That meant she was next. Elizabeth looked at the clock. Maybe the bell would ring and she'd have to wait until tomorrow to give her speech. She squeezed her eyes shut and prayed that Peter would take his time.

From behind the stage came the sound of very loud rock music. Elizabeth saw Amy standing in the wings, operating a record player. At that moment Peter burst through the curtain wearing dark sunglasses. To the beat of the music he said, "I'm Rockin' Peter, and I'm here to say, if you vote for me, you'll do OK."

Elizabeth's jaw dropped. *This* was Peter's speech? The audience started to clap and cheer, but Peter wasn't finished. He spun around and bent the mike to the ground. "I want to help, you bet I do, so if you vote for me, I'll see you through. I'm rock, rock, rock, rockin' Peter." He leaned backward until it looked like he was going to fall over, and then he hopped across the stage.

"Go, Peter," someone shouted. Two sixth-grade boys stood up on their chairs and whistled.

Elizabeth watched in amazement. Peter was

really good. And funny too. The audience loved him.

Peter fell to his knees. "I'll watch your cash, I'll guard your stash," he was saying. He bounced across the stage again, this time on his knees. Elizabeth recognized a few of the Boosters' moves and saw Amy signaling directions from offstage. So *this* was what she and Peter had been up to! She couldn't help being impressed, even though she knew it was going to make things much worse for herself.

Finally the song was finished. It took forever for the audience to calm down. Elizabeth kept looking at the clock and hoping that the bell would ring. But when Mr. Clark finally took the microphone there was just enough time left for her to do her speech.

Mr. Clark wiped the tears from his eyes. "Well," he said, "I can't remember when I've laughed so much at a campaign speech." He cleared his throat and the audience grew quiet. "We have one more speech scheduled for today," he said. "The other candidate for student council treasurer is Elizabeth Wakefield."

Elizabeth gulped and walked slowly to the podium. How was she ever going to follow Peter's act? She looked out at the sea of faces and smiled weakly. "I'm Elizabeth Wakefield and I'm running for student body treasurer," she began. The audience stirred restlessly. A big knot started to form in Elizabeth's throat. It just wasn't fair. "I think you should vote for me because . . ." Her voice quavered. "Because I'm very well-qualified for the job," she finished, taking a deep breath. Slowly, painfully, she was able to remember most of her speech, although it didn't sound the same as when she'd practiced it at home. After she sat down, there was a scattering of polite applause.

The bell rang and everyone immediately stood up. "Don't forget," called Mr. Clark as the students hurried out of the room. "Elections are tomorrow during lunch."

Elizabeth lowered her head and rushed out of the cafeteria, her cheeks still burning. "Lizzie!" she heard Jessica call.

Elizabeth kept walking until she reached the farthest stall in the girls' bathroom.

Jessica caught up to her. "Lizzie, what happened?" she said. "Your speech sounded so good when you rehearsed it at home."

Elizabeth was so grateful to see her sister that she forgot how angry she was with her. "Oh, Jess," she said. The tears started to roll down her face. "I was terrible, wasn't I? You won't believe what happened. I lost my speech." She blew her nose on a piece of toilet paper.

"How?" said Jessica.

Elizabeth shook her head. "I don't know," she said. "I put it in the front of my notebook this morning."

Jessica's face suddenly turned pale.

"What is it?" said Elizabeth.

"Nothing," Jessica replied quickly.

Elizabeth stared at her sister. "Are you sure?"

Jessica bit her lip. "Positive."

A look of horror crossed Elizabeth's face. "Jessica," she said slowly. "You wouldn't have my speech in *your* notebook, would you?"

Jessica gripped her book bag. "Of course not."

Elizabeth's eyes narrowed. "Let me see," she said.

Jessica hugged her book bag to her chest.

"I want to see," Elizabeth repeated.

Jessica knew she was cornered. "Lizzie, I didn't do it on purpose," she wailed. "I promise. You must have stuck the speech in my notebook by accident."

Elizabeth gritted her teeth. "How?" she asked.

Jessica swallowed. "Maybe when I borrowed your notebook to copy your math homework," she said in a tiny voice.

"Jessica!" howled Elizabeth. "What are you trying to do? Ruin my life?"

Several girls stopped talking and turned to watch.

Elizabeth's face got redder and redder. "You lied about the class money, and you stole my speech."

"I didn't," said Jessica. "That's not true."

Elizabeth shoved past her sister. "It is," she said. "Why don't you just leave me alone?"

Jessica leaned against the bathroom wall. Now she'd really blown it. "What are you staring at?" she said angrily to the other girls. Several of them whispered something and hurried out of the bathroom. "I'm not a thief," Jessica called after them. "I'm not."

Jessica found Ellen at the other end of the hall, getting some books out of her locker. "Ellen," she said. "We have to do something. Everybody hates us, and I've ruined Elizabeth's life. I'm giving you back the chest," said Jessica flatly. "I think we should tell the truth about the treasure."

Ellen swallowed. "But we'll have to return the

money," she said. "And we've already spent most of it."

"I don't care anymore," said Jessica. "I'll baby-sit. I'll walk Mrs. Bramble's dog. I won't spend my allowance for the next two years." She started crying. The class bell rang. "I'm coming over after school," Jessica said. "With the chest." She hurried off to class.

"Maybe we can think of something else," Ellen called after her.

"Forget it, Ellen," said Jessica. "It's not worth it anymore."

Eight

Peter and Amy were having a hard time maneuvering their way through the crowded hallway. Every time they managed to gain a few feet, someone else came over to congratulate them. Now as they worked their way toward their classrooms, Amy saw Jerry McAllister approaching.

"Good work, DeHaven," said Jerry. He gave Peter a friendly slap on the back and pulled out his ballpoint pen. "Watch this." He put the pen up to his mouth like it was a microphone. "Rock, rock, rock, rockin' Peter," he crooned into his pen.

Peter grinned. He felt someone else tugging on his arm.

"You were fantastic," said Janet Howell. "I didn't know you were so talented."

"Thanks," he said.

Amy stood protectively by his side. "Did you want something, Janet?" she asked.

Janet gave Peter a big smile, the one all the Unicorns used if they wanted something. "I just had the best idea," she said. "I think Peter should perform with the Boosters at our next game." Her smile broadened. "What do you think, Peter?"

"Uh, I guess so," he said.

"You'd be really great," Janet continued enthusiastically. "We could have you do some of the cheers with us. Maybe we could even get you a special uniform."

"That's really nice of you, Janet," interrupted Amy, "but don't you think you're being a little hypocritical?"

"What do you mean?" said Janet.

"Only a few days ago you were making fun of Peter," said Amy.

Janet's face turned red. "That was before this," she replied in a huffy voice.

"Oh," said Amy. "I see."

Peter coughed. "I'd like to perform with the Boosters," he said. "It sounds like fun."

Janet beamed at him. "Oh, good," she said. "Then it's settled." As she walked away, she glared at Amy.

"Those Unicorns are so two-faced," muttered Amy.

Peter shrugged. "I guess that's the way some people are," he said. He quietly opened his locker and exchanged his books. "Thanks for helping me on my speech," he said, closing the door. "Those cheers really helped."

"That's OK," said Amy. "It was your talent that pulled it off."

Peter nodded thoughtfully. "Why did you switch from Elizabeth to me?" he asked suddenly. "I thought she was your best friend."

"Yes," said Amy.

"Her feelings must be hurt," Peter added.

"I'm sure she'll recover," said Amy, turning away.

"I always wanted a best friend," Peter said quietly. He stared at his new shoes. "Maybe now things will be different."

A wave of guilt swept over Amy. Maybe she *had* been a little mean to Elizabeth. And what about Peter? Hadn't she been just as bad as everyone else about making fun of him behind his back? The only reason she'd taken a real interest in him was to make Ken jealous. What sort of a friend did that make her? "I've gotta go, Peter," she blurted.

Amy's next class was cooking, and her partner was Ken. When she walked into the classroom, she was surprised to see Julie sitting next to Ken. They appeared to be having a serious conversation.

As Amy approached her seat, Julie stood up. "Sorry," she said. "Ken and I were just talking."

Amy watched Julie leave. "Hi," she said to Ken.

"Hi," said Ken. He bent over the comic book he was reading.

"How've you been?" said Amy.

Ken didn't even look up. "OK," he replied.

Amy's heart sank. What was the matter with Ken? Wasn't he supposed to be jealous? Why wasn't he happy to see her?

For the rest of the class Ken barely paid attention to Amy. She started to feel guilty about all her scheming. What had she done wrong?

After the final bell rang, Amy headed for Mr. Bowman's room. The election issue of *The Sweet Valley Sixers* had to be run off and stapled before tomorrow.

"Just in time," said Mr. Bowman as Amy came through the door.

"For what?" said Amy. She noticed Elizabeth standing over Mr. Bowman's desk. Her eyes were red and puffy, as if she'd been crying.

"I'd like you and Elizabeth to go to the supply closet in the faculty room and bring me two more boxes of mimeograph paper," he said. "Here's the key."

Silently, the two girls walked down the hall. When they reached the supply closet, Amy fiddled with the key for several seconds before managing to unlock it. "After you," she gestured politely.

"No. You go ahead," said Elizabeth.

Amy fumbled with the light switch and then stepped inside. The supply closet was actually a small room that had been lined with shelves from floor to ceiling. A lot of extra school supplies were kept there.

"I don't suppose you know where the mimeograph paper is," said Amy.

"Mr. Bowman said it's on the left side of the closet near the floor," Elizabeth replied. There was a strained silence as the girls bent down to look. "I found it," Elizabeth said finally. She started to pull out the boxes.

Outside, in the faculty room, Mr. Nydick, the social studies teacher, had come in to put up a sign about a teacher workshop. He noticed the door to the supply closet open and frowned. "Someone being careless again," he grumbled. He tacked up his sign and then walked over to the closet. With a loud grunt he flipped off the light and slammed the door shut.

"People should be more careful," he said as he turned and left the room.

Inside the closet Amy and Elizabeth suddenly found themselves in the dark. "Hey!" said Amy. "What happened?"

Elizabeth groped across the floor. "Someone must've thought there was no one in here," she said. She managed to find the light switch and turn it back on. She reached for the doorknob and tried to twist it. "Uh-oh," she said.

Amy hopped up. "Here. I have the key."

Elizabeth looked at her. "There's no keyhole on this side," she said.

"There has to be," said Amy.

Elizabeth stood back and watched Amy inspect the knob. "Now do you believe me?" she said.

Amy pounded on the door. "Open up," she shouted. "We're locked inside here."

"I don't think there's anyone in the faculty room right now," said Elizabeth. She folded her arms and sat down cross-legged on the floor, a resigned expression on her face. "We might as well wait it out."

Amy stared at Elizabeth. "What's the matter with you?" she said. "Don't you even care? We could die in here. We could run out of air and they wouldn't discover our bodies until tomorrow." She pounded on the door again. "Help. Let us out of here."

Elizabeth's eyes filled with tears. "It doesn't matter anymore," she said bitterly. "Nothing matters."

Amy sat down and put her arm around her

friend. "Yes, it does," she said gently. "We don't want to spend the rest of our lives in the supply closet."

Elizabeth burst into tears. "Why don't you like me anymore?" she said. "Was it something I did?"

Amy felt terrible. Peter was right. She had hurt her best friend's feelings. How would she ever make it up to her? "Elizabeth, I'm sorry," she said. "I didn't mean it. I wasn't thinking. I never planned to hurt you. It's just that I didn't want to take the blame for the class money anymore. And then when Ken started to like you, I guess I got jealous."

Elizabeth sniffled. "Ken?" she said. "Why were you jealous of Ken and me?"

"Because he likes you," said Amy. "I thought if I paid attention to Peter, Ken would get jealous and like me again. Only now Ken doesn't like me either," she said, thinking about cooking class. She leaned unhappily against the shelf. "I've really messed things up."

Elizabeth reached over and opened a box of tissues. She blew her nose and wiped her eyes. "You're imagining the whole thing, Amy. Just like you imagined that everyone was blaming you for taking the money. Besides, Ken told Julie today that you like Peter now."

"Peter!" exclaimed Amy.

"Why else would you be spending so much time with him?" said Elizabeth.

Amy realized what an awful mistake she'd made. She was about to lose her two closest friends, and all because she'd thought only of herself. If she hadn't been so selfish in the first place, she would never have told anyone Elizabeth's secret about Jessica.

"You took advantage of me, of Ken, of Peter, and of Jessica," said Elizabeth. "All because of what you imagined." She turned away. "And now Peter is probably going to win the election," she said finally. "Not that he doesn't deserve it," she added.

"I thought your speech was very good," said Amy.

Elizabeth made a face. "What speech?" she said. "It was sitting in Jessica's notebook the whole time."

"It sounded good to me," said Amy. "I liked when you told about your qualifications."

"You did?" said Elizabeth.

Amy nodded. "What can I do so we can be friends again?" she said. "I've missed you."

Elizabeth smiled. "Me too." She reached over and gave Amy a hug. "Friends," she said.

"Forever," Amy replied solemnly.

Elizabeth sighed and looked around the room. "Now how do we get out of this place?"

Amy pointed to the shelves. "Think we can find a saw in here?" she said.

"It's worth a try," said Elizabeth.

The two girls immediately began digging through the shelves. "I guess there's not much need for a saw in middle school," observed Amy after several minutes. "What time is it?"

"Four-fifteen," said Elizabeth. "Our only hope is that Mr. Bowman comes looking for us." On a large piece of construction paper she wrote HELP! WE'RE LOCKED IN THE CLOSET. She slid it underneath the door.

"That's got to work," said Amy. "Some teacher will show up eventually."

"Let's hope so," said Elizabeth. She sat back down on the floor. Over in the far corner she noticed a stack of things they hadn't looked through yet. "Maybe there's something we can use in that corner," she said. She took a pile of art smocks off the shelf and gasped. "I don't believe it," she said. Hiding behind the smocks were several old math posters and a familiar-looking cigar box.

"What is it?" said Amy. "A saw?"

Elizabeth pulled out the cigar box and flipped open the lid. "Better," she said.

Amy's jaw dropped. "The class money?" she said. "You've got to be kidding!" She and Elizabeth quickly counted the contents. "It's all here," said Amy. "Every single cent."

"Ms. Wyler must have accidentally stuck it there when she was putting away these posters," cried Elizabeth.

"And then it got buried behind the art smocks," Amy added.

Elizabeth closed the lid and looked directly at Amy. "Jessica wasn't guilty," she said.

Amy swallowed. "You're right."

Elizabeth sighed loudly. "I'm so relieved," she said. "Poor Jessica. No wonder she was so upset when everyone blamed her. Wait till I tell her."

Just then the girls heard a key in the lock. A

moment later the door to the closet opened. "Aha!" said Mr. Bowman. He held up Elizabeth's note. "I understand you're looking for a locksmith."

Amy and Elizabeth cheered, and then dashed out the door. "Fresh air," shouted Amy. "Thank you, thank you, Mr. B. You saved our lives."

"I wouldn't go that far," said Mr. Bowman.

Still clutching the cigar box, Elizabeth said, "We need to talk to Ms. Wyler right away. It's an emergency."

Mr. Bowman raised his eyebrows. "Very well," he said.

"And after that," Amy added, "we have to go to Elizabeth's house. We need to talk to somebody. The paper can wait until tomorrow."

Mr. Bowman looked at Elizabeth and then at Amy. He walked into the closet. "Did something strange happen in here?" he said.

Elizabeth and Amy laughed. "You could say that," said Elizabeth. She grabbed Amy's arm. "Come on, Amy," she said. "I can't wait to see Ms. Wyler's face."

When Elizabeth and Amy arrived at the Wakefields' about twenty minutes later, Steven was the only one around. "Where is everybody?" said Elizabeth.

Steven spooned marshmallow sauce onto his bowl of ice cream. "What do I look like?" he said. "A bulletin board?"

"This happens to be an emergency," Amy cut in.

Steven put a big spoonful of his sundae into his mouth. "What'll you pay me?" he said.

"Steven!" said Elizabeth. "We're not kidding."

Steven tilted back in his chair. "Dad's at the office," he said.

"And . . . ?" said Elizabeth impatiently.

Steven dipped his spoon into his ice cream and watched the marshmallow sauce drip over the edge of the bowl. "Mom said something about going to school to talk to one of Jessica's teachers."

"We know that," said Elizabeth. "Ms. Wyler said we'd just missed them. She'd called Mom and Mrs. Riteman in because of all the rumors going around. She wanted to check out Jessica and Ellen's story."

"So what else do you want to know?" asked Steven.

"Where is Jessica?" said Amy.

Steven grinned. "If I were Jessica, I'd be hiding out with Ellen." He tilted his chair forward again and chuckled to himself. "Boy, is she going to get it."

Elizabeth and Amy dashed out the door. "Not if we hurry, Steven," called Elizabeth. "Jessica and Ellen are innocent, and we've got the proof!"

Nine

Jessica and Ellen sat on Ellen's front porch, waiting for Mrs. Riteman to get home from work. The treasure chest sat between them.

Jessica rested her elbow on the chest and sighed. "It's all for the best," she said.

"Right," said Ellen.

There was an uncomfortable silence. Neither girl was looking forward to telling the truth. "Do you think your mom is going to be mad?" said Jessica.

Ellen stared at the chest. "I'll probably be grounded for lying and for taking money that didn't belong to me," she said. "But I guess it's better to have one person mad at me than the whole school."

Jessica thought about what Ellen had said. If only they could think of some way to convince the class that they were innocent, and still keep the Walkman and earrings. "I have an idea," said Jessica. "What if we tell everyone that we found a buried chest and when we returned it to its owners, they gave us a reward?" She looked hopefully at Ellen.

"Do you think anyone would believe us?" Ellen said.

"It's possible," said Jessica.

"What would we do about Mark?" said Ellen.

Jessica frowned. "Maybe we could pay him some money to keep quiet." she said.

"I doubt it," said Ellen. "Besides, we'd have to hide the chest again." She paused. "And who would we say the chest belonged to?"

"Good point," said Jessica. She idly kicked her feet against the porch steps. "My mom's probably going to kill me for taking that money," she said finally. She thought about Elizabeth and all the trouble she'd caused her sister. "Maybe it's worth it, though," she added. She stared off into the distance and saw a young woman walking up the street. Jessica turned pale.

"What is it?" said Ellen.

The woman was closer now. She had dark hair and was very beautiful. She gazed at them and started in their direction. "It's her." Jessica gasped. "The girl in the picture."

Ellen watched in disbelief. "No," she said. "It can't be. She would be old now."

Jessica's eyes grew wide. "Ellen!" she said. "It's her ghost! She's come to get her things." She grabbed Ellen's arm.

Ellen leaned forward and strained her eyes. "Are you serious?" she said.

"It's exactly like my dream," Jessica replied earnestly. "I *knew* we shouldn't have taken that money. Now she wants it back."

Ellen stared at the figure moving silently up the street. She *did* look a lot like the photograph. Ellen moved closer to Jessica. "Can't we do something?" she whispered.

Jessica continued to squeeze Ellen's arm. "Go away," she called in a thin voice. "We didn't mean to take your money. Honest we didn't." Jessica had never felt more sorry. She was sorry she'd lied, sorry she'd bought the Walkman, even sorry she knew Ellen Riteman.

"We'll never do it again," Ellen added. "We promise."

The ghost kept walking. She reached the bottom of the Ritemans' driveway, stopped, and then continued up the walk. A faint smile crossed her lips.

"The chest," Jessica said under her breath. "Maybe she wants the chest."

Ellen grabbed the treasure chest and shoved it toward the ghost. "Here. Take it," she said. "We don't want it."

The ghost raised her eyebrows quizzically.

"We're really sorry about the money," Jessica added. "But the letters and the pictures are there just the way you left them. And we promise we'll return every cent of the money."

"Every cent," Ellen echoed.

The ghost looked puzzled. "I don't understand," she said. "There must be some mistake."

Jessica and Ellen huddled closer.

"Is this chest meant for me?" she repeated.

Jessica nodded, too frightened to speak.

"I'm Laura Wright," said the ghost. "My grandmother lived in this house."

Ellen and Jessica continued to stare.

"Her name was Jane McCreary," said the ghost. "She lived here as a girl. I just happened to be in

Sweet Valley on business and I wanted to come and visit the house."

Jessica leaned forward.

"Is anything the matter?" said the ghost.

It dawned on Jessica that maybe they'd made a mistake. A big mistake. "What did you say your grandmother's name was?" she asked.

"Jane," said the ghost. "Jane McCreary."

Slowly, Jessica released her grasp on Ellen's arm. "You're Jane's granddaughter?"

Laura laughed. "People say I resemble her." She smiled at the girls. "I hope I didn't frighten you."

Jessica and Ellen both took deep breaths.

Ellen opened the chest and pulled out the portrait of Jane. "You won't believe this, but we found this chest buried in the backyard a few weeks ago," she explained.

Laura examined the portrait. "That's Grandmother Jane," she said softly. She looked at the girls in amazement. "No wonder you two were acting so strange a minute ago. You must have thought I was Grandmother Jane. How in the world did you find this?"

Jessica and Ellen poured out the story about how they'd discovered the chest.

As Laura listened, she dug through the contents. "This is incredible," she said. "What an amazing coincidence."

Jessica and Ellen couldn't believe it either. They were dying to find out what had happened to Jane.

"Is your grandmother still alive," Ellen asked.

Laura shook her head. "She died about four years ago."

Jessica was just about to ask about William when she noticed her mother and Mrs. Riteman pull up in Mrs. Riteman's car. "Uh-oh," she said. "It's our moms, and they're together."

"Great," said Ellen.

The two mothers climbed out of the car, worried expression on their faces.

"Hi, Mom," Ellen called bravely. "Where've you been?"

Mrs. Riteman frowned. "With Ms. Wyler," she replied. She shut the car door. "We have some talking to do, young ladies."

"This is Laura," said Ellen. "Her grandmother used to live in this house. She's come back to see it, and you won't believe what happened."

Mrs. Riteman relaxed a little. "How lovely," she said. "If you'll forgive us, though, we really need to have a word with these two girls alone."

Jessica took a deep breath. "Mom, see this box?" she said. "We found it buried in the backyard a few weeks ago."

"Jessica," said Mrs. Wakefield, "please don't change the subject." She turned to Laura. "I must apologize," she said. "The girls are in a lot of trouble right now."

"But, Mom," Jessica interrupted, "this has to do with Laura. The box we found was full of letters to Laura's grandmother. Love letters." She threw open the chest and pulled out the packet of letters. "See?"

Mrs. Wakefield shook her head. "I still don't understand," she said.

Laura picked up the packet of letters and began reading them.

Mrs. Riteman looked sternly at Ellen. "Ms. Wyler told me you claimed that Aunt Jackie had sent you an expensive pair of earrings. Did she?"

Ellen shook her head. "No," she said quietly.

"Then what does finding some love letters have to do with this?" she demanded.

Jessica glanced at Ellen. They couldn't turn back now. "There was also two hundred dollars in that chest," she said, swallowing. "Laura's grandmother's boyfriend gave it to her so they could elope."

Laura looked up momentarily.

"And?" said Mrs. Wakefield.

Jessica gulped. "We split the money. I bought a Walkman and some clothes, and Ellen bought earrings," she said, staring at the ground. "We didn't think anyone would ever find out."

"So that's what Mark was trying to tell me!" said Mrs. Riteman. "He kept insisting he and the girls had found buried treasure."

"And the class money?" said Mrs. Wakefield.

"We didn't take that," said Ellen. "Everyone blamed us because of the Walkman and earrings."

Mrs. Riteman look dismayed. "Oh, Ellen," she said. "How could you take something that didn't belong to you?"

"We're going to return the money to Laura," said Jessica. "We've already promised her."

Mrs. Wakefield sighed. "I must say I'm relieved it wasn't the class money," she said. "I couldn't believe that you'd actually do something like that."

"Mother!" said Jessica. "How could you even *think* that?"

Mrs. Wakefield folded her arms. "That still

doesn't change the fact that you've taken money that isn't yours, young lady," she said.

"And I think you two girls owe some people apologies for the lies you told," Mrs. Riteman added. She frowned at Ellen. "Especially to your poor little brother."

Ellen grimaced. "But we were planning to tell the truth," she said. "That's why Jessica brought the chest back from her house today."

"That's still no excuse," said Mrs. Riteman. "Look at all the problems you made for yourselves by not being honest in the first place."

Ellen and Jessica squirmed. "I'm sorry," said Jessica.

"Me too," said Ellen.

Meanwhile, Laura had been busy reading the letters. Now she finished the last one and slipped it back into its envelope. Her eyes were misty. "Thank you, Grandmother Jane," she said quietly.

"What for?" interrupted Ellen.

Laura picked up the two portraits and gazed at them. "For helping me make the right decision," she said. She saw the girls' puzzled expressions and held up the portrait of the man. "This wasn't the man my grandmother married," she said.

"You mean she didn't choose William," said Ellen. "After all that?"

Laura shook her head sadly. "I loved my grandmother dearly," she said. "We were always very close. My grandfather was a nice man too. A successful lawyer. But there was always something missing between them." She paused long enough to look at the portrait of the man again. "Now I know why," she said softly. "My grandmother made the wrong choice. She let the one she really loved get away."

Laura picked up the letters once more and smiled. "But the story has a happy ending," she said. "Because right now I have to make a choice too. The same choice my grandmother had to make. To go with the man I love isn't going to be easy. My family's against him, my friends think I'm not being practical . . ." Her eyes misted over and again she looked at the girls. "But Grandmother Jane has helped me make up my mind," she said firmly. "If she were here right now, I know she'd approve of my decision."

For a moment no one said anything. Then Jessica sat down on the steps and hugged her knees. "How romantic," she said with a sigh.

"A perfect ending," Ellen said. She tried to imagine Laura's boyfriend. He was probably very handsome.

"I'd like you girls to keep the two hundred dollars," Laura added with a twinkle in her eye. "As reward money."

"Wow!" said Jessica. Things were beginning to work out even better than she'd expected.

"That's very generous of you, Laura," said Mrs. Riteman. "Are you sure?"

"Absolutely," she answered. "Consider it a gift from my grandmother."

Jessica and Ellen looked at each other and grinned.

Quietly, Mrs. Riteman turned to Ellen. "Wasn't Mark with you when you found that money?" she asked.

Ellen started to protest. "But—"

Mrs. Riteman gave her a stern look.

"OK," Ellen said reluctantly.

"Is there any money left?" said Mrs. Wakefield.

"I have about twenty-five dollars," Jessica admitted.

"Me too," said Ellen.

"Then I think that fifty dollars belongs to Mark, don't you?" said Mrs. Riteman.

It seemed like a small sacrifice to Jessica, considering the trouble they could have been in otherwise. "Fine by me," she said.

Ellen nodded her head in agreement. "It's OK with me too," she said.

At that moment Mark rode into the driveway on his bicycle.

"Perfect timing," Mrs. Riteman said to the girls. "Your first apology."

Mark's eyes popped out when he saw the treasure chest sitting on the front porch beside his mother. He threw his bike down on the lawn and hurried up the steps. "Mom, look!" he shouted, pointing.

Mrs. Riteman nodded. "Ellen and Jessica have something to say," she replied.

Ellen stared at the porch steps. "We're sorry we lied about finding the money," she said.

"We're going to give you fifty dollars," Jessica added. "Your share."

Mark threw his book bag in the air and let out a loud whoop. "Yippee!" he cried.

Ellen rolled her eyes. It was hard to give up that money, especially to Mark. But she and Jessica had learned an important lesson. She decided right then and there that no matter what, she'd never do anything dishonest again.

Ten

Elizabeth and Amy raced up the Ritemans' driveway. "Mom, Mom," Elizabeth called. "Don't get mad at Jessica. It was all a big mistake. Amy and I found the class money."

"We're serious," said Amy, panting from running so fast. "Call Ms. Wyler if you want. We just gave it back to her."

"You what?" said Mrs. Riteman.

"We found the money in the supply closet," Amy repeated.

Jessica could hardly believe the news. "You see?" she said triumphantly. "It wasn't us. That proves it!"

Elizabeth rushed over to her sister. "Jess, I'm really sorry," she said. "I should never, ever have doubted your word. Will you forgive me?"

Jessica stared stubbornly at the ground. She'd really earned this apology, and she wanted to drag it out for as long as possible. "Maybe," she said in an offended voice.

"Please?" said Elizabeth.

"You hurt my feelings a lot," said Jessica. She

looked up and saw her mother watching her. "But I guess I can forgive you," she added hastily.

"And I'm sorry too," said Amy. "I spread the rumor about you and Ellen taking the money because I thought everyone was blaming me."

"We accept your apology," said Ellen.

Elizabeth looked around the porch and suddenly noticed the stranger.

"This is Laura," said Mrs. Wakefield. "Perhaps Jessica and Ellen should tell you the rest of the story."

As the two girls explained about the chest, Amy and Elizabeth listened in amazement. When they were finished, Jessica sat back. "I owe you and the class an apology for lying about where I got the Walkman."

"And the earrings," Ellen chimed in.

"Apology accepted," said Elizabeth with a grin. "I'm so glad we're all friends again and that everything has worked out. Let's never do that again. It was awful."

"I know," said Jessica.

Mrs. Wakefield put her arms around both her girls. "Thank goodness you two are speaking to each other again," she said. "The house was beginning to sound like a library."

Jessica laughed. "Oh, Mom, I thought you liked the peace and quiet."

"Not *that* much quiet," said Mrs. Wakefield.

That evening at dinner Mr. Wakefield and Steven listened as Jessica and Elizabeth told about the surprising events that had happened that day.

"Laura sounds like a lovely person," said Mr. Wakefield after they'd finished.

"She is," said Mrs. Wakefield. "In fact, we've invited her and the Ritemans to dinner tomorrow night."

"We have?" said Jessica and Elizabeth at once.

"You two were so busy making up, you missed the invitation," Mrs. Wakefield said, laughing.

"Can we barbecue out by the pool?" asked Jessica.

"I don't see why not," said Mrs. Wakefield.

Jessica grinned. Everything was working out perfectly. She glanced over at Elizabeth and noticed there was something still troubling her. Jessica knew at once what it was.

Later that evening Elizabeth heard a knock on her door. "Lizzie, it's me," said Jessica. "Open up."

Elizabeth came to the door.

"There's something I want to say," Jessica began. "It's about your speech."

Elizabeth's face fell. "Yes?"

"I just wish there were some way I could make it up to you," Jessica blurted. "I've been thinking. How about if I make an announcement over the loudspeaker about you?"

Elizabeth's eyes grew wide. "Jess! You can't do that! No one except Mr. Clark can use the loudspeaker."

"Well, what if I sneaked into the office, tied up Mr. Clark, and then grabbed the mike?" Jessica said, trying to sound as serious as possible.

Elizabeth clapped her hand over her mouth and

gasped. Then she realized that Jessica was only joking, and broke into a howl of laughter.

"T-t-tie Mr. Clark up?" Elizabeth gasped, holding her stomach. Every time she looked at Jessica she cracked up all over again. "You're too much, Jess," she said finally. "What a crazy sister."

"I was only trying to help," Jessica replied.

"Thanks, but no thanks," Elizabeth giggled. She leaned her head forward and grinned mischievously. "I'll tell you what you *can* do," she said.

"What?" said Jessica.

Elizabeth playfully hit Jessica over the head with her pillow. "You can find my green sweater that you borrowed two weeks ago and never returned." She laughed. "If I'm going to lose, I might as well lose looking good."

The next morning Amy waited anxiously outside school. As soon as she saw Ken, she hurried over. "Did you hear the news?" she said. "Elizabeth and I found the class money in the supply closet."

"You're kidding!" said Ken.

Amy nodded and continued walking with Ken. "It was all a big mistake," she said. "Ms. Wyler misplaced it. Jessica and Ellen had nothing to do with it."

"That's great," said Ken. "I guess that means we get to go to Disneyland."

Amy took a deep breath. "I'm sorry I've been such a bad friend," she said. "It isn't even worth it to tell you why I was acting this way. I just want to apologize."

Ken stopped. "Really?" he said.

"Really," Amy replied.

Ken picked up his pace. "Are you coming to the game this weekend?"

"The Boosters are cheering," said Amy.

"Maybe we can go out afterward for ice cream," said Ken.

Amy's eyes lit up. "OK," she said. She remembered something else. "Can I invite a friend?"

Ken's face fell. "Who?"

"Someone I haven't seen too much lately," Amy continued with a sly grin. "Her name is Elizabeth."

Ken looked relieved. "Sure," he said. "Sounds good to me."

The news about the class money spread quickly, and by noon everyone in the school knew it had been found.

Despite all the excitement, there was one thing that Elizabeth hadn't forgotten about: student council elections. She wished she'd done a better job with the speech. She'd practiced it enough times that she felt she should have known it by heart.

Just before lunch she went into the cafeteria by herself to cast her vote. As she crossed the empty room, she noticed all the colorful posters lining the walls. Maybe next year she'd try again, she thought.

Elizabeth carefully filled out her ballot, being sure to mark a heavy X next to her name. "When will we know the results?" she asked a girl who was watching the ballot box.

"Mr. Clark will announce it over the loudspeaker this afternoon," said the girl.

Elizabeth nodded and quietly walked away.

That afternoon Elizabeth had English class with Mr. Bowman. As she slid into her chair and prepared to take out her notebook, Julie approached, her face red. "You won't believe what happened," she said in a confidential voice.

"What?" said Elizabeth.

Julie bent down to whisper in Elizabeth's ear. "Peter asked me to go to the Dairi Burger with him on Saturday," she said.

The bell rang and Julie sat down in the seat next to Elizabeth. Elizabeth grinned at Julie, wishing there were some way she and Julie could finish their conversation, but Mr. Bowman was very strict about talking. She tore a corner off a piece of notebook paper, wrote *Congratulations* and drew a happy face inside the *O*. She passed the note to Julie.

Julie smiled. "Thanks," she mouthed back.

Elizabeth nodded and bent over her textbook.

Mr. Clark's announcement didn't come over the loudspeaker until nearly three o'clock. Everyone could hear him tapping on the microphone before he spoke. "Shirley, is this thing on?" he asked Mrs. Knight, the school secretary. Elizabeth giggled to herself as she imagined Jessica crashing through the door, taking over the office. There was some more background confusion, and then Mr. Clark said, "We're pleased to announce our new student council members." The class grew very quiet. "President, Olivia Davidson." There was loud applause. "Uh, boys and girls, if you're applauding, please hold it until the end. Vice President, Tom Sleeter. Secretary, Virginia Walker. Treasurer, Elizabeth Wakefield."

Elizabeth's mouth fell open. How could she possibly have won? It must be a mistake.

"On behalf of myself and all the teachers, I want to thank everyone who ran this year," Mr. Clark was saying. "You were all fine candidates, and we had some very close races."

Elizabeth looked around the room. People were smiling at her now and applauding. The bell rang, and everyone stood up.

"You won!" said Julie. "You must be so happy."

Elizabeth had a puzzled expression on her face. "But Peter's speech was so good," said Elizabeth. "Mine was awful."

"*I* voted for you," said Julie.

"You did?" said Elizabeth.

"I thought you were better qualified," Julie answered. "You told us that in your speech."

"But didn't you like Peter?" said Elizabeth.

Julie blushed. "Peter's speech was the funniest thing I'd ever heard," she said. "But you were the person who would do the best job."

Elizabeth nodded slowly. "I guess I see what you mean," she said.

Julie and Elizabeth made their way out into the hall. Julie squeezed Elizabeth's arm. "Look who's coming."

Peter approached Elizabeth and stuck out his hand. "Congratulations," he said.

"Thanks," said Elizabeth. Julie stood awkwardly at Elizabeth's side.

"Where are you going?" he inquired.

Julie looked at Elizabeth. "Uh, my house," said Julie quickly. "To celebrate. Want to come?"

"Sure," said Peter.

Amy came crashing down the hall. "Elizabeth!" she squealed. "You won!" When she saw Peter standing there, she stopped.

"It's OK," said Peter. "If my best friend won, I'd be happy too."

"You're right," said Amy. She slapped Elizabeth on the back. "All right, Elizabeth," she said.

"We're just going over to my house to celebrate," interrupted Julie. "Want to come?"

Amy grinned. "Sure," she said. "Your mom makes the best chocolate chip cookies in the world. Let's go." Laughing and joking, the four friends headed out the door.

Later that evening Jessica was busy helping Mrs. Wakefield set the table for their dinner guests. As she raced around the patio, she listened to Toy Car on her Walkman. "Be mine, be mine," she sang loudly as she tossed down the forks and spoons.

"Jessica, be careful!" shouted Mrs. Wakefield from the other room.

Jessica nodded and spun around. She had a good reason to be in such a great mood. Laura had called that afternoon to say that after she'd told her boyfriend her decision, he'd decided to drive down from his home in San Francisco to spend the weekend with her. He'd be joining them for dinner that evening. Jessica was ecstatic. She and Ellen had already spent about an hour on the phone discussing it.

Jessica looked up and saw Elizabeth standing nearby. "Did you hear the good news?" she shouted. "Casey is coming to dinner!"

Elizabeth looked puzzled.

"Laura's boyfriend," Jessica explained. "He was so excited when Laura told him she would marry him that he's driving down for the weekend. He said he wanted to be with her. Isn't that the most romantic thing you ever heard?"

Elizabeth smiled and held up a fork. She said something Jessica couldn't hear over the noise of her Walkman. "What?" said Jessica, pulling off the earphones.

"You put two forks at Casey's place," Elizabeth said. "He's going to have a tough time with his steak."

Jessica looked horrified. "Thank you so much, Lizzie," she said. "I would have been so embarrassed." The door bell rang and Jessica shrieked. "It's them! They're here!" She and Elizabeth both raced for the door and threw it open.

Their faces fell. "Oh, it's just Dad," said Jessica.

Mr. Wakefield laughed. "That bad, huh?" he asked.

"We were hoping it was Laura and her boyfriend," Elizabeth explained.

Mr. Wakefield nodded. "I'm glad to see you two getting along again."

Jessica's eyes lit up. "*Now* is it time for us to hear the secret you told us about?" she asked.

"Not quite yet," said Mr. Wakefield with a twinkle in his eye. "I'm still waiting for the right moment."

"But when is the right moment?" said Elizabeth. Now that she and Jessica were speaking again, even she was getting curious.

"You'll see," said Mr. Wakefield mysteriously.

The barbecue was a big success. As it turned out, Laura and Casey were the last guests to arrive.

When Jessica, Elizabeth, and Ellen opened the door, Jessica's heart stopped. Casey was about the handsomest man she'd ever seen. Tall, blond, and blue-eyed, he looked just like Parker Smith on *Love and Lace,* Jessica's favorite soap opera.

As Laura introduced him, he kept his arm around her waist.

"He's so cute, I'm about to die," Ellen whispered to Jessica.

Jessica stood transfixed as Laura finished her introductions.

"We're so happy you both could join us tonight," said Mrs. Wakefield.

Casey grinned. "I wanted to meet the people who were responsible for changing Laura's mind," he said.

"Don't thank us, thank Grandmother Jane," exclaimed Jessica. She was instantly embarrassed for blurting out like that, but Casey and Laura didn't seem to mind.

Laura held out her left hand. On her ring finger was a shiny new diamond. "Casey's been keeping this in his dresser drawer for months." She laughed. "I guess he couldn't wait for me to get back to San Francisco to put it on."

Casey squeezed Laura's hand. "I didn't want

you to change your mind, sweetheart," he joked.

"Why don't we all go out by the pool?" said Mrs. Wakefield, smiling. She turned to Casey. "I'm sure the girls would love to hear where you and Laura met."

Jessica cringed. Why did her mother have to ask such embarrassing questions?

"At the Laundromat," Casey replied with an easy grin. "I couldn't figure out how to work the machines."

"What an excuse!" Laura interrupted gleefully.

"Actually," Casey admitted, "I'd seen her around the neighborhood for months, but couldn't figure out how to manage an introduction. One day when I saw her heading for the Laundromat, I ran home, pulled the sheets off my bed, and hurried after her."

"Here was this guy standing around the washing machines with no soap and no change!" Laura said.

"So then you fell in love?" said Ellen.

Laura and Casey exchanged glances. "Sort of," said Laura. "I was dating someone else at the time. David. I'd been going out with him since high school. His parents and mine were best friends and they were really pushing for us to get married."

Casey took Laura's hand. "Laura was never really happy with the idea, but she didn't want to rock the boat."

"Until now," Laura added.

"We're so happy everything has worked out," said Mrs. Wakefield.

"And how," added Mark Riteman, no doubt thinking about the money he'd been given.

Mr. Wakefield put on a blue barbecue apron. "I don't know about anyone else, but I'm getting hungry for those steaks," he said. Everyone laughed. Mr. Wakefield handed Steven and Sam Riteman some long-handled forks. "How about some help, boys?" he said.

Over dinner, Steven, Sam, and Mark enjoyed hearing Casey's college football stories. Laura told everyone about her grandmother and talked about how there had once been a chicken coop in the Ritemans' backyard. Everyone had a wonderful time.

After the guests left, Jessica leaned against the front door and sighed. "I'll never forget this night as long as I live," she said. "Come on, Lizzie," she said, laughing. "Mom and Dad worked hard all night. Let's go load the dishwasher."

"Let me get this straight," said Steven. "You're actually volunteering?"

Jessica sniffed and stuck her nose in the air. "What's so strange about that?" she asked.

Elizabeth put her arm around Jessica. "Yeah, Steven," she said. "What's so strange about that?"

Mr. Wakefield picked up a sponge and threw it at Steven. "Come on, son," he said. "If the girls are doing the loading, you can wipe down the counters." He grinned at Elizabeth. "You can help the new student council member in the family."

"That's right," said Jessica. She spun around and pointed to Elizabeth. "That's my twin!" She turned to face her father. "*Now* can we hear your secret?" she asked.

Mr. Wakefield laughed. "What did I tell you?"

"You're waiting for the right moment," the girls said in unison.

Mr. Wakefield nodded. "Exactly," he said. "And this isn't it."

Jessica carefully rinsed off a dinner plate and handed it to Elizabeth. What in the world could the secret be? She peeked over at her father again, but he was already busy putting away the grill. Jessica handed the last dish to Elizabeth and dried her hands with a dish towel. Maybe her father would even tell them tonight, or tomorrow! Jessica gave an excited little skip across the room as she imagined the far-off exotic place where her father was bound to be taking them!

SWEET VALLEY TWINS

Keeping Secrets

Written by
Jamie Suzanne

Created by
FRANCINE PASCAL

A BANTAM BOOK®
TORONTO • NEW YORK • LONDON • SYDNEY • AUCKLAND

To Jessica Ann Copskey

One

"I'm dying of curiosity!" Jessica Wakefield cried to her identical twin Elizabeth as they entered their house after school.

"Well, Dad should be home in about half an hour, and then we'll find out what this mystery is all about," said Elizabeth. She dropped her books on the counter of the Wakefields' Spanish-tiled kitchen and then poured herself a glass of milk.

"Did he give you any clue about what it is?" Jessica asked, her blue-green eyes sparkling.

Elizabeth sighed and threw up her hands. This was the third time that Jessica had asked her the same question. But Elizabeth could never stay annoyed at her sister for long. Being twins made them as close as any two people could be. From their long blond hair to the dimples in their left cheeks, they were exact doubles in appearance.

"All I know is that at breakfast this morning, after you left, Dad said he would tell us the secret tonight," Elizabeth said. "By the way, where did you go so early this morning?"

"I had Booster practice," Jessica told her. The Boosters were a cheering and baton squad that Jessica belonged to at school. "I just can't wait to hear this secret."

Elizabeth took her social studies book and sat down at the kitchen table. "Yes, I'm excited, too," she said, opening the book. "But right now I'm going to try to get some of my homework out of the way."

Her concentration was quickly broken by the sound of Jessica's fingernail tapping on the counter. Raising her head, she gave her sister a long, hard stare. "I'm trying to get some work done," she said.

But Jessica ignored her comment. She was much less concerned with things like homework than her hardworking twin. She never understood how Elizabeth could come home after a long day at school and start in immediately on her homework. "Maybe Dad's going to tell us that he's taking us on a trip to Europe!" Jessica declared. "Or maybe the secret is that we're finally getting a boat. . . ." She started to pace back and forth across the kitchen. "Maybe he's going to tell us that we have another twin—that we're really triplets!" she said, her blue-green eyes growing wide.

Elizabeth burst out laughing, remembering the time she and her sister pretended to have a triplet named Jennifer in order to pull a joke on their friend, Brooke Dennis. "I'm sure that would surprise Brooke!" she exclaimed, giggling. "Jessica, instead of letting your imagination run wild, why don't you try doing some of your homework?"

Jessica shook her head. "I'm too excited to sit still. I can't even think of doing homework right now!" She continued to pace across the room, her blond ponytail bouncing up and down with each step she took.

As she looked up at her sister, Elizabeth noticed the barrette that she'd just purchased. It was in Jessica's hair. "Hey, isn't that my barrette?" Elizabeth asked.

"Oh, this?" Jessica asked innocently, touching her hair with her fingers. Then, in her sweetest voice, she explained, "I noticed it sitting on your dresser for almost a week. I thought maybe you'd decided that you really didn't like it. . . ."

"You could have asked," Elizabeth said. Though she was used to Jessica borrowing her things without asking, it still bothered her.

"I promise I'll never borrow anything of yours again without asking first," Jessica assured her. "Here, you can have it back, big sister," she said, starting to remove the clip from her hair.

Elizabeth smiled. It was a running joke between the twins that Elizabeth was the "big sister" because she had been born four minutes earlier than Jessica. "That's all right, you can keep it. Besides, it looks better on you," Elizabeth said.

"How could it look better on me?" Jessica asked. "I mean, we look exactly the same."

"I'm not sure," Elizabeth admitted. "But if you say another word, I just might ask you to return it!"

Jessica smiled and clamped her hand over her mouth. "Don't worry, my lips are sealed!" she exclaimed.

I'll believe that when I see it, Elizabeth thought with a sigh.

Elizabeth started to read once again, and Jessica went over to the refrigerator and opened the door. "Look at this!" she exclaimed.

"What?" asked Elizabeth, closing her book. She wasn't going to get any work done with Jessica around.

"Look at all this food," said Jessica, opening the door wide enough for Elizabeth to see.

"I guess we beat Steven home," Elizabeth observed. Steven was the twins' older brother and a freshman at Sweet Valley High. Jessica and Elizabeth often joked that he could eat more than all of the Wakefields put together.

"Wow, this is great!" Jessica said as she removed a plate of brownies. "I'm glad we got here first!"

Jessica crammed a brownie into her mouth and was about to grab another one when Elizabeth warned her, "Don't spoil your appetite."

"Hmmm?" Jessica said.

"Dad's taking us out to eat because Mom's having dinner with a client," Elizabeth reminded her.

"Don't worry. I *never* lose my appetite," Jessica joked, reaching for yet another brownie. "Lizzie, what do you think the secret's going to be?"

Elizabeth shrugged.

"Don't you even have a guess?" Jessica asked.

Elizabeth had no idea about the secret, but just then another idea occurred to her. "Jess, why don't you and I make dinner for Dad? I think he'd really appreciate it. It'd be a real surprise and—"

"But we don't know how to cook," Jessica interrupted.

"That's not true. I can make spaghetti and you make a great salad."

Elizabeth could tell from the grimace on her sister's face that she wasn't exactly excited about the idea. "I want to go out," Jessica said firmly. "It'll be much more fun."

"OK, OK. It was only a suggestion," Elizabeth muttered.

When the twins had entered the sixth grade, Elizabeth noticed that their interests were beginning to take separate paths. Elizabeth liked to read and write and have long talks with her close friends. She was in charge of the *Sweet Valley Sixers*, the sixth-grade student newspaper at Sweet Valley Middle School. Jessica preferred cheering at basketball games and gossiping at meetings of the Unicorn Club, an exclusive all-girls club to which she belonged. She also loved to dance and took ballet lessons at Madam André's studio. But having different interests didn't stop them from being best friends. Though they'd grown in separate directions, Elizabeth felt there was no one in the world closer to her than Jessica, and she knew in her heart that Jessica felt the same way about her.

At that moment Elizabeth heard a loud noise and jumped up. At the same time Jessica gasped, her eyes growing wide and fearful. "W-what was that?" Jessica stammered in fright.

"I don't know," Elizabeth whispered, starting to tremble. Now she heard distinct footsteps coming up the basement steps. Someone was in the house! Was it a burglar? Elizabeth saw Jessica's tanned face instantly turn white as a sheet. She grabbed Jessica's arm tightly as the footsteps grew closer.

Then, to their horror, someone opened the basement door. They froze.

"What's going on? Are you two getting reacquainted?" Steven Wakefield asked as he walked in and saw his sisters with their arms around each other.

"Steven!" Elizabeth cried. "What are you doing here?"

"I live here, remember?" Steven replied.

"You mean you were home the whole time?" Elizabeth said, looking confused.

"We didn't think you were here. The refrigerator was full!" Jessica added. "You practically scared us to death!"

"I was downstairs doing my laundry," he reported matter-of-factly. Then he started dribbling an imaginary basketball. Aside from eating, basketball was Steven's favorite activity.

"You, doing laundry?" Elizabeth asked in disbelief.

"I didn't think you even knew how the washer worked," Jessica commented sarcastically.

"That's how much you know," Steven said, making a noise between a chuckle and a snort. Elizabeth thought Steven was the most immature fourteen-year-old she knew.

"I still don't understand why you were doing laundry," she continued.

"And I'd like to know why you didn't raid the refrigerator like you always do. Are you sick or something?" Jessica asked.

"Ha-ha. You guys think you're so smart. Since you're going out with Dad, I'm going out, too. I'm going to the Dairi Burger with some of the guys, and I wanted to save my appetite so I'd have room for at least two cheeseburgers, two chocolate shakes, and—"

"Stop!" Jessica cried as she bent over and clutched her stomach. "I'm getting sick just listening to this!"

"That still doesn't explain the laundry," Elizabeth observed.

"Can't a guy wear clean clothes? Mom's so busy these days that I have to do this myself. We all have to learn to help out." It was true that their mother, who had a job as a part-time interior designer, had been working long hours lately.

"Is this Steven Wakefield talking?" Jessica asked. "Mr. Big Deal High School Freshman? I remember when it was too much for you to carry a dish to the sink!"

Elizabeth was impressed. She'd never heard her brother sound this mature and responsible. He claimed that high school was changing him. Maybe, she silently admitted, he was right. The "old" Steven would never have given a moment's thought to helping out around the house.

"Now I've got to throw my stuff in the dryer," Steven announced, starting downstairs again. He turned around and added, "By the way, Mom said that you can wash sneakers in the machine, so I threw mine in with the rest of my clothes. Does that sound OK?"

"Oh, no!" Jessica exclaimed.

Elizabeth shook her head. "You're supposed to wash them separately," she explained, starting to laugh. Things hadn't changed as much as she thought. The "new" Steven was very similar to the "old" one. "Do you need any help?"

"Thanks, but the day when I need help from a sixth grader is a long time away," he shouted, then dashed back down to the basement, two steps at a time.

Just then Elizabeth and Jessica heard the front door open. "I'm home!" boomed a deep voice.

Mr. Wakefield came into the kitchen, a big smile on his rugged, tanned face. With brown hair and eyes, he looked like an adult version of Steven. "How are my favorite twins?" he asked. Jessica ran over and gave him a big hug. Just as Elizabeth was about to do the same, Mr. Wakefield noticed the whirring hum coming from the basement.

He looked startled. "What's that?" he asked.

"Steven's doing his laundry," Jessica informed him.

Mr. Wakefield looked surprised. "You're kidding. All of you are turning into such responsible—"

"That's right, Dad. We really are." Jessica interrupted, in case he had changed his mind about telling them the secret.

"And that's why tonight's the night. You girls have shown me that you're old enough to keep a secret. So, do you promise not to tell anyone?"

"I promise," Elizabeth assured him, placing her right hand over her heart.

"Me, too," Jessica said.

"'Me, too' what?" her father asked.

"I promise," Jessica declared.

"Good, then we have an understanding. I'll change my clothes and say hi to your brother, and then we'll go. How does Guido's sound?"

Guido's Pizza Palace was an old family favorite, and it also had the world's best pizza. "That's a great idea," Elizabeth told her father.

"To tell you the truth, I've had so much pizza lately, it's coming out of my ears!" Jessica whispered to her sister as they raced upstairs to get ready.

"It serves you right for not bringing your lunch to school and having to eat those awful mini-pizzas in the cafeteria!" Elizabeth scolded.

For once Jessica had to agree. "You're right. Besides, it's not every day that a handsome man wants to take me out for dinner," she said with a giggle.

Elizabeth opened the door and smiled as she glanced at her neat blue-and-cream bedroom and all her familiar belongings. It wasn't long ago that she and Jessica had shared a room and constantly got into arguments about keeping it clean and how to decorate it. But all that had changed once each twin had a room of her own.

Elizabeth changed her sweater and brushed her long blond hair vigorously. After applying a dab of clear lip gloss to her mouth, she was ready to go. She walked through the adjoining bathroom to Jessica's room.

Jessica called out, "I'll be ready in a sec. Have a seat, Lizzie."

That's easier said than done, Elizabeth thought, looking around her at Jessica's pink-and-white room. Piles of clothing were on every piece of furniture. She cleared a spot on Jessica's messy bed and sat down. Then she looked around the room and wondered how Jessica ever found anything in there.

"Jess, may I have my clip back, please?" Elizabeth asked. She wanted to reclaim it before it got lost in the room's confusion. "That is, if you can find it," she joked.

"No problem," said Jessica. She went straight to the pile of clothes on her desk, reached underneath, and to Elizabeth's amazement, found the clip immediately. Jessica might not be the tidiest person in the world, Elizabeth thought, but she knew exactly where everything was.

After trying on several different outfits, Jessica still wasn't ready. "Guido's is very casual," Elizabeth reminded her. "It doesn't matter what you wear."

Looking shocked, Jessica answered, "Of course it does! It matters to *me*. I always try to look my best." Before Elizabeth could respond, Jessica changed out of her sweater and into a light blue sundress. Then she tied a purple belt around her narrow waist.

Jessica always made a point of wearing at least one purple article of clothing. She did this because she was a member of the Unicorn Club, and every girl in the club did the same. The Unicorns were very exclusive, and considered themselves to be as beautiful and special as the mythical animal of the same name. Elizabeth made no secret of the fact that she was proud *not* to be a Unicorn. She thought that the club's sole purpose was to talk about clothes and boys and to gossip about girls who weren't Unicorns.

When Jessica was finally ready, the girls ran downstairs to meet their father.

"Now, Dad?" Jessica asked excitedly.

Mr. Wakefield chuckled and said, "I'll tell you one thing, this secret is older than you girls."

Hearing this made Jessica even more impatient. "Come on, Dad, please tell us," she pleaded. "I'll die if I have to wait a second longer. . . ."

"Don't do that, it'll ruin the secret," Mr. Wakefield joked. Then he grew serious. "Ithig*I* *th*ithig*ink* *th*ithig*is* *w*ithig*ill* *c*ithig*ome* ithig*as* ithig*a* *s*ithig*urpr*ithig*ise*."

"Huh?" Jessica asked, not understanding a word she'd just heard.

"What did you say?" asked Elizabeth. It sounded like a mixture of pig latin and Greek.

Their father continued, "This is a secret language called Ithig. I learned it when I was just about your age. I'm going to teach it to you, but I want it to be just between the three of us. It'll be our private way of communicating."

In a million years Elizabeth would never have guessed that this was the secret. Jessica looked a little disappointed, which was understandable since she'd been expecting something more like a trip to Europe. But as Mr. Wakefield continued to talk in Ithig, she seemed to grow more curious.

Suddenly Jessica was full of questions. "What does *ithig* mean?" Jessica asked. "How long will it take for us to learn it?"

"I promise you one thing," said Mr. Wakefield, "you'll be speaking it fluently by the time you go to bed tonight. And I'll tell you everything you need to know as soon as we get to Guido's."

Two

When the waiter came over to their table, Mr. Wakefield ordered a large Guido's Deluxe. Then he began his story. "When I was a boy I had a friend named Billy Fantana. Billy and his family lived across the street. We were practically inseparable. Just like you two, especially when you were little. We had a secret tree house in the woods, and we—"

"Dad," Jessica interrupted, "what about Ithig?"

"Don't worry, I'm getting there. First, I'm giving you a little background. Now then, where was I? So Billy and I . . ."

Mr. Wakefield told them that Billy had learned about Ithig from *his* father. Mr. Wakefield and Billy spoke Ithig all the time and nobody knew what they were saying. Elizabeth was fascinated. She tried to imagine her father as a little boy, and listened closely to everything he said.

But Jessica was definitely less interested. She rolled her eyes and played with her knife and fork, twirling them between her fingers like a baton. It was good practice for the Boosters, she told herself.

Then Mr. Wakefield looked at Jessica and said, "*J*ithig*essi*ithig*ca w*ithig*ants* ithig*to l*ithig*earn th*ithigis *l*ithig*ang*ithig*uage*."

Jessica looked up, thinking that she'd heard her name, but she wasn't quite sure.

Elizabeth was just as confused as her twin. She concentrated on what her father was saying. Certain sounds were familiar. And "ithig" was repeated over and over again.

"It's really very simple," Mr. Wakefield said, switching back to ordinary English.

"It doesn't sound it," said Jessica doubtfully.

"Listen closely," their father instructed them. "This is how it goes. First, each syllable of a word has its own 'ithig.' That is, you simply insert an 'ithig' *inside* each syllable. For example, let's take the word twin. In Ithig, it would be 'twithigin.'"

Elizabeth stared at her father, trying to follow what he was saying.

"Now you try it. How would you say the word girl in Ithig?"

After a few moments Elizabeth answered, "I think it would be '*g*ithig*irl*.'"

"Very good!" exclaimed Mr. Wakefield. He continued, "But words of two letters or less, like I, it, and am, *start* with ithig. Ithig*I*, ithig*it*, ithig*am*, and so on. Basically, that's the secret. Give it a try, Jess."

"Yes, try," urged Elizabeth. "I mean, *Y*ithig*es*, *tr*ithig*y*!"

"*G*ithig*ood w*ithig*ork, L*ithig*iz*." Mr. Wakefield laughed and patted her on the back.

"*Th*ithig*anks, D*ithig*ad*," Elizabeth replied.

"This was supposed to be between the three of us!" Jessica protested. Elizabeth could already speak this new language and she could barely understand it. It wasn't fair!

"Honey, you'll pick this up in no time," her father reassured her.

"Think of how much fun it's going to be!" Elizabeth exclaimed. "Everyone will go absolutely crazy. Think how upset Lila will be!"

Lila Fowler was a Unicorn and a good friend of Jessica's. She was the daughter of one of the wealthiest men in Sweet Valley. Elizabeth thought she was a big snob and spoiled rotten. She really wasn't concerned with what Lila thought, but she knew that her sister cared a great deal.

Jessica took a moment to concentrate, trying to remember the rules to Ithig. Just then she saw Caroline Pearce walk into the restaurant with her mother. Caroline wrote the gossip column for the *Sweet Valley Sixers* and was known as the biggest blabbermouth in school. She had very long red hair and always wore her shirts buttoned all the way up to the top.

Jessica blurted out, "*Carol*ithig*ine Pearce*ithig ithig*is here*ithig!"

Mr. Wakefield smiled at her effort, even though it was a little mixed up. "At first everyone has a little trouble with Ithig," he commented. Then he asked Elizabeth if she knew the correct way to say "Caroline Pearce is here" in Ithig.

After thinking it over for a moment, Elizabeth replied, "*Car*ithig*ol*ithig*ine* Pithig*earce* ithig*is h*ithi*gere!*"

"Very good!" Then he turned to Jessica and repeated the rules. "You see, every syllable gets an 'ithig.' With short words, put the 'ithig' first."

"But Caroline really *is* here," Jessica insisted.

Elizabeth looked over her shoulder. Sure enough, Caroline was standing there.

"Pretend you don't see her," Jessica whispered. "I don't want her coming over here. She's always sticking her nose in where it doesn't belong."

At that moment Caroline spotted them, waved, and started walking toward their table. "Ithig*oh* ithig*no*!" cried Jessica.

"Shhh," Elizabeth urged, putting her finger to her lips.

When Caroline reached their table, she asked suspiciously, "Did I hear something strange going on at this table?"

Jessica smiled sweetly. "You heard us speaking a different language."

"Oh, really?" Caroline said, her eyes widening in surprise. "What is it? French? Spanish?"

"I'm sorry, Caroline, but I can't say. It's a secret language that's only between the three of us," Jessica told her.

But Caroline wasn't about to let the subject drop. "Why is it a secret?" she persisted.

"This is sort of a family matter, Caroline," Mr.

Wakefield said. "You must have secrets in your family. . . ."

"None like this," Caroline retorted, and walked toward the next table.

"Ithig*I* ithig*am* *pr*ithig*oud* ithig*of* *y*ithig*ou,* *J*ithig*ess,* *f*ithig*or* *n*ithig*ot* *t*ithig*ell*ithig*ing,*" Mr. Wakefield said to Jessica.

Just then the waiter appeared, carrying a steaming pizza high above his shoulder. He placed it on the table and suggested they let it cool off for a few minutes before they started eating But Jessica, who rarely paid attention to advice, immediately pulled a slice toward her and took a bite. "Ouch!" she cried.

"Jessica, why didn't you listen to the waiter?" Elizabeth scolded. "You have the patience of a flea!" She quickly pushed a glass of water toward Jessica.

"Ithig*I* ithig*am* *s*ithig*orry,*" apologized Jessica after downing the whole glass of water in three gulps.

"Pretty good, Jess," Mr. Wakefield commented. "Just remember, each syllable has its own 'ithig.' If a word has more than one syllable, you continue in the same manner for each."

Jessica corrected herself, "Ithig*I* ithig*am* *s*ithi-g*orr*ithig*y*."

Mr. Wakefield smiled. "Both of you are very quick learners. It took me days to get the hang of this."

"*Th*ithig*anks*, *D*ithig*ad*," said Elizabeth.

"Ithig*we* *l*ithig*ove* *th*ithig*is* *se*ithig*cr*ithig*et*!" Jessica declared.

"Ithig*I* *kn*ithig*ew* *y*ithig*ou* *w*ithig*ould*," Mr. Wakefield said with a grin.

Three

The next morning Elizabeth sat at the kitchen table eating a bowlful of cereal while Jessica painted purple stripes on each of her pink fingernails. Although Elizabeth thought the end result looked a little ridiculous, the process was fascinating. With deft fingers Jessica applied each stroke. She dipped the brush in the polish, wiped off the excess on the side of the bottle, then made a single, careful line lengthwise down the nail. She repeated the exact same procedure for each fingernail.

"You're a real artist when it comes to fingernail painting," Elizabeth told her sister.

"*Th*ithig*ank* *y*ithig*ou*, *b*ithig*ig* *s*ithig*is*," Jessica said with a smile. She waved her hands back and forth and started to blow on her fingertips.

Steven sauntered into the kitchen with his books under his arm. He took one look at Jessica's outstretched hands and made a face. "Oh boy!" he exclaimed. "What happened? Did you get your fingers slammed in the door?"

"No one asked you, Steven," Jessica snapped.

"Too bad," he remarked.

Mr. Wakefield came into the kitchen, briefcase in hand. "I'm in a hurry," he said, "Anybody need a ride?"

"Sure," said Steven.

"What about you two?" Mr. Wakefield asked the twins.

"Thanks, Dad, but I'd rather walk," said Elizabeth.

Jessica nodded in agreement and said, "Ithig*we* *b*ithig*oth* *w*ithig*ant* ithig*to* *w*ithig*alk*. . . ."

Putting his fingers to his lips, Mr. Wakefield said, "Shhh. Remember, this is a secret."

Steven shook his head and looked confused. "This family's getting really weird," he said, following Mr. Wakefield out the door.

As soon as they left, Jessica broke out laughing. "The best part about Ithig," she said, "is that Steven doesn't know it!"

"Well, he will soon if he keeps hearing you

speak it," Elizabeth warned. She got up and said, "Ready?"

Jessica lightly touched her fingertip to see if it was dry. "Lizzie, would you do me a favor and carry my books?" she asked. "My nails are still damp, and I don't want them to smudge."

Elizabeth had the feeling that once again Jessica was trying to con her. But before she could give her an answer, Mrs. Wakefield walked in, yawning. She had on her favorite terry robe, and her pretty blue eyes looked as if they weren't quite awake yet.

"Morning, Mom," Elizabeth said brightly.

"*M*ithig*orn*ithig*ing, M*ithig*om*," said Jessica.

Mrs. Wakefield looked surprised. "Is that the language your father was talking about?" she asked.

"*Y*ithig*es* ithig*it* ithig*is*!" Jessica declared with delight.

"Oh, my! Dad taught you that?"

"Yes. But the thing is, Mom, it's sort of a secret just between Dad and us. You see, when Dad was our age he had this friend—" Elizabeth began. She didn't want to hurt her mother's feelings.

"Honey, there's no need to explain. I understand completely. I think it's wonderful that you girls and your father have something private and special."

"Thanks, Mom. You're terrific." Elizabeth turned to her sister and said, "Are your nails dry yet? I really don't want to carry your books. I have enough of my own." Jessica looked surprised. She wasn't used to being turned down by her sister.

At this point Mrs. Wakefield noticed Jessica's hands. "How interesting," she commented. "I don't believe I've ever seen anything quite like that."

"Thanks, Mom. I came up with this design all by myself."

"Are you girls hungry?" Mrs. Wakefield asked. "Can I fix you some breakfast?"

"No, thanks. We're in a hurry," Jessica answered. She turned to Elizabeth. "Lithig*ets* githi*get* githigoithig*ing*."

Elizabeth followed her to the door, surprised to find that Jessica had agreed to carry her own books. "Bye, Mom. Have a good day."

"Githig*oodb*ithig*ye*, Mithig*om*," Jessica sang out.

Elizabeth and Jessica strolled down the tree-lined streets of Sweet Valley, California, a town which both twins thought was the most perfect place on earth. As always, the sun was shining in a blue sky that was dotted with only the tiniest puffs of clouds.

"Ithig*I* *w*ithig*ond*ithig*er* *wh*ithig*at* *ev*ithige-*ry*ithig*one* *w*ithig*ill* *th*ithig*ink* *wh*ithig*en* *th*ithig*ey* *h*ithig*ear* ithig*us*?" said Jessica.

"Remember, Jess, this is supposed to be a secret," Elizabeth said.

"I know that," Jessica said indignantly.

"Well, then, I don't think we should blab it all over school."

"Lizzie! I have no intention of doing that. Ithig*I* *c*ithig*an* *k*ithig*eep* ithig*a* *se*ithig*cr*ithig*et* ithig*as* *w*ithig*ell* ithig*as* *an*ithig*y*ithig*one*!"

Elizabeth looked doubtful, and Jessica started to get angry. "Ithig*I* *w*ithig*ould* *ne*ithig*ev*ithig*er* ithig*go* *b*ithig*ack* ithig*on* ithig*my* *w*ithig*ord*!" she declared loudly. "*Wh*ithig*at* ithig*do* *y*ithig*ou*—"

Just then a familiar-sounding voice called out their names. Elizabeth and Jessica stopped and turned around. It was Amy Sutton, one of Elizabeth's friends. "Wait up!" she called, running toward them.

"What's going on?" Amy asked when she caught up with the twins. Her pale blue eyes were bright and curious.

"Not much," Elizabeth answered. "What's going on with you, Amy?"

Amy was a smart girl, and she was also very direct. "I thought I just heard Jessica say something weird."

"Oh, Jessica was just fooling around," Elizabeth told her. But she felt terrible about fibbing. Aside from Jessica, Amy was her best friend, and Elizabeth hated not being able to tell her about Ithig.

Amy pressed on. "Are you sure? I could've sworn I heard—"

"Well, you didn't!" snapped Jessica, cutting her off.

"You don't have to get nasty," Amy snapped back. Before Elizabeth could apologize for her sister's rudeness, Amy said, "I'll see you later, Elizabeth." Then she took off and ran down the block.

Jessica turned to Elizabeth with a big smile on her face. "Aren't you proud of me? I didn't say a word about the secret."

Elizabeth couldn't believe what she was hearing. "Proud of you? I'm furious with you!" she cried. "How could you speak to Amy that way?"

"What do you mean?" Jessica asked, looking confused. "First you don't want me to speak Ithig in front of anyone. Then you get angry at me when I don't. . . ."

They were half a block away from school, and Elizabeth didn't want to start an argument. Already she could see groups of students milling around on the lawn in front of the sprawling brick building. "Let's just forget about Ithig for now," she suggested. "We can talk about this later."

"Fine," Jessica agreed.

As they approached the entrance to Sweet Valley Middle School, a group of Jessica's Unicorn friends came over to the twins. Lila Fowler was at the head of the group, and she looked upset.

"Hi, Lila," Jessica called out cheerfully, waving to her friend.

But Lila just tossed her shoulder-length brown hair and flashed a cunning smile. "There's something we want to discuss with you," she said.

"What's that?" Jessica asked.

"Caroline told us that you two have a secret language," Lila said.

Jessica giggled nervously. "That girl is always saying all sorts of things that aren't true," she said, trying to make light of the situation.

"So she made this whole thing up?" Lila asked suspiciously.

Jessica looked down at the ground. Then she glanced at Elizabeth, clearly looking for help. But Elizabeth just shrugged her shoulders. In a very small voice, Jessica answered, "No."

"Ha! She was right! How could you tell Caroline about this first? This is a huge insult to the Unicorns!" Lila hissed, sounding angrier with each word she spoke. Her brown eyes looked as if they were on fire.

"I didn't tell Caroline anything!" Jessica cried in a desperate attempt to explain herself. "She just happened to overhear us speaking. . . ."

"Speaking what?" Lila pressed on.

"Yeah, speaking what?" Janet Howell chimed in. Janet was Lila's first cousin and the president of the Unicorn Club.

"Tell us, Jessica," insisted Ellen Riteman, who could be just as demanding as Lila.

All of the Unicorns were pressing in on Jessica. It was a difficult position to be in, and she didn't know how to get out of it. If she told them about Ithig, she'd be breaking the promise she'd made to her father and Elizabeth. But how could she keep a secret from the entire Unicorn Club?

Elizabeth spoke up, coming to her sister's defense. "It's a special language that our father taught us. He made us promise not to tell anyone," she explained simply. As she spoke, Elizabeth noticed Amy sitting on a nearby bench. It was clear from the look on her face that she'd heard everything.

Elizabeth went over to her friend, but Amy immediately got up and started walking away. "Amy!" Elizabeth yelled, but Amy didn't turn around. Elizabeth ran after her and called her name again.

Finally, Amy faced her. "Elizabeth, you lied to me," she said, her lips trembling.

"I'm sorry, Amy. I didn't mean—"

"You lied to me," Amy repeated. "I asked what you and Jessica were up to, and you said nothing. And then you had the nerve to admit everything to those dumb Unicorns." Amy pushed her straight blond hair out of her face. Elizabeth could see tears welling up in her eyes.

"Amy, I never meant to hurt you," Elizabeth said honestly. "Let me explain. You see, my dad taught us this special language and made us promise to keep it a secret, you know what I mean? So, last night at Guido's, Caroline overheard us speaking it, and now she's telling everyone. The only reason I said anything about it to the Unicorns was because they were giving Jessica such a hard time. You know how awful they can be. . . ."

Just then the bell rang. Elizabeth put her arm around her friend and said, "We can talk more later, OK?"

Amy wiped her moist eyes with the edge of her sleeve. "OK," she said with a tentative smile.

Four

It was lunchtime, and Elizabeth was on her way to the cafeteria. Someone tapped her on the shoulder, and she wheeled around and saw Amy.

"I've been looking all over for you," Amy told her.

"I had to see Mr. Bowman and give him the master for next week's issue," Elizabeth said. Mr. Bowman was their English teacher and supervisor of the *Sweet Valley Sixers*.

"Do you want to eat lunch together?" asked Amy.

"Sure," Elizabeth replied enthusiastically. After what happened that morning, Elizabeth was pleased to see Amy acting like her old self again.

As they walked down the hall, Elizabeth said

to her friend, "I'm sorry about what happened earlier. I never thought that a silly secret could cause so much trouble. It doesn't seem that Lila is ever going to forgive Jessica."

"Why is it silly?" Amy asked.

Elizabeth hesitated for a moment. "It just is. If you knew the secret, I'm sure you'd agree."

"It all sounds so mysterious," Amy remarked. "You and Jessica must be having a lot of fun with this language."

Elizabeth thought it would be best to change the subject. "We need more articles for the next *Sixers*. I was hoping you'd have some ideas."

But Amy wasn't about to let the subject drop. "Liz, since you don't want to tell me the secret, maybe you could just say something in the language. . . ."

Elizabeth shook her head. "It's not that I don't want to tell you. The point is, I gave my word that I wouldn't."

"How about if you write it down?" Amy persisted. "Then you really wouldn't be telling me, would you?"

Though she was half joking, Elizabeth knew that Amy was also half serious. "Amy, can't we forget about this?"

"Couldn't you at least tell me the name of the language?"

Elizabeth was growing annoyed. "I don't understand why you're making such a big deal out of this," she said. "It's not like you."

Amy's mouth grew tight and she appeared to be getting upset all over again. Her tone became angry as she looked Elizabeth in the eye, and said, "Why? I'll tell you why. We're supposed to be best friends, and best friends aren't supposed to have secrets from each other. Sometimes I think that you already have a best friend, and her name is Jessica!"

Elizabeth was speechless. She had no idea that Amy was the slightest bit jealous of Jessica. "That's not true!" she cried.

Amy just stared at Elizabeth, a hurt look in her eyes. Elizabeth didn't know what to say. "I guess I sort of have two best friends," she muttered finally.

"Oh, yeah? Well, from now on you only have one!" With that Amy stomped away.

Elizabeth stood in the hall in a state of shock, too stunned to follow the crowd of students heading for the cafeteria. She'd never known Amy to be so unreasonable.

"Hey, Elizabeth, are you coming to lunch?" a friendly voice called out.

Elizabeth turned around and saw Julie Porter and Mary Robinson waiting for her. "Uh, yes, in a minute. Why don't you go ahead and I'll meet you there," Elizabeth told them. At the moment she was too upset even to think about eating. Maybe going outside for some fresh air would help.

As she walked downstairs she heard two girls arguing on the landing above her. Elizabeth couldn't see them, but their voices were loud and clear, and very familiar. Jessica and Lila Fowler.

"If you don't tell me your secret, I'll never speak to you again for the rest of my life!" Lila shouted.

"How can I? I promised my father and sister!" Jessica pleaded.

"That's not my problem," Lila said nastily. She could be very unpleasant when things didn't go her way.

Then Elizabeth heard a door slam and a whimpering sound, like someone crying. She ran up the stairs as fast as she could. Jessica was sitting on the steps with her head in her hands, sobbing quietly. Elizabeth put her arm around her sister's shoulders.

Through her tears Jessica said, "How did this happen? I didn't do anything to hurt anyone."

Elizabeth understood completely. She felt exactly the same way. Their closest friends had suddenly turned against them for no good reason.

"What are we going to do?" Jessica asked after she had calmed down.

"Let's first go eat lunch," she suggested, hoping that perhaps some food would make them feel better.

Jessica stood up and straightened her skirt. She ran her fingers through her hair and pulled up her socks. Then she pulled a tissue from her purse and dabbed her damp eyes. "Lizzie, do I look OK?" she asked.

"You look absolutely *f*ithig*ine*!" Elizabeth said, putting on her brightest smile. Jessica broke into a wide grin and gave her a hug.

They raced downstairs to the cafeteria. At the top of her lungs, Jessica yelled, "Ithig*I'm s*tithig*ar**v*ithig*ing*!"

Jessica hadn't brought her lunch to school, so Elizabeth waited with her on the cafeteria line. Then they walked out to the seating area.

Carrying her tray, Jessica glanced at the table

where the Unicorn Club always sat. She was surprised to see that Amy and Caroline, who weren't in the club, were sitting right at the center of the long table. Jessica felt a pang of sadness. The Unicorns hadn't even saved a seat for her.

Elizabeth was also surprised to see Amy with the Unicorns. She was chatting and giggling as if she sat with the club every day. Elizabeth knew Amy didn't like spending much time in the company of the Unicorns. *What is Amy up to*? she asked herself.

Trying to ignore the Unicorns, Jessica scanned the room, looking for a place to sit. The only free seats were at a table not far from the Unicorns, with people she and her sister hardly knew. Having no alternative, they went over and sat down.

Jessica ate her sandwich quickly and nervously, while Elizabeth just nibbled at hers. She overheard their names being mentioned at the Unicorn table, but tried not to pay attention.

Jessica, however, became enraged. She shot a dirty look across the room, but no one seemed to notice. They were too busy whispering among themselves. Then she got an idea. "I have the perfect way to get back at them," she told Elizabeth.

Jessica pushed her wispy bangs out of her face and cleared her throat. "*Th*ithig*is* *w*ithig*ill* *m*ithig*ake* *th*ithig*em* *ang*ithig*ry*," she said at the top of her voice. But the girls at the Unicorn table still didn't pay any attention to her. Raising her voice even louder, Jessica continued, "*N*ithig*ow* *y*ithig*ou* *s*ithig*ay* *s*ithig*ometh*ithig*ing*, *L*ithig*iz*."

"Later," Elizabeth insisted.

Jessica's scheme wasn't working. The people sitting nearby stared at her, but still no one at the Unicorn table even bothered to look up. They just continued to whisper as if they hadn't heard a thing out of the ordinary. It made Jessica furious.

She stood up and went directly over to the Unicorns table. As she approached, the whispering stopped. All the girls at the table turned their heads away and pointedly ignored her.

Jessica had never felt more humiliated in her life. There was no way she was going to let the Unicorns get away with it, she decided.

"How long is this going to last?" she asked, trying to stay calm.

"Till you tell us the secret to your language," Lila said flatly.

"I can't, Lila. Do you expect me to break the promise I made to my father and sister?"

Lila just stared back at her. None of the other girls breathed a word. Apparently that's exactly what they did expect.

Five

Elizabeth was rummaging through her locker, getting ready to go home for the day, when Amy passed by. "Hey, Amy," she called.

"Yes?" Amy replied, a distinct chill in her voice.

Trying to ease the tension between them, Elizabeth said, "Um, I was wondering . . . would you like to come over today? Jessica won't be there—she has a Unicorn meeting. I thought maybe you and I could talk."

"Sorry, I'm busy," Amy said curtly, going over to her locker.

"Well, how about tomorrow?" Elizabeth persisted, following Amy as she walked away.

"I have plans," Amy replied.

"Amy, don't you think you're being a bit unreasonable?" Elizabeth said.

But before Amy had a chance to reply, Lila Fowler came breezing around the corner, a mischievous grin on her face. She ran directly over to Amy and shrieked, "Have I got news for you! I just spoke to my father and he's arranged for Chris Crosby to be the star at the benefit for the hospital. It's going to be at my house on Saturday, and Daddy told me to invite all of my friends. I hope you can make it, Amy."

"Make it? Are you kidding? Chris Crosby is my favorite tennis player in the world! I absolutely adore him! You mean, I'm actually going to see him in person?" Amy was practically screaming with delight.

Lila glanced at Elizabeth, but made no effort to include her in the conversation. Elizabeth went to her locker and pretended she was looking for something. She was suspicious about Lila's sudden interest in Amy. Everyone knew that they only talked to each other because of the Boosters.

"I have so much to do," Lila was saying. "I have to send the invitations, figure out what I'm going to wear . . . do you want to help me, Amy?"

"Sure. I'd love to," Amy replied.

"Great," Lila said. Then she lowered her voice and added, "By the way, do you think I should invite Jessica and Elizabeth? I mean, since they won't tell us their secret."

Elizabeth shut her locker with a loud bang and wheeled around just in time to see Lila link her arm through Amy's as they walked down the hall. Amy was talking, but Elizabeth couldn't hear what she was saying. She wondered if Amy was agreeing with Lila's spiteful plan.

Elizabeth didn't mind missing a party. Missing the chance to see Chris Crosby didn't bother her either. But it broke her heart that she was losing her best friend, especially to someone as phony as Lila.

When Elizabeth walked outside, she was surprised to see Jessica sitting alone on the steps. "Hi," she said. "I thought you had a Unicorn meeting today."

"It was cancelled," Jessica said with a frown. "Besides, I'm not attending another meeting until they start acting nicer to me. I couldn't believe that scene at lunch."

"I know what you mean," Elizabeth replied. She sighed sympathetically. "Amy won't even talk to me."

As they walked across the lawn, Elizabeth didn't mention Lila's party, fearing the news might send Jessica into a rage. But just as they were leaving the school grounds, Amy and Lila strolled right across their path, talking loudly. Lila was saying, "This is going to be the greatest party ever. The twins will turn absolutely green!"

When Jessica heard the word "party," she stopped in her tracks. "Lila," she called, "what were you just saying?"

"I'm sorry, Jessica, but I can't tell you. It's a secret," Lila answered haughtily as she and Amy faced the twins.

"Did you say something about a party?" asked Jessica.

"Oh, you mean the one I'm having this weekend? It's going to be very special," Lila bragged.

"Why is that?" Jessica asked.

"Only because Chris Crosby is going to be there, and my dad's arranged for him to play a match in the afternoon. It'll be a big event but *I'm* having my own private party. . . ."

"Chris Crosby?" Jessica gasped, her mouth falling open.

Lila continued, "Yes, it's a benefit, and all the proceeds are going to the hospital. The adults have to make donations, but my friends can come for free. Of course, I'm only inviting my closest friends." Then she paused, grinned maliciously, and added, "I guess that means you two won't be coming."

"Lila, how could you do this to me?" Jessica demanded, outraged.

"Well, look what you two did to her," Amy declared.

Elizabeth looked her friend directly in the eye. "Amy, I didn't hurt your feelings on purpose," she said. "If I could tell the secret, you'd be the first person I'd—"

"Ha!" Lila interrupted. "Don't believe that for one minute, Amy. Now they'll get a taste of their own medicine and see how it feels! Come on, Amy, we have lots to do," she said, grabbing Amy's arm.

Amy looked at Elizabeth, but followed Lila. As they walked away, Lila looked over her shoulder and said to Jessica, "If you tell me your secret, maybe I'll change my mind about inviting you to the party." Then she and Amy hurried off together.

"Can you believe this?" cried Jessica. "What are we going to do?"

Elizabeth just shook her head.

The twins walked home in silence. They didn't even feel like speaking Ithig. "I think this has been the worst day of my life," Jessica declared.

"Don't worry. I'm sure this will blow over," Elizabeth said hopefully. "In a week no one will even remember that we had a secret."

"Maybe," Jessica said, not sounding convinced. "But I'll just die if I can't go to that party. Everyone's going to be there. I wish we'd never even heard of Ithig!"

Later that afternoon, when Mr. Wakefield came home and walked into the kitchen, the first thing he said was, "*D*ithig*id y*ithig*ou k*ithig*eep* ithi*gour se*ithig*cr*ithig*et*?"

"*Y*ithig*es, D*ithig*ad*," Elizabeth answered with a groan.

"Ithig*is s*ithig*ometh*ithig*ing wr*ithig*ong*?" Mr. Wakefield asked, sounding concerned.

"*W*ithig*ell* . . ." Jessica started to say, but Elizabeth immediately cut her off.

"Ithig*no*," she said flatly. She didn't want to spoil her father's good mood. Maybe she and Jessica could figure out a solution to their problem on their own.

"I've got a few calls to make," Mr. Wakefield announced. "Ithig*we* *c*ithig*an* *t*ithig*alk* *l*ithig*at*ithi*ger*," he said as he left the room.

Steven walked in, his books under his arm. He dropped them on the counter and went directly to the refrigerator. He grabbed as many things as he could hold in one arm, carried them over to the table, and started making a sandwich.

"Hey, did you hear about Lila's party?" he asked his sisters, spreading mayonnaise on a slice of bread.

"Yes," Jessica sighed.

"It sounds really great. I can't wait to go," he said.

"Since when are you going to a party of Lila's?" Jessica asked, surprised. Most of the time Steven made fun of Lila.

"Since she started inviting famous tennis players. This is one party that I'm definitely not going to miss."

"So, how did you manage to get yourself invited?" she prodded her brother.

"Lila just found me after school and invited

me. I guess she wanted to have some older men there for decoration," he joked.

"*I* guess she wanted to rub it in some more," Jessica muttered under her breath.

"What did you say?" Steven asked.

"Never mind," said Jessica. "It's just that Elizabeth and I aren't going."

Steven looked surprised. "What's the matter? You always go to Lila's parties. Did you have a fight or something?" he asked.

"It's a long story," Jessica said wearily.

"Well, I think you should try and make up," Steven advised, "because this is supposed to be the party of the year. They're having TV stars, photographers—"

"TV stars? Who?" she asked, her lower lip trembling.

"Lila said someone named Brett Carter's going to be there—"

"Brett Carter! I adore Brett Carter," Jessica screamed. He was one of her favorite soap opera stars. "I can't miss this party. I just can't!" Jessica cried. Then she turned and ran upstairs, bursting into tears.

Six

The staff of *Sweet Valley Sixers* was assembling their latest issue in Mr. Bowman's classroom. Amy and Sophia Rizzo collated the freshly mimeographed pages, Pamela Jacobson stapled, and Mary Robinson stacked the copies neatly. Julie Porter counted them and handed the finished copies to Elizabeth.

While they worked, the girls chatted and caught up on recent happenings. No one seemed to notice that Amy and Elizabeth weren't talking to each other.

"I've got some real exciting news," Mary reported. Mary was in the seventh grade, but she sometimes volunteered to help out the *Sixers* staff.

"What's that?" Elizabeth asked eagerly.

Mary put down the papers in her hand. "My mom's got a new boyfriend," she said, her eyes sparkling brightly. "She's been seeing a lot of him. . . ."

"How does your mother feel about him?" Elizabeth asked, hoping that Mrs. Robinson had found a nice man. She was a divorcée and new to Sweet Valley, and Elizabeth imagined that it was lonely for her.

"She says they're getting serious," Mary said with a big smile.

"That's great!" everyone chorused. Though they'd never discussed it, Elizabeth suspected that Mary would be thrilled to have a father. She'd spent most of her life in foster homes, as Mary Giaccio. It was only recently that she became reunited with her real mother and became Mary Robinson.

Mr. Bowman strolled into the room. "How's it going?" he asked with a wink.

Pointing to the tall stack of finished *Sixers*, Elizabeth replied, "We're almost done."

"Does anyone have ideas for the next issue?" Mr. Bowman asked, sitting down at his desk. "I don't think we have enough articles."

"Chris Crosby is going to be appearing in Sweet Valley," Amy replied eagerly. "It's going to be a benefit for the hospital, and it's taking place at the Fowlers'. I think it would make a great story."

"So do I," said Mr. Bowman, stroking his chin. "Are any of you going?" he questioned them.

"I am," everyone said in unison—everyone except Elizabeth.

"Well, who do you think should get this assignment?" Mr. Bowman asked Elizabeth.

Elizabeth paused for a moment to think about the question. She was sure that Amy would love the job, but when she looked over at her, Amy lowered her eyes nervously. Elizabeth suspected that Amy thought she wasn't going to be chosen because of their argument. But Elizabeth wouldn't do that to Amy.

"I think Amy should do it. After all, she knows more about sports than any of us," offered Elizabeth.

Amy broke into a smile. "Thank you," she said, though she didn't look at Elizabeth.

"Fine. Any other ideas for articles?" Mr. Bowman asked.

"How about a story on the Sweet Valley Symphony? My father could arrange an interview," suggested Julie, whose father was a professional musician.

"That's a great idea!" Elizabeth said. "You're such a good piano player. I think you'd be the perfect person to do this piece."

Julie smiled shyly. "I'll talk to my dad tonight," she said.

"That's a great idea, Julie. Any others? What about you, Elizabeth?" Mr. Bowman asked.

"Um, uh, not really . . ." Elizabeth admitted apologetically. Most of the time she had plenty of ideas, but now she was still upset over her argument with Amy. "But I'll come up with something for our next meeting," she promised.

"Then we'll call it a day," announced Mr. Bowman, handing a stack of papers to each girl.

Usually Amy and Elizabeth distributed copies of the *Sixers* on the first floor, leaving stacks in the sixth-grade homerooms, and the other girls brought them to the cafeteria and auditorium. But today Amy started to follow Julie out of the room. "We'll take care of the cafeteria," Julie called as they left.

Though Elizabeth tried not to show that anything was wrong, inside she felt it strongly. She missed Amy's company more and more. But what could she do? If she made up with Amy by telling her secret, she would be going back on her word. She wished Amy would try to understand. . . .

Out in the corridor with a stack of *Sixers* under her arm, Elizabeth walked down the quiet hall. Most of the kids had already left for the day, and a lot of the classrooms were already locked. From where she stood, Elizabeth saw that the music room was still open and the lights on. As she headed in that direction she heard loud voices coming from within. It sounded like a party. She wondered if Mr. Garvin, her music teacher, knew about it.

Elizabeth poked her head in the door and discovered a group of teachers standing around Mr. Garvin's desk with small paper cups in their hands. They were all laughing and smiling. Feeling surprised and out of place, Elizabeth stood in the doorway without saying a word.

Mr. Garvin was the first to notice her. "Elizabeth! How long have you been here?" he asked, a big grin on his face.

"I just came to drop off the *Sixers*. I didn't mean to interrupt," Elizabeth said apologetically. She plopped a stack of papers down on the desk nearest the door. But as she turned to leave, Mr.

Garvin stopped her. "Please stay for a little while."

On Mr. Garvin's desk Elizabeth noticed a bottle of champagne, a carton of orange juice, and a stack of paper cups. "What's going on?" she asked.

"We're celebrating the birth of Mr. Garvin's first baby," Mrs. Arnette announced.

"Mr. Garvin had a baby?" said Elizabeth, surprised. She didn't even know he was married.

"I think it was his wife that had the baby," Mr. Nydick, the white-haired man who taught social studies, said with a chuckle.

"That's right. This morning at thirteen minutes after eleven," added Mr. Garvin, shaking his head as if he still couldn't believe it had actually happened.

"Gee, Mr. Garvin, congratulations!" said Elizabeth. She had always liked Mr. Garvin, and she was sure he'd make a great dad.

"Here," said Ms. Wyler as she handed Elizabeth a cup of orange juice. "Let's drink a toast to young Michael Jay Garvin. Here's to his health and happiness." She held up her cup and took a sip.

"Michael? I like that name," Elizabeth said to Mr. Garvin. She was so happy for her teacher that for a moment she forgot all about the trouble she was having with Amy.

When Elizabeth arrived home that day, a letter was waiting on the hall table. The envelope was addressed to her. She tore it open excitedly and read:

> Dithig*ear* *El*ithig*iz*ithig*ab*ithig*eth*,
> *Y*ithig*ou* ithig*are* *inv*ithig*it*ithig*ed* ithig*to*
> ithig*a* *t*ithig*enn*ithig*is* *p*ithig*art*ithig*y* . . .

It went on to give the date and time of the Fowlers' tennis benefit and was signed by Lila—all in Ithig! How in the world had Lila learned to write in Ithig?

It didn't take long for Elizabeth to realize that Jessica must have told Lila the secret. How else could Lila have learned the language?

Elizabeth ran up to her room and waited for her sister to return home. Too upset to read or write, she threw herself on her bed and just lay there, staring at the ceiling. When Jessica got home, Elizabeth was really going to let her have it!

Soon Elizabeth heard her sister's footsteps on the stairs. Whistling and humming to herself, Jessica sounded as if she were in a good mood. *Too good,* Elizabeth thought angrily.

Sticking her head in Elizabeth's doorway, Jessica said cheerfully. "Hi, Lizzie. How was your day?"

"Not good," Elizabeth replied. She got up and waved the invitation. "What do you know about this, Miss Benedict-Arnold Wakefield?"

"I don't know what you're talking about," Jessica answered innocently. She took the card from Elizabeth and read it. Her cheeks paled. "I can't believe it!" she exclaimed. "This time Lila's gone too far. . . ."

"Why is it Lila's fault?" Elizabeth said sternly. "You're the one who squealed!"

"But Lila told me she wouldn't tell anyone!" Jessica said defensively. "She promised that if I told her the secret, she wouldn't breathe a word. Now look what she's done! I never should have trusted her!" Jessica cried.

"What about yourself?" Elizabeth demanded. "You blabbed our secret, didn't you?"

"Well, not exactly," said Jessica, a thoughtful look crossing her face. "I had to do something, Lizzie. Our best friends were turning against us! I couldn't just sit back and let that happen."

"You just wanted to get invited to Lila's party!" Elizabeth cried angrily. "Isn't that right, Jess? You told her just so you could go to her stupid party!"

"Don't be so dramatic, Lizzie. You're making too much of this—"

"We promised. Or don't you remember?"

"Of course I do," Jessica insisted.

"Then admit what you did was wrong!" Elizabeth demanded.

"Why was it so wrong?" Jessica asked innocently. "You got invited to the party, didn't you? So what's the big deal?"

"You broke your word. You went back on a promise. Doesn't that mean anything to you?" she said, her voice rising.

"Sure it does. But so do friends and having fun," Jessica cried, her lower lip trembling. Large tears started to run down her smooth cheeks. "You don't have to act so high and mighty!" she cried out.

"Hey, what's going on up there?" Mr. Wakefield called from the foot of the stairs.

Clearing her throat, Jessica jumped up and called back, "Nothing, Dad." Then she closed her sister's door.

But a second later they heard a knock. "May I come in?" Mr. Wakefield asked.

"Sure, Dad," Elizabeth called as Jessica quickly wiped her eyes.

Mr. Wakefield walked in and said, "I could hear you two all the way in the den. What's going on? Maybe I can help."

At first neither Jessica nor Elizabeth said a word. Then Jessica, who had been trying to act as if nothing were wrong, could not hold back her tears any longer. Mr. Wakefield immediately went over and put his arm around her. "There, there, honey," he said comfortingly. "Why don't you tell me what the problem is."

At this, Jessica broke down and started to sob uncontrollably. "Oh, Dad, whatever I do, it's always wrong."

"What do you mean?" her father said with concern.

Between sobs Jessica told him the whole story. "First Lila and Amy found out about our language, and they got really upset with me and Elizabeth because we wouldn't break our promise and tell them the secret," Jessica explained. "Then Lila decided not to invite us to this really great party that she's having. I'm sure even you've heard about it. You know, the benefit the Fowlers are having with Chris Crosby—"

"Yes, Steven did mention something about that," Mr. Wakefield interrupted.

"Anyway, the only way Lizzie and I could get invited was to teach Lila how to speak Ithig," Jessica explained.

"So what did you do?" Mr. Wakefield asked.

"I told her the secret," Jessica answered softly. "But only after she promised not to tell anyone," she added.

"I see. And how do you feel about this, Elizabeth?" Mr. Wakefield asked.

"I think it would have been nice if she told me that she planned on letting Lila know. I mean, we all three promised that we wouldn't tell, right?" Elizabeth looked at her father for an answer.

Mr. Wakefield shook his head. "I'm sorry Ithig has caused such problems for you girls," he said. "I certainly never intended that. There's nothing good about something that causes this kind of trouble between sisters and friends."

"Then you think I did the right thing?" Jessica asked eagerly.

"Well, not exactly," he said. "But I think I understand. However, I do think you owe your sister an apology. You should have told her first, and me, too, for that matter. It really wasn't fair."

Jessica turned to her sister and said in her most sincere voice, "I'm sorry Lizzie. What I did was wrong, but I just wanted everything to be all right again. Please forgive me." She gave her sister a big hug and added, "I promise I'll never squeal on a secret again."

Knowing her twin as well as she did, Elizabeth wasn't totally convinced of this. But she smiled and forgave her nonetheless. She could never stay angry at Jessica for long. And maybe now that the secret was out, life would start returning to normal.

Seven

"Oh, Lizzie, it's going to be so much fun! I wish you'd come," Jessica urged. She was browsing through her sister's closet, looking for a sweater to wear with her new dress.

"No, thanks," Elizabeth said firmly. "I'm going to spend a quiet day alone, trying to write a story."

"But you can write a story any time," she protested. "How often will you have the chance to see Chris Crosby?" She pulled Elizabeth's yellow cardigan off its hanger. "Can I borrow this one?" she asked.

Elizabeth nodded. "I'm not going to Lila's party. I just don't want to have anything to do with her," she said.

"OK, have it your way. But I think you're

making a big mistake," Jessica warned. She twirled in front of the full-length mirror on the bathroom door, checking to make sure her sundress looked all right. Then she ran a comb through her long blond hair and was ready to go. As she walked out the door she said, "I'll see you later, Lizzie. If you happen to change your mind—"

"I won't," Elizabeth insisted. Sometimes Jessica didn't understand her at all, she thought.

As soon as Jessica was gone, Elizabeth began her work. But as she reread what she'd written, she decided that she didn't like it. She tore the sheet of paper from her typewriter, crumpled it into a ball, and tossed it in the trash basket. Using a fresh sheet, she started her story again. But she didn't like her second attempt any better. For some reason her ideas just weren't flowing. Maybe it was because the house was too quiet. She wasn't used to that. Normally Steven's stereo would be blasting and Jessica would be barging into her room every five minutes.

Elizabeth sighed and stared at yet another blank piece of paper in front of her. She was desperately trying to come up with an idea when she heard a knock at her door. "Honey, may I come in?" called Mrs. Wakefield.

"Sure, Mom," answered Elizabeth.

The door opened and Mrs. Wakefield walked in, her purse under her arm and sunglasses perched on her head. "I'm going to the mall, and I wondered if you'd like to take a ride with me," her mother asked.

It sounded like fun, and Elizabeth hesitated for a moment. "I don't think so. I'm trying to write a story, and I'm having trouble getting started," she explained.

"Then maybe you need to take a break. Sometimes it helps to clear your thoughts for a while," her mother suggested. "Also, I thought you might want to get a card for Mr. Garvin."

"Hey, that's a great idea!" Elizabeth exclaimed, her face lighting up. She had wanted to do something for her teacher, but until now she wasn't sure what. Deciding that a break might be just what she needed, Elizabeth jumped up and followed her mother outside to the car.

When Jessica arrived at the Fowlers' house a butler greeted her at the front door and escorted her out back. There, Jessica was dazzled by what she saw. Newly constructed bleachers framed the Fowlers' tennis court, a huge tent had been erected on the grounds, and people of all ages were milling about. And in the middle of the lawn, surrounded by adoring fans, cameras, and reporters, stood Chris Crosby. Jessica gasped. It was incredible seeing someone so famous in person.

Just then Lila came over to Jessica. "Ithig*so* *n*ithig*ice* ithig*to* *s*ithig*ee* *y*ithig*ou*," she said with a broad smile as she linked arms with Jessica.

Jessica grinned back, happy that they were friends again. "Would you like something to eat?" Lila asked. "There are all sorts of things under the tent." She pointed to the long tables heaped with delicious-looking food. But before Jessica could answer, Ellen Riteman came running up to them, so excited she could barely speak.

"Look at this!" she said breathlessly, holding up a napkin that bore Chris Crosby's autograph. "I can't believe it!" she shrieked. "He actually signed my napkin!" Several of the other Unicorns, including Janet, Mary, and Betsy Gordon, gathered around to take a look. They were all very impressed. Celebrities were high on the Unicorns' list of important people.

Tapping Jessica on the shoulder, Julie Porter asked, "Where's Elizabeth?"

"Uh, she wasn't feeling well," Jessica fibbed, not knowing what else to say. She was sure Elizabeth wouldn't want her to tell everyone why she really stayed away.

"That's too bad," Julie said, her friendly brown eyes showing concern. "Tell her I hope she feels better."

"Sure," said Jessica with a grin. Then she spotted her brother coming in with his friend Ted Rogers. Having a bit of a crush on Ted, Jessica excused herself and walked over. "Hi, guys," she greeted them.

"Hi, Jessica," said Ted. "Where's your sister? I told her I'd give her some riding pointers soon." Ted worked after school at Carson Stables and was always helpful to Elizabeth, who loved horses.

"Uh, she's not feeling well," Jessica repeated.

"I'm sorry to hear that. Well, as soon as she gets better tell her to come down to the stables—"

"She's sick?" Steven interrupted. "When did that happen? She seemed fine when I saw her this morning."

Shooting him a mean look, Jessica discreetly nudged him with an elbow.

Mr. Fowler announced through a microphone that the match would be starting soon. The grown-ups were taking their seats in the bleachers. "We have our own special section," Lila informed her friends, pointing to the folding chairs that had been set up on the grass. The Unicorns and all the other kids from school rushed to get seats.

Jessica sat in one of the chairs next to Lila, and Amy sat in the other. Frowning at Jessica, Amy said to Lila, "What's she doing here?"

"I changed my mind and invited her," Lila said, brushing off the question. Then Lila turned to Jessica and said, "Ithig*I g*ithig*ot* ithig*to m*ithig*eet Chr*ithig*is earl*ithig*i*ithig*er*."

"*W*ithig*ow*! *Wh*ithig*at d*ithig*id* ithig*he s*ithi-*gay*?" Jessica asked.

"Ithig*he s*ithig*aid, 'N*ithig*ice* ithig*to m*ithig*eet y*ithig*ou*,'" Lila said proudly.

"*W*ithig*ow*!" Jessica repeated.

"By the way, where's Brett Carter?" Jessica whispered.

"Unfortunately, ithig*he c*ithig*ould*ithig*n't m*ithig*ake* ithig*it*," Lila said.

When Amy heard the two of them speaking Ithig, she became very upset. "Hey, when did you learn to speak that language, Lila?" she asked angrily, her voice rising. "Why didn't you tell me?"

"I was just about to," Lila informed her. "There's nothing to it. All you do is stick an 'ithig' in each syllable of a word. *S*ithig*ee h*ithig*ow* ithi*gea*sithig*y* ithig*it* ithig*is*?" she told her.

"Is that all?" Amy asked, surprised. "*Th*ithi*gat s*ithig*eems r*ithig*eal eas*ithig*y*," she added, getting the hang of it.

After overhearing Lila, everyone around them picked it up. Soon they were all speaking Ithig. "*Th*ithig*is* ithig*is f*ithig*un*!" Jessica heard Janet say.

"Ithig*it s*ithig*ure* ithig*is*," Ellen answered.

Then the game started and they all quieted down. Chris Crosby's opponent was a local talent from the Sweet Valley Tennis Club. But he was no match for a professional like Crosby. Whenever he scored a point, everyone in their section would jump up and yell, "*Y*ithig*ea, Cr*ithig*osb*ithig*y*!"

By the end of the afternoon, after winning three out of five sets, Crosby won the match. The moment he scored the winning point, the crowd rose to their feet, breaking into cheers and applause. Crosby lifted his arms up in the air and took a bow while the spectators cheered him on.

Though not a big sports fan, Jessica thought this was one of the most thrilling moments of her life. Joining the others, she stood and clapped until her hands hurt.

When Jessica arrived home she ran straight upstairs to Elizabeth's room. "How did it go?" Elizabeth asked, looking up from her typewriter.

"Oh, Lizzie, it was fantastic! Chris Crosby is an unbelievable player. It was almost like being at Wimbledon! You really should've come. Have you been writing all day?"

"On and off. But I'm almost done." Elizabeth sighed. For once maybe Jessica was right. Perhaps she should have gone to the party. She could have put up with Lila for something so special. But it was too late to worry about it now, she thought.

Elizabeth turned around in her chair and forgot about her book for the moment. "Tell me everything," she urged her sister. "Wait a minute. Before you start, I want to show you something," Elizabeth interrupted herself. "I took a ride to the mall with Mom earlier and got this card for Mr. Garvin." She pulled out the card and showed it to Jessica.

Jessica cooed, pointing to the picture of the baby swaddled in a blue blanket. She opened it.

"'Congratulations from the two of us,'" she read aloud. "Oh, Lizzie, it's just perfect!"

Elizabeth handed her a pen, and Jessica quickly signed her name under her sister's. Then Elizabeth put the card in its envelope and looked at her attentively. "OK, continue," she said.

"Well, Crosby won, of course," Jessica began. But before she could go on, the phone rang. Jessica leaped up, ran into the hall, and picked up the receiver. "Hello?" she said.

"Is that you, Jessica?" a voice asked angrily.

"Amy?" Jessica guessed.

"Please put your sister on," Amy requested coldly.

Jessica called for Elizabeth. As she handed her the phone, she covered it and whispered, "It's Amy, and she sounds upset about something."

"Hello, Amy?" Elizabeth said into the receiver, unable to imagine why Amy was suddenly calling her. It had been nearly a week since they'd last spoken.

"Hello, Elizabeth. I just wanted to tell you that your dear sister told Lila about Ithig. What do you have to say about that? I mean, if Jessica told Lila, why couldn't you tell me? Apparently it wasn't such a big secret after all. . . ."

"Amy, we've got to talk. Listen, I'll be happy to tell you the secret whenever you like. It's really simple."

"It's too late," Amy interrupted. "I already know your dumb secret. And so does everybody else. Thanks, but no thanks," she yelled as she slammed down the phone.

What did Amy mean? Had Jessica told everyone? Elizabeth wondered. But more important, would Amy ever be her friend again?

On Tuesday afternoon Elizabeth walked into the music room for her weekly music class. She expected to find everyone sitting at their desks and Mr. Garvin at the front of the room. Instead she found a noisy group of kids. "Where's Mr. Garvin?" she asked as she walked over to her desk.

"Nobody knows," Sophia answered, shrugging her shoulders.

"Maybe he's sick," suggested Charlie Cashman, who also sat near Elizabeth. "Wouldn't it be great if class was cancelled?" he added hopefully.

"You want Mr. Garvin to be sick? That's terrible, Charlie," Elizabeth said, raising her voice over the noise in the room, which was getting louder and louder. Kids in the class were yelling, walking around, sitting on their desks, and in general taking advantage of the fact that no teacher was present.

Then a tall, young-looking woman entered the room. Everyone turned to look at her as they scrambled to their assigned seats. The woman went to the front of the room, stood behind Mr. Garvin's desk, and faced the students. "My name is Ms. McDonald," she announced, smiling nervously.

"As you all know by now, Mr. Garvin and his wife just had a baby. Mr. Garvin has since decided to take a leave of absence so he can help out at home. I'm pleased to announce that I'm going to be his substitute for the remainder of the year," she informed them.

Elizabeth was happy to hear that Mr. Garvin and his new family were doing well, but she was also saddened that he wouldn't be teaching any longer. She hoped that Ms. McDonald, with her wavy brown hair and pretty blue eyes, would be as nice as he was.

Elizabeth heard people groan and mutter,

"Oh, no!" She guessed that almost everyone would miss their old teacher as much as she would.

"Guess we don't have to worry about any tests today," Charlie joked loudly.

His best friend, Jim Sturbridge, called out, "Since it's your first day, we won't have any homework, right?"

Then Elizabeth saw a paper airplane glide right past her nose.

Picking up a ruler, Ms. McDonald rapped it against her desk, saying, "Boys and girls, please settle down." For a brief time the room became totally silent. Then Ms. McDonald started the lesson she'd planned. "Mr. Garvin was teaching you the history of different musical instruments, correct?" she began. No one answered her question, but she continued. "Today I'm going to play several different recordings and I want you to tell me which instruments you hear."

She walked over to the record player and put on an album. But as soon as she turned her back, the kids started talking and laughing.

"Hey, Charlie, catch this," Jim Sturbridge shouted, throwing the purse he'd just snatched off Lila's desk across the room.

"Jim! How dare you!" Lila cried. She rose from her seat and ran over to grab her purse from Charlie's hands. But by the time she got there, Charlie had already tossed it back to Jim. When Ms. McDonald turned around, Lila was standing in the middle of the center aisle.

"Just what do you think you're doing?" Ms. McDonald asked her.

"I'm trying to get my purse," Lila answered, pointing to the object that Jim was holding under his desk.

"Is that her purse?" the teacher asked Jim.

But Jim, a bully and a class clown, didn't say a word. Instead he pointed to his throat and silently mouthed, "I can't speak. I've got laryngitis." All the kids immediately burst out laughing.

Elizabeth saw Ms. McDonald's face turn red as she looked furiously at him. "Answer me!" she demanded, losing her patience. "If you don't give me an answer, I'll be forced to give you a week of detention," she threatened.

With this, Jim spoke up. "I'm sorry, Ms. McDonald, ithig*I* *r*ithig*eall*ithig*y* ithig*and* *tr*ithig*u*-*l*ithig*y* ithig*am*." He got up and gave Lila her purse.

"What?" the teacher asked, looking confused.

"*Nithigevithiger mithigind,*" Jim replied with a cunning smile.

Elizabeth was shocked that Jim Sturbridge knew Ithig. She remembered Amy saying that the secret was out and everybody knew it. At the time she thought Amy was exaggerating, but now she knew it was true. Most of the other kids were laughing hysterically at what was going on. Ms. McDonald's face was red and she looked as if she were about to start crying. She pounded her desk, trying once again to bring the class to order, but it was no use.

"*Hithigere, cithigatch thithigis,*" Charlie yelled to Jim as he tossed him an apple that he'd taken from his book bag. Then Jim threw the apple to Jerry McAllister, who started to eat it.

"*Cithigan ithigI hithigave ithiga bithigite?*" someone called from the back of the room.

"*Ithigme tithigoo!*" shouted someone else.

Elizabeth couldn't believe her classmates could be so cruel. After all, there didn't seem to be anything wrong with Ms. McDonald. The way the kids were acting was terribly unfair. No one even gave her a chance.

Ms. McDonald was so upset, she couldn't say a word. Everyone was speaking Ithig, and she couldn't understand a word they were saying. She sat at her desk with her head in her hands as the students continued to carry on. When she looked up, her eyes were red and her face was sad. Elizabeth desperately wanted to help her, but how?

Eight

"Oh, I'm sorry, I was looking for Mr. Bowman. . . ." Amy apologized as she opened the door to his empty classroom and found Elizabeth sitting alone, working at one of the desks.

"He already left. He said something about a dentist's appointment," Elizabeth explained as she looked up.

"I had a question about our next assignment, but it can wait till tomorrow. . . . I didn't mean to disturb you." Amy started to close the door.

"No problem," Elizabeth called, trying to be friendly. "By the way, I just read your article, and I think it's terrific."

"Oh, thanks. Thanks a lot. I worked really hard on it," Amy said, her face beaming with pride.

"Well, you did a great job. Your descriptions were so clear, I almost felt like I was there myself," Elizabeth complimented her.

"That's a really nice thing for you to say," Amy volunteered, adding, "especially after some of the things I've said to you recently."

Then both girls opened their mouths at the same time. "I've been thinking—" Elizabeth started. "I wanted to tell you—" Amy began. Breaking into laughter, they smiled at each other for the first time in more than a week.

With her head down, Amy walked over to where Elizabeth was sitting. "Listen," she said softly, her blue eyes misting over. "I've acted really silly. I don't know why I got so upset. I wouldn't blame you if you never forgave me. Things just aren't the same without you, though."

Elizabeth was so happy, she felt like crying. Forgiving Amy at once, she said, "I've missed you, too, and I'm really sorry about—"

"Shh," Amy interrupted, holding her finger to her lips. "I'm the one who should apologize. I'm the one who acted like a spoiled brat. You didn't do anything wrong, Elizabeth. If you and Jessica have a secret, that's your business. Lila had me convinced that there was something more behind it—"

"I'm willing to forget the whole thing if you are. *Frithigiends*?" Elizabeth asked, grinning warmly.

"*Frithigiends*!" Amy declared, throwing her arms around her friend and hugging her.

"We should celebrate," Elizabeth suggested brightly.

"How about getting sodas at the Dairi Burger?" said Amy.

"Sounds good to me." Elizabeth gathered together the papers on her desk. This was one time when the *Sixers* would just have to wait, she told herself happily.

Leaving school, Amy and Elizabeth walked outside and saw Lila, Charlie, and Jim on the lawn. They were all excitedly discussing something. As Elizabeth and Amy walked over to them, they heard them saying, "This'll really do her in! She's going to learn her lesson the hard way!"

When Lila saw them she called out, "Amy, Elizabeth, come over here! We want to tell you our plan."

"What's going on?" Amy inquired.

"What are you talking about?" said Elizabeth, puzzled.

"We're talking about that awful Ms. McDonald," Lila said, and sneered. "We've got the perfect plan for ruining her future in Sweet Valley," she continued meanly.

"But how do you know she's so bad? Nobody even gave her a chance. Maybe she's really nice," protested Elizabeth. Even before hearing the plan, she knew she wasn't going to like it.

"What do you mean? You saw how she acted!" Charlie shot back.

"If she'd yelled at you, believe me, you'd hate her, too," Lila cried. "She's so nervous, she doesn't know what she's doing!"

"I think she was the one who didn't give *us* a chance," Charlie added.

"And do you know what I heard?" Lila said. "This afternoon when I was in the office, I heard the secretary say that the district supervisor is coming to our music class next week. Ms. McDonald is probably being reviewed for a permanent position here—"

"So this is the plan," Jim interrupted, looking at Elizabeth and Amy. "When the supervisor comes to our music class we'll only speak Ithig, got it? Ms. McDonald's gonna go crazy, and she'll probably get fired right then and there," he explained, smirking.

"That's a horrible idea!" Elizabeth exclaimed.

"You can count me out," said Amy.

"I think it's brilliant," Lila declared. "Are you saying that you're not going to help us?" she asked.

"That's right!" Elizabeth and Amy shouted in unison.

"There are always one or two party poopers in the group," Lila hissed back at them.

"It doesn't matter," Jim commented with a snort. "We can pull it off without them."

"Why don't you think about what you're doing? It's an awful thing to do!" Elizabeth pleaded. But her classmates didn't pay any attention. She and Amy turned away and left. But all the way down the block they could hear Lila shouting, "Party poopers! Party poopers!"

When Elizabeth got home from the Dairi Burger that afternoon, she ran upstairs, dropped her books on her desk, and immediately went back outside. She climbed into the huge pine tree in the backyard and sat on the lowest branch. This was her "thinking seat," the spot she came to whenever she needed to be by herself and do some serious thinking.

In her mind all Elizabeth could see was the frustrated expression on Ms. McDonald's sad face. To Elizabeth, the teacher seemed young and inexperienced, not mean and nasty. It was almost unbearable to think about what the class had planned for her. Nobody deserved to be treated that cruelly, Elizabeth thought.

Suddenly she had a terrific idea. If she told Ms. McDonald the secret of Ithig, Lila's plan wouldn't work. The more Elizabeth thought about it, the more excited she became. Of course, if Lila or the others found out, they'd be furious with her. But that was a chance she'd have to take. It was the only way to help Ms. McDonald.

"Hi, Jessica," Elizabeth called, jumping up and waving as she saw her sister approaching the back door.

"Hi, Lizzie. What's new?" Jessica called.

"Nothing," replied Elizabeth. Though this wasn't exactly the truth, she had no intention of telling Jessica her secret. If Jessica slipped and told Lila, the plan would be ruined. She couldn't risk telling a single person.

Nine

Elizabeth was standing in front of the music room before school started the next morning. Taking a deep breath, she raised her hand and rapped loudly on the door. When she heard, "Come in," she turned the knob and entered. Ms. McDonald was sitting at her desk.

"May I have a word with you, Ms. McDonald?" Elizabeth said softly.

"Yes, of course," the teacher replied.

"I'm Elizabeth Wakefield," Elizabeth said, walking across the room.

"I know," smiled Ms. McDonald, "and you have a twin sister named Jessica. Why don't you have a seat?" the teacher offered. Elizabeth liked her more already. She was really very friendly.

Elizabeth pulled up a chair and cleared her

throat. Trying to be delicate, she said, "You're probably aware that some of the kids, well . . . uh, they don't seem to get along with you. . . ."

That brought a smile to Ms. McDonald's face. "I would say that's putting it mildly," she admitted.

Elizabeth continued, "I hate to squeal, and it wasn't easy for me to do this, but the other kids are planning something really bad when the district supervisor comes. They hope you'll get fired. . . ."

Ms. McDonald remained calm. "What are they planning to do?" she asked.

Elizabeth kicked at the trash basket with the toe of her shoe. "Well, remember when they were speaking that strange language last week in class? It's called Ithig, and when the supervisor comes, that's *all* they're going to speak."

To Elizabeth's complete surprise, Ms. McDonald broke out laughing. "Ah, yes, the dreaded Ithig," she said, continuing to chuckle to herself.

"But I thought of a way to help you," Elizabeth explained. "If I told you how it works, you'd be able to understand what they were saying. Then you could explain to the district supervisor—"

Ms. McDonald interrupted with a question, "Yithig*ou* withig*ant* ithig*to* tithig*each* ithig*me* Ithig?" She finished her sentence, folded her hands on her desk, and looked at Elizabeth.

Elizabeth couldn't believe her ears. *How did Ms. McDonald ever learn to speak Ithig?*

Sensing Elizabeth's surprise, the teacher explained, "I certainly hear it enough around this place. You kids seem to be obsessed with it. So I just figured out how it works by hearing it around school. It's really quite simple."

Elizabeth was very impressed that Ms. McDonald could pick up the language just by hearing it. Most people got so confused. . . .

Ms. McDonald laughed and said, "Elizabeth, how do you think children learn to speak? Or how do you think people learn foreign languages?" Ms. McDonald winked at her and added, "But I have a pretty good ear, if I do say so myself. After all, I'm a music teacher."

After a minute's thought Elizabeth realized that it made perfect sense—of course someone could figure out Ithig if that person had a good ear. Ms. McDonald was certainly proof of that.

"Now I feel silly," Elizabeth confessed.

"Whatever for?" the teacher asked.

"I had no idea you could speak Ithig," Elizabeth explained.

"Well, I couldn't a few days ago. But now I think I've got the hang of it," Ms. McDonald told her.

Then she rose to her feet and said, "Thank you for wanting to help me, Elizabeth. It's nice to have a friend."

"It only seemed fair," Elizabeth replied shyly as she got up to leave. She smiled to herself, thinking of the surprise that her classmates were going to have when they discovered that their secret language wasn't so secret after all!

Ten

When Elizabeth's class filed into the music room the following week, the short, balding district supervisor had already arrived and was talking to Ms. McDonald.

Putting her hand to her head as if she had a headache, Amy groaned. "I'm not looking forward to this. Poor Ms. McDonald," she whispered in Elizabeth's ear as they took their seats.

Elizabeth nodded sympathetically. Meanwhile most of the other kids were giggling and looking at each other with mischievous glints in their eyes.

After everyone had taken a seat, Ms. McDonald stood up and said, "Hello, class. Say hello to Mr. Carruthers, the district supervisor. He'll be observing our class today." Already Elizabeth could hear the students snickering. But she was pleased to see that Ms. McDonald seemed much more relaxed and confident than she had during their first class.

"Hello, Mr. Carruthers," everyone said in unison, obeying their teacher like well-behaved students.

Ms. McDonald took attendance and then got down to business. "Now, did you all read the assignment?" she asked. Everyone nodded, indicating that they had. Elizabeth had never seen her classmates look so eager to get on with a lesson.

"The chapter described all the different types of string instruments. Are there any questions?" the teacher asked.

Immediately a sea of hands waved in front of her. But Lila Fowler raised her hand the highest and shook it the hardest. "Yes?" said Ms. McDonald, calling on Lila.

Lila cleared her throat, "I was wondering," she said, "Ithig*are* ithig*a* *p*ithig*ian*ithig*o* ithig*and* ithig*a* *h*ithig*arps*ithig*ichord* *t*ithig*he* *s*ithig*ame*?" By the time she got the whole sentence out, everyone was laughing hysterically.

But Ms. McDonald acted as if nothing was the slightest bit out of the ordinary. She patiently listened to Lila. Then she answered, "That's a very good question, Lila. *T*ithig*he* ithig*answ*ithig*er* ithig*is* ithig*no*. *B*ithig*ut th*ithig*ey're b*ithig*oth str*ithig*ing* ithig*instr*ithig*um*ithig*ents*. Does that answer it for you?" she said matter-of-factly.

Lila was so shocked, her mouth hung open. Elizabeth smiled. Her classmates were all looking at one another with wide eyes. She overheard Lila hissing at Jim Sturbridge, "What happened?"

"Someone must have snitched, but it wasn't me," Jim shot back.

"I want to know who it was," Lila whispered, enraged. She looked around the class accusingly. But, of course, no one admitted to being the culprit. Sitting back in her chair, Elizabeth was pleased with the way things were going.

The teacher continued, "Sorry about this little interruption, Mr. Carruthers. We just had an exchange in a language called Ithig. It's a secret language the sixth graders have. I'd teach it to you, but it's their secret," she said, pointing to the students.

What a nice thing for her to do, thought Elizabeth. Even Charlie was surprised.

"Can you believe it?" he muttered under his breath. "She didn't even tell."

"I have some recordings that I want to play for you now," Ms. McDonald continued, going over to the record player. "Let's see how many different string instruments you can hear," she instructed, putting the needle on the record.

The orchestral sounds of a beautiful symphony filled the classroom. Soon, everyone was listening closely, interested in the lesson. And no one said another word about Ithig. Maybe Ms. McDonald wasn't such a bad teacher after all.

After class, while most of the kids rushed for the door, Amy stopped by Elizabeth's desk and sat on the edge as Elizabeth collected her things. "I guess Lila's plan was a real bomb!" Amy chuckled. "I thought I was going to die laughing when Ms. McDonald started speaking Ithig! Lila was so mad, I thought smoke was going to come out of her ears!"

"I know." Elizabeth laughed. "Lila looked as if she didn't know what hit her!"

"But isn't it strange that Ms. McDonald suddenly knew Ithig? I mean, she didn't know it last week. Somebody must have told her. Was it you?" Amy wondered out loud, tugging at her hair absentmindedly.

Elizabeth shook her head. "No," she said truthfully. "Maybe Ms. McDonald heard it enough to figure it out for herself."

"Hey, want to come over to my house this afternoon?" Amy asked as they walked to the door.

"Sure. I don't even remember what your house looks like," Elizabeth joked. She'd missed hanging out at Amy's ever since their big argument over Ithig.

"Oh, Elizabeth," Ms. McDonald called as the girls were walking into the hall. When Elizabeth turned around, the teacher was standing with Mr. Carruthers, a big, warm smile on her face. "Thank you again," she said, looking straight at Elizabeth. She winked. Elizabeth just smiled back at her as she left the room.

"Huh? What did she mean by that?" Amy asked suspiciously as soon as they were out in the hall.

Elizabeth just smiled mysteriously and pointed to the group of kids gathered in the corner. Lila was at the center of the group, making a big fuss about her foiled plan.

"When I find the squealer, there's going to be big trouble," Lila threatened, her pretty face twisted into an angry scowl.

"Aw, come on Lila," said Jim Sturbridge. "Just forget it. The plan didn't work, that's all. You don't have to get nasty about it."

Ellen Riteman agreed with him. "We'll probably never know who the backstabber was," she said, shaking her head.

"I don't think she's so bad after all. It was really neat that she kept our secret," Charlie Cashman remarked.

"That's not the point," Lila hissed.

At that moment the door to the music room opened and Mr. Carruthers came out. Recognizing the sixth grade students, he walked up to them and said in a friendly voice, "How do you like your new music teacher? I think she'll be a nice addition to the school. What do you think?" he asked earnestly.

Lila's face lit up in a cunning grin. Straightening her shoulders, she stood up tall. "If it were up to me, I'd get someone else," she told the supervisor.

He raised his eyebrows, looking concerned. "Is there something I don't know about Ms. McDonald that I should?" he said, bending his head attentively.

"Mr. Carruthers," said Lila, "I just don't like

her. Personally, I think she's a bore. Even the music she played was boring. . . ."

Elizabeth was furious at Lila for acting like a spoiled brat. She was so outraged that she was about to say something.

But Mr. Carruthers beat her to it. His friendly smile disappeared and he said in a sharp tone, "Young lady, I'm not interested in your musical preferences. Do you have any valid reasons for not liking Ms. McDonald?"

Lila seemed stunned by his change of manner, and just stood there stammering and clearing her throat.

"Does anyone else have anything they want to say?" Mr. Carruthers asked the group.

"I think she's very good," Amy immediately volunteered.

"Yeah, she's not so bad," Charlie admitted.

Lila whipped her head around and glared at them, horrified that no one was sticking up for her. Even Ellen, who usually agreed with everything Lila said, didn't come to her defense.

"If I were you, I'd spend more time with my books and less time causing trouble," the supervisor told Lila sternly. With that he turned on his heel and walked away.

Lila's face turned bright red. "No one talks to me that way," she sneered as soon as he was out of earshot.

"Let's get out of here," Jim said to Charlie, slapping him on the back. Then he called to Lila, "Next time you have a great plan, don't call me!"

The boys scooted around the corner and ran down the stairs, hooting and hollering at the top of their lungs. "*Wh*ithig*at* ithig*a d*ithig*umb* ithig*id*ithi-*gea*!" shouted Jim.

"Lila," Ellen said softly, trying to put her hand on Lila's shoulder.

But Lila snapped nastily, "Leave me alone!" and ran down the hall.

On their way to Amy's house, Amy turned to Elizabeth and said, "You *did* teach Ms. McDonald Ithig, didn't you?"

Elizabeth looked her best friend directly in the eye. She wanted to be honest, but she also didn't feel that she had to defend herself. "No," Elizabeth replied. And that was the truth, because the teacher had figured it out on her own. But that was Ms. McDonald's secret.

"Then what was she thanking you for?" Amy asked suspiciously.

"For being a friend," Elizabeth answered simply.

They were walking past Mary Robinson's house when they heard someone shout. "Did you hear that?" Elizabeth gasped.

"It came from Mary's house," said Amy.

"I think we should check this out," Elizabeth said.

The two girls walked hesitantly up the path to the front porch. "Anybody home?" they called as they knocked on the door.

Just then the door flew open. Mary stood before them, her face red and tears streaming down her cheeks.

"Mary! What's wrong?" Elizabeth cried.

Mary took one look at their frightened faces, then burst into hysterical laughter.

"What's the matter with you?" Elizabeth cried, alarmed.

"It's not what you think. . . ." Mary stammered. "I just heard the most wonderful news. . . ."

Mrs. Robinson poked her head out of the kitchen and called out cheerfully, "Elizabeth, Amy, come in. We have some great news to tell you!" She came to the door and invited them into the sitting room.

Until recently Mary and her mother were separated for many years. Mary spent most of her life in foster homes, but she always believed that her real mother would return. And, miraculously, she did. Now they lived happily together in Sweet Valley.

"Tell them," Mary excitedly urged her mother as the girls took seats.

Mrs. Robinson sat on the arm of Mary's chair and started to giggle. "Well," she began, giving Mary's hand a squeeze. "Tim has asked me to marry him, and I've accepted. We're finally going to have a real family."

Amy and Elizabeth jumped out of their seats and ran over to hug Mrs. Robinson. "Congratulations! That's wonderful!" they screamed.

"And they're going to have a beautiful wedding and both of you are invited," Mary declared, her eyes gleaming.

"That's right. Elizabeth, I want your parents and your sister to come. Your family's been so kind and helpful to us ever since we moved here," said Mary's mother with a sweet smile.

"I'm sure they'll be honored," Elizabeth said warmly. She had a special feeling for Mrs. Robinson. With her blond hair and blue eyes, she reminded Elizabeth of her own mother. "Especially Jessica. She adores weddings," Elizabeth added.

"Will you do me a favor?" Mrs. Robinson asked her.

"Sure," Elizabeth replied eagerly. "What is it?"

"I was going to ask you to keep quiet about this just till we send out the invitations and make it official. It won't be long, because Tim and I want to get married as soon as possible," said Mrs. Robinson, then held her face in her hands and started giggling all over again.

The girls laughed at her, but in a good way. Her girlish joy made her seem more like a friend than one of their mothers.

Elizabeth was happy for both of them, but most of all for Mary. Her life had changed remarkably in the last few months. It wasn't long ago when Mary thought she might not have any family in the world.

"I won't say a word," Amy assured everyone. Then she added, "But it won't be easy, because this is incredible news!"

"And I'm good at keeping secrets," Elizabeth promised. It was lucky that Jessica wasn't there, Elizabeth thought with a grin. In a million years

Jessica wouldn't be able to keep quiet about a secret this big!

After walking home from Amy's later that day, Elizabeth burst through the door of the Wakefields' house. "Anybody home?" she called out.

Jessica came out of her room and called back from the head of the stairs, "Hi, Lizzie. Where have you been?"

As Elizabeth ran up the steps, she casually replied, "With Amy and Mary." Every time she thought about Mary's mother, she had to bite her lower lip to keep from grinning. She dropped her books and sat down on the top step next to Jessica. Though she was overflowing with excitement about the wedding, she didn't dare let on.

But Jessica wasn't fooled for a moment. She took one look at her sister's face and said, "Something happened. Tell me."

But Elizabeth just shrugged her shoulders as if she didn't know what her sister was talking about.

"Elizabeth Wakefield!" Jessica yelled, playfully pinching Elizabeth's arm. "I know you better than you think! You're keeping something from me, I know it."

"All right, I won't deny it. But it's a secret, and I can't tell you," Elizabeth confessed.

"A secret?" Jessica shrieked. "What do you mean you can't tell me? You can't tell your own flesh and blood? Your only twin in the world?" Jessica went on in dramatic outrage.

"You'll find out soon enough," Elizabeth said with a mischievous smile.

"Please, Lizzie," Jessica pleaded in her sweetest voice. "I promise I won't tell anyone."

Elizabeth broke out laughing. "With your track record? You expect me to believe that?" she kidded Jessica.

A week later Jessica and Elizabeth came home from school and found two ivory-colored envelopes, one addressed to each girl, waiting on the hall table.

"I wonder who they're from?" Jessica cried excitedly as she tore open her envelope.

"We'll soon find out," declared Elizabeth, opening hers at the same time. Though she knew exactly whom it was from, she didn't let on.

"Maybe these are the invitations to Mrs. Robinson's wedding," said Jessica. "Yes, I'm right! This is so exciting!" she exclaimed.

Elizabeth was shocked. "You knew about the wedding?" she asked.

"Oops," said Jessica. "I wasn't supposed to tell. You see, Mary swore me to secrecy. But I guess it doesn't matter now," she went on.

Just then the front door opened and Mr. Wakefield entered, carrying his briefcase. He'd just gotten home from work. *"H*ithig*ow* ithig*are* ithig*my f*ithig*av*ithig*or*ithig*ite tw*ithig*ins*?" he asked with a smile.

"Guess what? Mrs. Robinson's getting married and we're all invited to the wedding," Jessica shouted. There was another invitation for Mr. and Mrs. Wakefield, which Jessica grabbed and showed to her father.

"*Th*ithig*is* ithig*is gr*ithig*eat*!" he exclaimed, looking it over. "*W*ithig*e'll h*ithig*ave* ithig*a b*ithi-g*all*!"

"I can't wait. I just love weddings," said Jessica, holding the invitation to her chest.

"Why don't you two speak Ithig any more?" he wondered out loud as he took off his coat.

"It's not a secret, so it's not nearly as much fun," Jessica mused.

"Personally, I'm sick of secrets," admitted

Elizabeth. But at least Jessica was learning how to keep them, Elizabeth thought proudly.

"Besides, Dad, we've got much more important things to discuss than Ithig," Jessica announced.

"Oh, really? What's that?" asked Mr. Wakefield, looking slightly amused, but a little hurt.

"What we're wearing to the wedding, of course!" laughed Jessica.

Mr. Wakefield smiled understandingly. "Well, maybe you've lost interest in Ithig, *b*ithig*ut* ithig*I* sithig*ure* *h*ithig*av*ithig*en't*!" he declared.

SWEET VALLEY TWINS

Stretching the Truth

Written by
Jamie Suzanne
Created by
FRANCINE PASCAL

BANTAM BOOKS
TORONTO • NEW YORK • LONDON • SYDNEY • AUCKLAND

To Molly Jessica W. Wenk

One

"I don't care what anyone says," Jessica Wakefield announced, tossing her blond hair. "*Dream Chaser* is positively the best movie in the world!" She challenged her sister Elizabeth to disagree.

Jessica and Elizabeth were identical twins. Facing each other across one of the old-fashioned marble tables in Casey's ice cream parlor, the two girls looked like mirror images. They both had long blond hair, blue-green eyes, and dimples in their left cheeks. But though the pretty sixth graders looked alike, they hardly ever agreed on anything. "I don't know," Elizabeth replied, pausing to sip her root-beer float. "Tom Houston is a good actor, but the plot was completely unbelievable. Everything worked out so perfectly. It wasn't like real life at all."

Jessica loved romance and glamor. She couldn't understand her twin at all. "Oh, Lizzie!" she cried. "Why do you always have to be so practical? That was the most exciting, wonderful movie ever made. Tom Houston is the cutest guy in the universe!" She sighed in tribute to her latest heartthrob. "Honestly,

Lizzie, I don't see why you bother going to the movies at all. If you want to see 'real life,' you could save your money and watch Lois Waller eat three desserts at school everyday!"

"Or Charlie Cashman shooting spitballs," Mary Robinson interrupted. Mary was a seventh grader and a good friend of both twins. With a laugh she squeezed into the booth beside Elizabeth and signaled the waitress. She ordered two Casey's specials. "Lila's joining us," she explained. "She's just calling home to say she'll be late." Lila Fowler was a pretty and popular sixth grader who was Jessica's very best friend in school.

A minute later Lila strolled into Casey's, looking as perfectly groomed as a model. "Hi, you three," she said, sitting next to Jessica. "Wasn't that movie incredible? Tom Houston was gorgeous!"

Jessica gave her twin a triumphant grin. "You see!" she crowed. "Now maybe you'll listen to your baby sister." The twins often joked about Jessica's being born four minutes after Elizabeth. "Everyone in the world except Lizzie knows *Dream Chaser* is a masterpiece!"

"I just wish it had been a more realistic story, that's all. Happy endings like that don't happen to real people."

"They most certainly *do*!" Jessica insisted. "Just look at Mary. She lived in foster homes almost all her life, and just this year she found her own mother."

Like everyone else in Sweet Valley, California,

the Wakefield twins had been thrilled when Mary, separated from her mother as a small child, had been reunited with her.

"And in case you've forgotten, Mary and her mom found each other in our very own living room." Jessica sighed again. "Just like in a fairy tale!"

"It *was* like a dream come true for me," Mary remembered, her eyes shining. "I've never felt so happy."

"Well, that *was* a pretty special adventure," Elizabeth admitted. She smiled at her friend as the waitress brought Mary and Lila's three-scoop specials.

"And Mary's getting happier all the time," Jessica continued, delighted to be proving her point. "Her mom just got married again, and they're all living happily ever after. Aren't you, Mary?"

Mary stared at her ice cream without touching it. "Sure," she said quickly. "We're really happy."

"If your stepfather's so wonderful," Lila asked, "how come I haven't gotten to meet him?" Lila never wasted any time being tactful. "What does he do, anyway?" Lila's face took on a suspicious look.

"He works on houses."

"*My* father owns three houses." Bragging was one of the things Lila Fowler did best. "He also owns a condominium and an apartment building."

"Well, Tim works on houses and apartments, and skyscrapers, too," Mary said, looking flustered. "He's a . . . a sort of architect."

"I knew it!" Jessica looked delighted. "You see, Lizzie? It must be great to have a dad that builds office buildings and skyscrapers."

"My mom would never choose anybody ordinary," Mary insisted again, her voice firm. She paused, staring into Lila's dark eyes. "Tim is very, very special."

"My father is sending me to Europe next summer," Lila said, daring Mary to top her.

Mary looked uncomfortable. She saw Jessica and Elizabeth watching her. "Oh, Tim says Europe is boring," she announced. "He says Africa makes a better vacation." Her eyes shone and a big, broad smile covered her face. "Just before he moved to Sweet Valley, Tim designed a palace for an African king."

"Wow!" Jessica exclaimed. "A palace!" She looked at Mary with admiration. "I guess you must be the happiest person in the world, Mary. You've got just about everything anyone could ask for."

"Except good grades," Mary admitted, frowning. "My report card looks like a national disaster area. Two of my teachers called our house Friday. They want my parents to come in for a conference."

"But, Mary," said Elizabeth, "you've always done so well in school!"

"Well, uh . . . I haven't had much time for homework lately. It just seems like there's always so much else to do."

"I know exactly what you mean," Jessica told

her. "When you have to choose between fun and work, you'd be crazy to choose work. No offense, Lizzie."

Elizabeth laughed. Jessica never *did* see the point of spending time on homework when she could be cheerleading or talking with her friends. But Elizabeth didn't ever feel comfortable until her nightly assignments were completed. "That's OK," she said. "I don't mind being the bookworm in our family." Still, she appeared concerned as she turned back to Mary. "I can't understand why you're having problems doing your work. We used to go all sorts of places together. Lately, though, we've hardly seen you at all."

"Yeah," added Jessica. "Mom asked us about you the other day. She said she hasn't seen you since your mother's wedding."

Mary shifted uncomfortably in her seat. "I just don't have much time anymore. You see, my stepfather always wants to go places with Mom. I mean with Mom and me. So I like to stick around." She looked at Jessica's expectant face. "You wouldn't want me to miss something exciting, would you?"

"Like what?"

"Well . . ." Mary closed her eyes. It was hard to tell what she was thinking. Then she looked straight at Jessica with a big, bright smile. "Like a big dinner out. Tim always wants the three of us to go out to dinner."

"That's nothing," Lila countered. "My dad and I eat out more than we eat in."

"Or shopping," Mary added quickly. "Tim loves to take us shopping and buy me presents."

"He does?" Jessica loved her own father very much. But the idea of a dad who came home every day itching to buy his family presents sounded absolutely terrific.

"Uh, sure. He's bought me so much stuff I can barely fit it all into my room!"

Mary was wearing a great big smile and looking just like a fairy-tale princess. But Elizabeth couldn't help thinking that it sounded too good to be true.

"Wow!" Jessica was thrilled and dying to hear more. "I guess with a stepfather that rich, you won't be staying much longer in that little house your mother rented, huh?"

"No." Mary dipped her spoon slowly into the mound of whipped cream on top of her ice cream. "I mean, of course not. Tim says we're moving to a much bigger house."

"Sure. And how many servants are you going to have?" Lila challenged.

"Well, not any right away." Mary took a bite of the strawberry scoop on her special. "It won't be for quite a while because . . . because Tim is just designing the house now. Naturally, he wants everything just the way Mom and I want it. He's very picky."

"You mean you get to help plan your own house?" Now Lila sounded just the tiniest bit jealous. "Gee, Daddy always moves into houses that are already built. He says it saves time."

"Not Tim," Mary told her. "He likes to take charge of everything himself."

"Oh, great!" Jessica cried. "You should ask for big French doors for your bedroom, with a formal rose garden right outside. And a tennis court," she added.

"Well, I don't know." Mary stopped eating. "I mean, I haven't really thought about it."

"Haven't thought about it! Mary, what is the matter with you?" Jessica rolled her blue-green eyes. "I can see you need someone to help you with this project. How about if I help plan your room?"

"I don't think—"

"First we'll have a big dressing room off the bathroom," Jessica said. "The pool should be right off the rose garden. We'll make it just like the one in *Dream Chaser*."

"Oh, no!" Elizabeth interrupted, exasperated. "Whose house is this, anyway, Jess? Don't you think we should let Mary's stepdad build his own home?"

"And how about a long terrace with a sweeping view of the nine-hole golf course?" Lila suggested.

Mary looked alarmed. "Lila, I really don't think my house is going to be *that* special."

But Jessica and Lila were too carried away to pay any attention. "You'll definitely need a guest cottage," Jessica declared.

"Yes!" agreed Lila. "With its own pool. Something small yet tasteful, full of class. . . ."

"Speaking of class," Elizabeth said to Mary, glad

to change the subject, "are you going to take the jewelry-making classes Mr. Sweeney and Ms. Lacey are giving on Wednesdays?" Even though they had very different interests, the twins had signed up for the after-school jewelry workshop. Lila was also planning to take the course. But Elizabeth hadn't seen Mary's name on the list posted in the main hall. "Ms. Lacey says we're going to start out with silver bracelets!"

"Gee, I'd really like to," said Mary, "but I have to get right home after school."

"Mary, you've just got to come! All the Unicorns have signed up."

"Oh, we were hoping you would come," said Lila. "We're going to make official club bracelets."

Mary, Jessica, and Lila were all members of the Unicorn Club. Elizabeth thought most of the girls in the club were snobs and that the only purpose to their meetings was to talk about boys and clothing. But Jessica loved being a Unicorn more than anything else in the world. The Unicorns were all pretty and popular. They did everything and went everywhere together. And they always wore a lot of purple. Purple was the Unicorn club color. But Mary hadn't been to meetings in quite a while, so she didn't know anything about the club's plans. "Er . . . that's great, Lila. But I still can't come."

Jessica couldn't imagine anyone turning down the chance to make their own jewelry. "You don't have to make the same thing as everyone else, Mary," she explained. "Mr. Sweeney told our art class that you can do anything you want. I'm going to make my bracelet look like two roses twined together. I already did a drawing in class."

"You can't have *that* much homework," Lila insisted.

"I—I can't come," Mary told her, looking very uncomfortable again. "I know just about everybody in school has signed up, and it *does* sound like fun. But I have to get home right after school now. It's the only time I have with Mom all to myself. If I spent it making jewelry or . . . or doing homework, things would never be like they were before."

"What do you mean, 'like they were before'?" Elizabeth asked gently.

"Oh, you know. Before I got a stepfather and Mom got a new husband. It used to be special, just the two of us. Just Mom and me." For an instant Mary's eyes misted over, but then her face broke into a wide grin. "Not that things aren't great now," she insisted. "It's just that I have to give up some things because we're so busy." She set her chin firmly and looked at her three friends with determination. "But I'm *not* going to give up my mom!"

"So that's why you haven't been able to type those articles for us!" Until Mary's stepfather had moved in, Elizabeth, who organized the *Sweet Valley Sixers,* the sixth-grade class paper, had been able to count on her friend to help with the typing. Lately, though, Mary always seemed to have an excuse when Elizabeth asked her for help.

"And that's why you haven't been coming to

the Dairi Burger with the Unicorns?" Jessica asked in surprise.

"I—I've missed being with you," Mary admitted. "But I just can't give up my mom. Things are different now. I hope you understand." She looked at her watch and struggled quickly with her sweater. "Gee, I didn't realize it was so late. I've got to get home. Mom and Tim said they were driving up the coast, but they're probably back by now."

Jessica looked down at Mary's bowl. "But you've hardly touched your ice cream."

"You eat it for me, Jessica." Mary was already headed for the door. "I want to tell Mom all about the movie. See you tomorrow!"

"Boy, Mary sure has changed lately," observed Jessica as she watched their friend race off.

"Yes," Lila agreed. "She's turned into a regular hermit!"

Elizabeth frowned. She missed spending long *Sixers* work sessions with Mary, the two of them typing and laughing for hours on end. "The only thing is, hermits usually *want* to be alone," she told Lila and Jessica. "But I don't really think Mary wants to choose between her family and us." She looked up as Mary slipped out the door. "I wonder why she thinks she has to?"

Two

Jessica and Elizabeth entered the Wakefield home through the sunny, Spanish-tiled kitchen. In his usual position by the open refrigerator, the twins' brother, Steven, was assembling the ingredients for one of his enormous sandwiches.

"Hey, guys!" he greeted them as he pulled a head of lettuce from the crisper. "Guess which mature, sophisticated freshman has been picked to be chairman of the entertainment committee for the next Sweet Valley High dance?" Steven's eyes were twinkling with excitement.

"Today is Sunday, dummy," Jessica reminded him. "How could you get picked on the weekend?"

"Well," he admitted, "the election really isn't until tomorrow. But I talked to Cathy Connors, and she says she's sure everyone's going to want me to be chairman. The whole committee was crazy about my idea of making the dance theme *Dream Chaser*. I want to get a DJ to play all the songs from the movie, and have all the girls dress like Leslie Morgan."

"Ugh!" Jessica looked disgusted. "I didn't like

her clothes at all!" She paused, remembering the movie. "Of course, a room full of Tom Houstons would be wonderful. Your idea's only half bad."

"Thanks a lot," Steven told her sarcastically. "Now, if you two will excuse me, I have some serious work to do." He carried his plate into the family room, where he could watch a football game while he ate his colossal sandwich.

The twins followed Steven, and found Mr. and Mrs. Wakefield already watching the game in the next room. Eyeing Steven's sandwich warily, Mrs. Wakefield commented, "I certainly hope that leaning tower of turkey is more stable than it looks."

"It's ham," Steven corrected. "And it's built to last."

"Sure." Elizabeth giggled. "About as long as anything edible lasts near you—two seconds!"

"You know," said Mr. Wakefield, his brown eyes shining. "I think Steven holds the all-county title in munching out!"

"Hey," Steven protested, laughing with the rest, "what do you mean all-*county*? I defy anyone in the state to make a better sandwich!"

Mrs. Wakefield rolled her eyes and turned to the twins. "How was the movie, you two?"

Jessica sank to the floor with a dreamy expression. "Tom Houston is the ultimate!"

"I suppose that means he's good," her mother guessed.

"Good? He's perfection. He's super. He's—"

"Someone who could use a better movie," Elizabeth finished for her. "Mom, you should have seen how silly this script was. Women threw themselves at him every second, and he never made a single mistake. I mean, you'd think he was playing Superman instead of a race-car driver. He didn't even come close to losing a race in the whole movie!"

"Why should he?" Jessica challenged. "He's not supposed to be an ordinary human, anyway. He's . . . he's . . ." She sighed and waved her hands in the air helplessly. "He's Tom Houston."

"Well, nobody asked me," their father announced, "but I think I agree with Elizabeth. I like to watch stories with which I can identify. And I'm afraid I've made too many mistakes and lost too many battles to identify with perfection!"

"Besides," Elizabeth added thoughtfully, "I'll bet perfection can be pretty hard to live with." She remembered the discussion at Casey's after the movie. "According to Mary, it's nearly impossible!"

Her mother looked concerned. "Elizabeth, what do you mean? I thought everything was going well for the Wallaces."

"For the Wallaces. But maybe not for Mary." Elizabeth remembered how sad Mary's face was when she described her "perfect" stepfather.

"Oh, I'm sure Mr. Wallace will be adopting Mary as soon as it's legally possible," said Mrs. Wakefield. "Then they'll all have the same name."

"Yes," Mr. Wakefield agreed. "These things take

time, but as soon as they've located Mary's real father and made the proper application, they can all become Wallaces."

"That would be great," said Jessica. "After all, Mary can't miss her real father very much. He and her mother got divorced when she was just a tiny kid."

"Yes," admitted Elizabeth. "But don't forget that Mary just found her mother and her real name. I'm not sure she's ready to give all of it up for anyone else."

"That's silly, Liz," Jessica assured her. "Why, with the spectacular house her stepfather is building, everything will be perfect!"

"The Wallaces are moving?" asked Mrs. Wakefield. She had a part-time job as an interior designer and was always interested in finding new clients. "Maybe Andrea would like some help planning her new home."

"Oh, don't worry about that, Mom," said Jessica. "I've already given her lots of good advice."

"I don't think a new house is going to make much difference to Mary," Elizabeth insisted. "There's something really bothering her, Mom. I've asked her over here at least a dozen times in the past month, but she always says no. She never goes anywhere anymore."

"Not even to Unicorn meetings," Jessica added. "We've been operating without our treasurer for weeks now."

"From what I hear," Steve teased, "you don't

have much use for a treasurer anyway. I mean, any club that holds all its meetings at the Dairi Burger has got to be broke!"

"For your information, Steven, Sweet Valley High isn't the only group that can sponsor a dance!" Jessica declared. "It just so happens the Unicorns are planning a big party with a band and everything."

"A band?" Elizabeth sounded surprised. "Do you know how much that will cost?"

"Isn't it fabulous?" Jessica smiled smugly at her twin. "I bet you wish you'd joined the Unicorns after all!"

"And spend my life painting my fingernails purple and gossiping about everyone in school? No thanks." Elizabeth had gone to one Unicorn meeting at the beginning of the year. For her, one was enough. She decided that the Unicorns did nothing but dream up new clothing fads and laugh at girls who didn't follow them. In fact, Jessica and Mary were just about the only two club members Elizabeth respected. "Maybe Mary's just decided she's had enough of the Unicorns."

"No," Jessica insisted. "Mary really loves the club. She's always had lots of fun at meetings, and she comes up with the best fund-raising ideas. Or at least she used to," she corrected herself.

"She *used* to do a lot of things, including spend time visiting her friends." Elizabeth was getting more and more upset, remembering Mary's big, phony smile that afternoon.

"It's true. I haven't seen Mary for weeks," Mrs.

Wakefield said. "I wonder where she's been keeping herself?"

"She just stays home with her mother," said Elizabeth. "She's afraid to let her out of her sight." Elizabeth felt her voice catch a little. "Meanwhile, I feel like I'm losing a friend."

"Hmmm. I haven't talked to her mother in a few weeks. Maybe I'll give her a call and see how things are going."

Elizabeth felt much better. Mrs. Wakefield had a knack for fixing things. She had been the one who helped Mary's mother find a job so she could stay in Sweet Valley. "Gee, thanks, Mom. It just seems like Mary's problems are bigger than she can handle."

"Well," Jessica observed, "if having a stepfather who's going to build her a mansion with a pool and tennis court is a problem, I wish I had some problems of my own!"

Elizabeth remembered the way her twin had taken charge of Mary's future home. "Jessica, you were so busy building that house yourself, you didn't let Mary get a word in edgewise."

"Well, somebody had to get excited about it, didn't they? All you and Mary wanted to do was sit around and mope about her grades!"

"Grades? Is Mary having trouble in school, too?" Mrs. Wakefield asked, looking concerned.

Elizabeth hadn't wanted to mention how badly Mary was doing in school, but now that Jessica had let it slip, it seemed important to explain things. "You know how terrific Mary's grades have always been, Mom. I just know something is bothering her. I mean, if her new stepfather is so wonderful and everything is going so well, why is Mary afraid to leave her mother's side—even to do homework?"

"I'm not sure, Elizabeth." Mrs. Wakefield exchanged glances with her husband. "But I'm going to try to find out."

Three

"Hi, Mom. Has the carpet come yet?" Mary rushed into the living room of the small, cozy house Mrs. Robinson had rented when she got a job in Sweet Valley. It was Monday, and Mary's classmates were eating lunch in the school cafeteria, but she'd remembered that her mother had taken off work today. Mary was sure she would have her mom all to herself without her stepfather around. She stopped short when she saw the slender, bearded man in the kitchen. "Hello, Tim," she said slowly. "What are you doing here?"

Tim Wallace smiled and joined them in the living room. "I live here, remember?"

Mary remembered, all right. She also remembered what it had been like before her stepfather moved in. After years of hoping, after nights filled with tears and prayers, she had found her mother at last. At last she didn't need to be jealous of her friends. She no longer looked at their mothers, wishing she was their little girl, too. She had a real mother of her very own. For a short time, anyway.

She watched her new stepfather circle her mother's waist with his broad arm. She watched him pull her close to him. And worst of all, she watched her mother smile up at him, looking as though he was everything she needed. Maybe he was. Maybe they didn't need her at all. Maybe she was just in the way.

"I thought Tim was working on a house today," Mary whispered to her mother. "I thought you were going to be home alone, Mom."

Mrs. Wallace hugged her daughter. "I thought so, too, honey. But it seems I've got two terrific friends who decided to visit me while I wait for our new dining room carpet." She smiled again at Tim, who now put his arm around Mary, too. But Mary stepped away, ducking from under his hand. She didn't feel like being part of a threesome.

"Actually, I just came back for a minute," Tim explained, stopping to retrieve a battered guitar case from under the couch. "I wanted to tell your mom about my big purchase."

Mrs. Robinson smiled with enthusiasm. "Oh, yes, Mary. Wait'll you hear what Tim bought this morning!" She led Mary to the couch and sat down beside her. "Come on, Tim, sing her the song you wrote about our new boat!"

Tim sat down on the other side of Mary, his old guitar in his lap. Mary looked at them in disbelief. "Our new *what*?" she asked.

Tim smiled at her, but Mary was sure it was only to please her mother. "You've just become part owner of a magnificent ocean-going vessel, young lady." He winked at Mary, but her expression made it clear she wasn't at all interested in what he had to say. "And," he continued, "in honor of this occasion, I've just composed a suitable song!"

Mary had heard enough of her new stepfather's songs—especially the sticky-sweet love songs he was always singing to her mom. Every time Tim took out his guitar, Mary's mother looked at him with a shy, loving smile that made Mary feel more left out than ever.

"It's true," Mary's mother told her. "Tim actually bought a boat for us today. And you'll never guess what kind!" She looked as proud and happy as Mary had ever seen her. "It's a tugboat! You know how Tim's been working on refinishing a kitchen for that family over on Bellevue Drive? Well, it turns out the father used to work at a naval shipyard. He's had this old boat for years and years."

"That's right," Tim said, strumming a few chords. "He liked the work I did on his house so much, he said he'd love to see me try my hand at restoring the tug. One look and I fell in love with the old boat." He laughed and then began to sing a silly song called "I Think I Can," about a decrepit old boat. The boat got into a race with a sleek yacht, and in the last verse chugged its way to victory.

When the song was over, Mrs. Wallace clapped loudly. She thought her new husband a very talented musician. "Oh, Tim, you're wonderful! Mary and I are so lucky to have you in our family. Right, Mary?"

Mary didn't answer. She pulled closer to her mother on the couch, holding her hand tighter than ever. Her stepfather's voice was pleasant to listen to, but his song had made her lonely and frightened.

"It'll take time to fix the old tug up, but it's something we could all do together—a real family project." Tim smiled hopefully.

Mary felt them both looking at her. She knew they expected her to be pleased with their big surprise. But it was just one more thing she'd been left out of. They'd been talking about it, planning it together. It wasn't really hers at all. And having a tugboat was pretty embarrassing. In Sweet Valley almost every other family owned a sailboat or a cabin cruiser. Why did her new stepfather go and buy some leaky old boat?

"Yep! A chance like this doesn't come along too often." Tim was beaming, his arm again around his wife. "I haven't seen a tug like this since I was a kid."

A tugboat! What would the girls in the Unicorn Club think? A lot of them had wealthy parents who loved expensive clothes and houses. She had already boasted to her friends about her stepfather and how he was going to change their lives. How he was going to move them out of this small house into a fancy mansion he was designing. How his architectural firm built skyscrapers and office buildings.

"Of course, the sanding and painting will take time," Tim continued. "And it'll be hard work!"

"Won't it be fun?" A shadow crossed her

mother's pretty face as she looked at Mary. "It'll really be something when we've got it all fixed up!"

"Something" is right, thought Mary. *Just wait until my friends find out we've got a tugboat instead of a yacht. Just wait until they find out I've got a handyman for a stepfather!* She knew she should have felt guilty about saying that Tim built houses instead of fixed them. But actually, it had been sort of fun to talk about a glamorous, make-believe stepfather instead of the person who was trying to take her mother away. And maybe what she'd said wasn't a lie anyway. Maybe her *real* father was more than an ordinary carpenter. Maybe he was like the fathers of the girls she'd met in Sweet Valley; he might be a doctor, a lawyer, a banker—anything by now. If only her parents hadn't gotten divorced when she was a baby. If only she didn't have to get used to a brand-new father who just pretended to like her to please her mother!

"Your mother and I decided that you should name our boat, Mary. What do you think we should call her?" Tim asked.

But Mary couldn't stop thinking how much better things used to be. If only they had stayed the same. If only her mother were still Andrea Robinson instead of Andrea Wallace. Now she didn't even have the same name as her mother. She didn't feel like part of this new family at all. "Why don't we call the dumb boat just what it is," she said angrily. Bolting from the couch, she ran upstairs toward her room. "A rotten wreck!" she shouted. Quickly, before they could see the tears streaming down her cheeks, Mary disappeared into her room.

At first Mary tried not to listen to the voices in the living room below. But soon, as the conversation drifted up to her, she found herself straining to catch the words. "I don't know what's come over her," she heard her mother tell Tim. Her voice was tired and sad. "Mary never acts like this, Tim. I just don't know what to think anymore. She's changed so much. I feel like I hardly know her."

"That's according to *you*." Tim, too, sounded tired. "Ever since I've known her, though, Mary hasn't changed at all. She's still doing poorly in school, she's still angry at the world. And she still doesn't seem to like me at all!"

"Please, Tim, be patient with her. It takes time to get used to big changes like the ones we've been through. I know the two of you will get along together if you just give her a chance."

"There's nothing I want more than for us to be a real family, honey. But I'm afraid you have things a little mixed up." Tim started to walk across the room. "If this thing is ever going to work, it's *Mary* who has to give *me* a chance."

"She will. I know she will." Now Mary could hear her mother following her stepfather to the front door. She covered her ears with her pillow, but she could picture Tim kissing her mother good-bye before he hurried out the door to his next job.

When she was absolutely certain that Tim had left, Mary dried her eyes and went downstairs.

"I'm afraid we didn't have much of a lunchtime together, sweetheart," her mother told her.

"We never have any time together anymore," Mary complained. "Alone, I mean."

"We have lots of time to be mother and daughter, Mary. We've got the rest of our lives. My loving Tim doesn't change that at all."

"But it does. Don't you see?" Mary wanted to make her mother understand just how much everything had changed. At first the idea of her mother getting married had seemed exciting. The two of them had picked out dresses for the ceremony and talked about plans for the honeymoon trip. But then her mother and Tim had left her alone with the Altmans, the foster family she'd lived with before she'd found her mother. It was only for two weeks, but each night she woke up tossing and crying, convinced that she'd lost her mother once more.

"What I do see, young lady, is that it's time for you to get back to school, and you haven't eaten a thing." Quickly Mrs. Wallace grabbed an apple and some slices of cheese and slipped them into a plastic bag.

Mary was glad that Jessica and Elizabeth had not been able to come to her mother's wedding. They had had to cancel at the last minute. At least she didn't have to introduce them to Tim. If only her mother would send him away. If only she could put everything back the way it used to be. Just the two of them. No handyman for a stepfather, no broken down boat, no crying in bed while Tim and her mother whispered downstairs.

"Here, silly," her mother was saying as she put a twist tie around the bag of fruit and cheese and handed it to Mary. "Maybe you can sneak a bite or two in between classes."

Mary looked sullenly at the bag. Her mother never used to forget about making her lunch. Mary dropped the bag on the counter. "I'm not hungry," she said, then scooped up her books and headed for the door. "I lost my appetite!" She slammed the door behind her, glad that for once she'd forced her mother to think about her instead of Tim.

Four

Janet Howell, the Unicorn Club president, was furious as she scanned the faces around the cafeteria table. "I scheduled this meeting at lunchtime just so Mary could be here. This is the fourth meeting in a row she's missed." A bossy eighth grader, Janet wasn't used to club members skipping meetings. She liked to think that the Unicorns were the most important thing in the whole middle school—in fact, in the whole world. "Does anyone know where she is?"

Sitting at the end of the table next to Lila, Jessica raised her hand. She had seen Mary in the hall just before lunchtime. "Mary went home," Jessica told Janet. "She needed to talk to her mother. I'm sure it was important."

Janet frowned. "Well, how can we have a meeting about fund-raising without our treasurer?" She glanced around the table again. Everyone was still eating.

At the end of the table Lila groaned. "Look, Janet," she spoke up. "It's not exactly a federal offense to miss a few meetings." Lila was Janet's first cousin and one of the few Unicorns who ever stood up to her.

"I think Mary has shown she's not ready to be a club officer," Janet replied.

"The way she runs this club," Lila whispered to Jessica, "you'd think it was the United Nations or something!"

"Well, all I know," Jessica whispered back, "is if this meeting isn't a short one, I'm going to be in a lot more trouble than Mary. I've got math next period, and if I show up without my homework one more time, Ms. Wyler is going to kill me!"

"You are pushing Wyler to her limits," agreed Lila. "Last week, when you were passing notes to Helen Bradley, she got so angry I thought her eyes were going to pop out of her head!"

As Jessica and Lila laughed, Janet banged her fork on a cafeteria tray as if she were a judge in a courtroom. "This meeting had better come to order," she announced, glaring at the two sixth graders, "or we'll never find out how much money we need to raise for our big party next month."

Kimberly Haver, a seventh grader, raised her hand. "Janet," she said, "we don't need Mary to tell us we have no money left in the Unicorn treasury."

"That's for sure," agreed Tamara Chase, another seventh grader. "We used all our money for those purple sweatshirts we bought for the club."

"I've got a great idea," Betsy Gordon piped up. "And it won't cost us a cent. Why don't we let my brother's high school band play for our party? He says they need the practice. I bet they'd play for free."

Jessica sighed loudly, and some of the other girls put their hands up to their mouths to hide their smiles. Everyone knew how horrible Johnny Gordon and the Waves sounded. "We'd be better off with no music at all," Jessica whispered to Lila.

"Uh, thanks, Betsy," said Janet. "But I think we need something different for this party. My bunkmate from camp, Judy Walker, is coming to visit me, and I already told her we're sponsoring a dance. Anyway, Judy is president of a club at her school. They call themselves the Shooting Stars and they give really terrific dances all the time."

"How about a singer?" asked Lila. "We need a really dreamy singer for our party."

"Yeah!" Ellen Riteman, another friend of Jessica's, agreed. Her brown eyes flashed, and her voice got high and excited. "Lila's absolutely right. Why, if we had a romantic singer, we might get boys to dance more."

"How about someone who knows the songs from *Dream Chaser*?" Jessica suggested. "That's what the high school is planning for its next dance." Jessica gave a knowing smile. The Unicorns always like to be filled in on what the older kids were doing.

"That's a terrific idea, Jessica," exclaimed Kimberly. "Do you think we could give the party at your house, by the pool, Lila?"

Lila's pool was, without a doubt, the biggest,

most luxurious swimming pool in all of Sweet Valley. "Sure," she agreed readily. "Daddy won't care." Mr. Fowler was usually so busy traveling on business that he let Lila do just about anything she wanted.

"This is dreamy!" Ellen declared. "I'm going to dress just like Leslie Morgan."

"Well, *I'm* going to dress a lot better than that!" Jessica assured them. "I'm going to wear my blue sundress with the beige jacket. And my new Unicorn bracelet. We're bound to have finished them by then."

"Me, too." Soon everyone was planning their outfits and discussing decorations. But Jessica had still another surprise planned.

"I just might have a very special dance partner, too," she said in a mysterious voice.

"Who?"

"Oh, just Tom Houston, that's who."

"Are you kidding, Jessica?" Ellen stopped describing Leslie Morgan's gold lamé jumpsuit and stared at her friend in astonishment.

"Well, I've been writing to him every week, and he's even sent me a photo."

"Is this photo 'personally signed,' just like the one you got from Johnny Buck?" Janet asked, sounding very superior. She hadn't forgotten the time Jessica boasted to everyone that the famous rock star had autographed a photo just for her. It had turned out that the picture had been signed with a rubber stamp and passed out to a concert crowd with hundreds of identical photos.

"Not everyone is as caring and wonderful as Tom Houston," Jessica replied haughtily. "I'm going to write him and tell him about our club's *Dream Chaser* party. I'm going to ask him if he'll sing the theme song for us."

"He'd never come in a million years!" Betsy Gordon exclaimed. But her expression showed that she hoped he would.

"Maybe not," Jessica told her coolly. "But it never hurts to try." She was sure all the Unicorns, especially Janet, would be incredibly impressed if she could get Tom Houston to come to the party. Why, Janet might even put her in charge of the whole dance.

"Well," concluded Kimberly, "if we're going to count on Tom Houston to entertain, we might just as well give up the idea of a party."

"What?" Janet declared. "And let the Unicorns be shown up by the Shooting Stars?" She wasn't about to let her friend from camp laugh at her or her club. "Let's let Jessica try." She smiled hopefully at Jessica. "I nominate Jessica Wakefield for chairman of our entertainment committee. All in favor, raise their hands."

Jessica's heart started to pound as all the hands at the table went up. What would she do if Tom Houston turned her down? She smiled confidently and decided to worry about that later. "What about decorations?" she asked Janet.

Janet frowned again. "Hmm . . . I don't think we have any money for decorations." She sighed.

"And speaking of money, I think we'd better elect a replacement for Mary. In fact, I'm not so sure Mary even deserves to be a Unicorn."

"Oh, come on!" Lila whispered just loud enough so Janet could hear her.

"After all," Janet went on, ignoring her cousin, "if she's not responsible enough to attend meetings, why should she be in our club at all?"

Jessica was furious, but she didn't dare challenge Janet. Janet was too popular and important to cross. Still, it wasn't fair to push Mary out of the club when she wasn't even there to defend herself. Jessica poked Lila in the ribs. "Janet's your cousin," she whispered. "Do something!"

"Why not give Mary one more chance?" Lila asked. "After all, she did most of the work typing up the celebrity cookbooks."

Janet looked around the table. It was clear that most of the girls agreed with Lila. "All right," she conceded. "We'll continue this meeting after school at the Dairi Burger. But if Mary's not there, she's out of the club." She tapped her pencil impatiently on the tray. "This meeting of the Unicorns is now adjourned."

As the club members were getting up from the table and piling up their empty trays, Jessica looked toward the other end of the wide, windowed cafeteria. Thank goodness—Elizabeth was still there! She raced over to tell her twin about Janet's ultimatum.

Elizabeth and three of her friends—Amy Sutton, Julie Porter, and Sophia Rizzo, were planning the next issue of the *Sweet Valley Sixers*. Munching on the last bites of their sandwiches, they reviewed the latest student council news, discussed the poetry column, and wondered how they were possibly going to get everything into print before next week.

The four girls stopped talking when they saw the expression on Jessica's face. "What's wrong, Jess?" asked Elizabeth.

Jessica poured out the story of the Unicorn meeting. Even though Elizabeth didn't have much use for the Unicorns, Jessica was sure she understood how much the club meant to Mary. "We've got to talk to her before the end of school today," she explained. "If we don't get her to that meeting at the Dairi Burger this afternoon, Mary will be out of the club." Jessica shuddered, thinking about it. "She'll be a total reject!"

"Speaking for all us non-Unicorns," Julie Porter replied, "I think things could be worse, Jessica!"

"Oh, sure," Jessica said apologetically. "But not for someone like Mary. She likes to be popular and have fun and do neat stuff."

"I think you just made us feel worse," commented Amy.

Sophia smiled. She understood best of all what Jessica was trying to say. Before Elizabeth had befriended her, Sophia had known just what it was like to feel left out. "I think Jessica's right," she said. "Mary needs the Unicorns just like we need each other."

"How can Janet be so ridiculous?" Elizabeth said. "It sounds so unfair!"

"Well, you know how bossy Janet can be," said Jessica.

"Does anyone know what classes Mary has this afternoon?" asked Julie.

"Sure," said Jessica. "Elizabeth and I have history class, and there's a seventh-grade science section right across the hall. I always wave to Mary during class."

"OK, Jess. I guess we're the ones to tell Mary." A frown knit Elizabeth's brow. "But you know how she is lately. She'll probably want to rush right home."

"Not this time. Not if I tell her she's going to be kicked out of the Unicorns," said Jessica.

"I guess you're right," Elizabeth agreed. She stood up to take her tray to the front of the room. "The rest of you keep an eye out for her, too. Mary's had enough changes in her life lately. She sure doesn't need to become an ex-Unicorn!"

Five

Jessica and Elizabeth were relieved when they saw Mary walk out of the room across the hall from history class. Elizabeth winked at her twin as Jessica got up from her seat and scooped up her books.

"And just where do you think you are going, Miss Wakefield?" Mr. Nydick asked sarcastically as Jessica headed for the door.

"But the bell rang, Mr. Nydick." Jessica looked around, embarrassed to see that the rest of the class was still seated. "Isn't class over?"

"You're right on one count." Mr. Nydick smiled as Jessica sank back into her seat. "The bell *has* rung. But I'm afraid your teacher hasn't quite finished talking." He rubbed his chin, then ran one hand through his gray hair. "Now, let's see . . . where was I?"

Jessica felt desperate. Mr. Nydick almost never kept his students after the bell. Why did he have to turn into a chatterbox today of all days?

". . . Oh, yes. I was going over your assignment for tomorrow. The real builder of the Roman Empire was Augustus. . . ."

Would he ever stop talking? Jessica turned in her seat and caught Elizabeth's eye. She pointed out the door to where they could both see Mary. She had stopped to talk to a girl in the hallway just outside Mr. Nydick's room. Jessica waved and tried to signal to her, but Mary didn't see.

"So, I want you to list as many of Augustus's accomplishments as you can, but I'd like you to write a detailed paragraph on your favorite one." Mr. Nydick watched Jessica waving, and frowned. "Would you like to invite your friend in for a refresher course, Miss Wakefield?" Blushing crimson, Jessica stopped signaling Mary and shook her head. With the whole class watching, she sighed quietly and faced the front of the room.

"All right, then. I'm not asking for a polished essay. Just your thoughts on one of the great Augustan triumphs." Again he stared at Jessica. "Is that clear?"

"Oh, yes, sir!" Jessica sat up straight, looking bright and eager.

When Mr. Nydick dismissed the class, Jessica darted into the hall and looked left and right. She caught sight of her tall, blond friend leaving the building. "Mary! Mary!" she shouted, and hurried after her, clutching her books in one hand and waving frantically with the other. "Wait up!"

But Mary didn't look back. Just as she ran through the front doors, Jessica collided with Bruce Patman and Rick Hunter, two seventh graders who were standing at the top of the steps with their arms full of oaktag posters. The three of them and a pile of books and cardboard ended up in confused heaps all over the stairs.

"Hey! What's the hurry?" The two boys stood up and helped Jessica to her feet.

"Next time you decide to rush a guy, give him some warning, will you?" Bruce Patman smiled at Jessica.

Jessica thought Bruce was the most gorgeous boy in the whole middle school. "Sorry," she said. "I was so anxious to get to our Unicorn meeting, I wasn't watching where I was going."

Rick was the seventh-grade class president, and though much quieter than Bruce, he was just as cute. "Are you all right?" he asked, looking a little worried.

"Sure," Jessica assured him, delighted to be talking to the two most popular boys in the school. "Gee," she said, turning her brightest smile on them, "I guess you never saw anyone so clumsy."

"Well," Bruce replied quickly, "if that accident was just a trick to get us to ask you to help us with these posters, it worked."

"Yeah," added Rick, stooping to retrieve the big cardboard sheets that lay scattered around them. "We could use some help. Mr. Sweeney wants us to hang them all over."

"I'd like to," Jessica replied. "But I really have to get to a meeting." She looked worriedly toward the path where she'd seen Mary just a minute before. She wasn't anywhere in sight.

"Well, if we don't want a lot of kids showing up at the wrong jewelry classes, I guess we'd better get started," Rick said to Bruce. The two boys started back toward the building.

"What do you mean?" Jessica asked, chasing after them. "What are those posters?"

"Sign-up sheets," Bruce told her. "The jewelry class next week is so crowded they had to add extra sections."

Jessica lowered her eyelashes. "Are *you* taking the class, Bruce?"

"I sure am. My mom's birthday is coming up and I thought maybe I could make something for her."

"That's so thoughtful," Jessica cooed. "What are you making her?"

"I thought a silver charm for a necklace might be neat," Bruce suggested.

"What a fabulous idea! I love charms. Maybe I could help."

"Great! Let's make sure to sign up for the same class. I was going to make a big silver letter P. What do you think?"

"I think you had better stop gabbing, Jessica, or we'll miss the Unicorn meeting," Lila Fowler interjected, coming up to them. "Did you forget about it?" Lila's father didn't get along with Bruce's father, so Lila thought a lot less of Bruce than Jessica did. "Come on. Let's get going."

"OK," Jessica agreed, waving at Bruce and heading down the steps with her friend. "I already told Bruce and Rick I couldn't help."

"Rick Hunter?" Lila stopped at the bottom step and turned to see Rick stapling a poster onto a bulletin board. "Why didn't you say so?" Lila didn't think much of Bruce, but Rick Hunter was an entirely different matter! The shy, popular boy had a way with everybody, and besides being handsome, he was one of the best tennis players in the school. Lila loved tennis, and she liked flirting, too.

Lila quickly headed back up the steps to join Rick and Bruce. Jessica followed frantically behind her. "Wait a minute, Lila. We don't have time for that now. We have to find Mary and tell her about the meeting."

"Don't be such a party pooper," Lila scolded. "The meeting's not until three-thirty. We've got plenty of time." Her long brown ponytail swished from side to side as she strode up the stairs. "Oh, Rick, do you need help?"

While Lila held posters, Rick stapled them. Jessica knew that her friend expected Bruce and her to form another team. Still, she couldn't help thinking about poor Mary. After a few minutes she tapped Lila's shoulder and told her she wanted to speak to her alone.

"You can stay if you want to," she said when they'd walked around the corner from the boys. "But I have to go look for Mary."

"Don't you dare leave me alone!" Lila's brown eyes blazed. "That would make everything look too obvious. Jessica Wakefield, if you walk away now, I'll never speak to you again."

Even though Lila was her best friend, Jessica knew that she could carry grudges forever. She also knew better than to cross Lila when she was determined. So the four of them worked together for half an hour, replacing all the old signup sheets with the new posters. Stapling the last board in place, Rick announced, "I guess that does it." He smiled easily and effortlessly, the way he did at everyone, but Lila seemed to think it was just for her. "Thanks a lot. If there's anything we can do in return, just let us know."

"There is," Lila told him, giving Jessica a knowing glance. "Walk us to the Dairi Burger. You could probably use a sundae after all that work."

Jessica was practically floating by the time they approached the Dairi Burger. She couldn't wait to see the Unicorns' faces when she and Lila walked in with the two most popular boys in school! But as they entered the popular after-school hangout, Bruce asked a question that brought Jessica quickly down to earth. "So, what's this special emergency session all about, anyway?" he said.

Jessica stopped short just inside the door. Oh, no! Mary! Because of Lila they'd never gotten the chance to catch up with Mary. Now, if her friend didn't come to the meeting, she'd be out of the Unicorns. *And it would be all my fault,* Jessica thought. Frantic, she surveyed the crowded room. She saw Ellen Riteman sitting at a table with Kimberly Haver and Tamara Chase. She saw Janet and two of her eighth-grade friends at the table across from them. But she didn't see Mary anywhere.

Just then Bruce spotted some friends across the room. "OK, girls," he said, "see you two later." Before Rick could say a word, Bruce had grabbed him by the elbow and led him toward his friends, leaving Lila and Jessica alone at the door.

What a mess! They hadn't found Mary, and Bruce and Rick had walked off so quickly that none of the Unicorns had seen them together. Jessica followed Lila dejectedly toward Ellen's table, but then the door opened behind them and a familiar voice stopped Jessica in her tracks.

"Jessica! Lila! Wait up." Mary, panting, rushed up to her friends. Her face looked anxious and worried. "Has the meeting started yet?"

Jessica sighed with relief. "Boy, am I glad to see you! How did you find out about the meeting?"

"Elizabeth stopped me on the way home and told me all about Janet. Thanks for spreading the word, Jessica."

Jessica never let an opportunity pass to take credit for something. "No problem. What are friends for?" she said breezily, then steered Mary to the two tables where the others sat. "Look who's here!" she announced cheerfully.

"Mary! Are we glad to see you," Kimberly told her.

"We thought you'd forgotten all about us," added Ellen.

"Of course I haven't," Mary told them. "It's just

that I've been really busy." She helped Jessica and Lila bring up extra chairs, and the three girls squeezed in to form a tight circle around one of the Unicorn tables.

"So what have you been up to?" asked Ellen. "We haven't seen you in ages!"

"She's been having an incredible time," Jessica answered excitedly. "Her stepfather is handsome and rich and he's building them a brand new house."

Mary felt embarrassed. Maybe she'd been carrying her boasting too far. "We're not moving yet, Jessica," she cautioned. "But we have been keeping pretty busy. Tim has all kinds of new projects. Today we bought a boat."

"A boat!" Kimberly exclaimed. "That's fabulous! Is it a yacht?"

"Uh . . . kind of. I mean it might not be *that* big. I haven't even seen it yet."

"Can we all go for a ride?" Jessica could picture herself on board a luxurious yacht, her hair streaming in the wind.

"Gee, I guess so." Mary was glad her friends still wanted to be with her. But how would they feel if they knew Tim was only a carpenter? What if they found out her "yacht" was really a tugboat? She wasn't at all sure they would feel the same way about her if she told them the truth. She wasn't sure about anything anymore.

"Attention, everyone." Janet banged on a table

with her spoon. "I think everyone knows why I've called this special meeting," she said, glancing at Mary. "I hope that we can finally have our treasurer's report."

Mary stood up quickly. "I'm afraid I really can't be of much help, Janet," she announced. "If we're going to hire a band with the money in our treasury, we're going to have to find one that will work for three dollars and ten cents!"

The girls at both tables looked dejected. "That won't even pay for decorations," said Jessica.

"I'm sorry. But we spent just about everything on our club sweatshirts."

"Are you absolutely sure that's all the money we have?" asked Janet. "I mean, you *have* been away a lot lately, Mary. Maybe there's something you left out."

"I'm sure," Mary replied. "I double-checked the figures."

"And that's not all the bad news," Lila added. "I called home after lunch today. The housekeeper says Daddy's put the pool off-limits until the filter's fixed."

"Oh, no!" Ellen cried. "You mean we can't have the party at your house?"

Lila nodded sadly.

"Oh, Mary, I just wish your stepfather would hurry up and finish your new house," said Kimberly. "It would be perfect!"

Mary looked embarrassed. "I'm afraid it won't

be ready for a long time," she insisted. "I . . . told you how picky Tim is."

"It's going to be terrific," Jessica told the Unicorns. "It's going to have a swimming pool and tennis courts and—"

"Maybe not all that terrific," interrupted Mary quickly. "It's just a new house." It wasn't exactly a lie, she told herself. After all, Tim *did* keep talking about buying the house they were renting and adding on a couple of rooms. "It'll be just like new," he was always saying.

"Well, what about a fund-raiser?" Janet suggested. "Do you think we could raise enough by next month, Mary?"

"Maybe. We'd have to work really hard, though. If not, we couldn't possibly—" A shocked expression passed over Mary's face and she stopped talking. She stared at the entrance to the Dairi Burger. "Oh, no!" she gasped. The other girls looked up to see Mary's mother and a thin, bearded man walk through the door.

Smiling when they spotted Mary and the Unicorns, Mrs. Wallace and Tim walked straight to the tables where the girls were gathered.

"Hello, darling." Mary's mother was beaming with pleasure. "What a nice surprise! What are you doing here?"

Mary wanted to sink into the floor. She wanted to go to sleep and not wake up for a million years. "I was just going to ask you the same thing," she told her mother, wishing that Elizabeth hadn't found her and that she'd missed the club meeting after all. As Jessica and the other girls gathered around to meet her new stepfather, Mary wished she'd never joined the Unicorns at all.

Six

Mary stared at her mother and stepfather in disbelief. How could they have appeared in the Dairi Burger, of all places? "I thought you were going out to dinner," she told them.

"We were," Tim explained. "But we hadn't driven two miles before your mother got a craving for a chocolate shake." He winked at the girls clustered eagerly around them. "So here we are. Sorry if we crashed your party."

"It's not a party, Mr. Wallace," Jessica told him. "It's a Unicorn meeting."

"A what?" Tim looked confused.

"I'll explain everything on the way." Mary was already on her feet, easing away from the table. "As long as you're here, we may as well all go out and eat together."

"All right, honey," her mother agreed. "Let me just order our shakes and we'll take them with us." She turned toward the counter at the back of the room. "Why don't you introduce your friends to Tim? I'll be right back."

Now Mary looked plainly miserable. "Tim," she said in a voice that was barely audible, "these are my friends Jessica, Lila, Ellen, and Tamara." She gulped as she saw Janet and the other Unicorns approach her table. "They're all members of our club." She remained standing, but her stepfather pulled up a chair and joined the group at the table.

"Hello, girls," he said agreeably. "I'm glad to meet some of Mary's friends."

"Oh, Mr. Wallace," Jessica told him, "we've heard all about the exciting work you do." She smiled charmingly. "I'd love to hear about your latest skyscraper."

Tim look confused. "I'm not sure what you mean, Jessica. The last job I had was in an apartment house, but I wouldn't call it a skyscraper."

Mary felt dizzy and faint, and thought her whole world was about to collapse around her.

"Have you named your new boat yet?" Ellen asked eagerly. "How many people does it sleep?"

Now Mary's stepfather laughed. "Well, the sleeping quarters aren't exactly luxurious, but it looks as if she had a working crew of about six."

"A crew?" Tamara was impressed. "Your boat must be the biggest one in Sweet Valley!"

"Can you tell us all about the summer palace?" Tamara piped in, eyes shining with admiration.

"Ohh!" Mary suddenly doubled up and collapsed into a chair. She looked very pale and held her stomach. "Ohhh!"

Mrs. Wallace was at her daughter's side in an instant. "Mary, what's wrong?" she cried.

Mary was pale and trembling as she struggled to her feet. "I feel awful," she told her mother. "Really sick."

Tim looked at his wife, then stood up. "I think we'd better get you home right away, young lady," he told Mary. "Jessica, Lila, all of you—it was nice to meet you, and I hope you'll come visit us soon."

"We'd love to," Jessica replied enthusiastically. "We haven't visited Mary in ages." Not, she realized, since Tim had appeared on the scene. "Hope you feel better, Mary."

Holding tight to her mother's arm, Mary looked terribly frightened and unhappy. "I'll be OK," she said. "Just as soon as I get home and into bed." She smiled weakly up at her mother and clutched herself still tighter. As the three of them left the Dairi Burger, Tim reached out to pat Mary's back. But she shook off his hand and shrank still closer to her mother.

Mary felt better as soon as they were safely in the car. But Mrs. Wallace was too worried about her daughter to go straight home without a stop at their family's doctor. Tim drove the car past the turnoff for their house and took them to Dr. Costa's office.

"What are we doing here?" Mary asked. She had been almost lulled to sleep as she lay against her mother's shoulder, and was surprised to see the doctor's familiar parking lot.

"I don't want to take any chances with my only

daughter." Mrs. Wallace laughed. "You've been acting strange lately, anyway. I think it's time for a checkup."

It didn't take Dr. Costa long to determine that Mary was as healthy as could be. In just a few minutes she was sent outside to the waiting room while the doctor, her mother, and stepfather had a discussion.

But she couldn't resist trying to listen to the words that drifted from the doctor's office. "It's not easy," she heard Dr. Costa say, "to deal with as many life changes as Mary has had to confront recently. Have there been any other problems?"

Mary couldn't hear everything they said, but she heard enough to convince her that her mother and Tim were telling the doctor the same things they'd said to each other that afternoon. Mary heard her mother mention the two teachers who called to schedule a conference about her poor grades, and she heard Tim describe the way she constantly rejected his affection and how discouraged he had become.

"I don't have any magic formula for you," Dr. Costa said a few minutes later. "But I can tell you one thing. That child needs to feel she counts in this new family of yours. She needs to be reassured that no one's taken her place. I've been seeing Mary since she first moved in with her foster family," he continued. "The Altmans are fine people, but for Mary there was only one person who mattered in her life: her mother. You can't expect that to change overnight, Tim. You have to let Mary find out for herself that there's enough room in her heart for you, too."

Mary thought it strange to hear Dr. Costa talking about her being able to accept Tim, when all along she'd been worrying about Tim accepting her. Maybe things *were* partly her fault. Maybe Tim really did care about her.

The phone was ringing when the three arrived home. It was Jessica, calling to find out how Mary was feeling. Anxious to make sure her mother and Tim didn't hear the conversation, Mary took the call on the upstairs phone. That gave her mother and Tim a chance to have a conversation that Mary didn't overhear. If she had, she might have felt better about her stepfather's feelings toward her.

"You know, honey," Tim said to his wife when Mary was safely upstairs. "I think the doctor's right. Mary *is* afraid I'll take you away from her. That's why she doesn't like us being alone together and why she won't leave your side."

"There must be some way we can make her feel needed and special, Tim. I know that's all she wants."

"What about her birthday?" Tim said softly. "That's coming up in a few weeks. Maybe we could give a big party. You know, invite all her friends and show her how important she is to us?"

"Oh, Tim! That's perfect!" Mrs. Wallace declared.

"And I've got a better idea still," Tim said proudly. "While you were getting our shakes at the

Dairi Burger, Mary's friends were pumping me for information about our new boat. It seems Mary's already told them all about the tug." He shook his head. "Boy, from her reaction earlier today, I never would have guessed she was so proud of it. Anyway, why don't we have the party on the boat?"

"Great!" Mrs. Wallace's eyes were shining with enthusiasm. "We can fix up the boat secretly in the next few weeks. I'll put up lots of decorations. Oh, Tim, she'll be thrilled!"

But when Mary walked into the living room from upstairs, she didn't look thrilled at all. "What are you two whispering about?" she asked sourly. Once again it seemed as if the two of them were leaving her out of things.

"Oh, nothing at all," her mother sang out, squeezing Tim's hand happily.

Just a minute ago, when she was sick, her mother had been cuddling her, Mary thought. Now she was paying attention only to Tim.

"Don't you have homework, honey?" Mrs. Wallace said, winking at Tim.

"Not really," Mary said grumpily. She wasn't going to leave them alone again, to whisper and plan things without her. "Besides, I feel sick again."

Her mother reached over to feel Mary's forehead. She stroked her daughter's hair and pulled her against her.

Smiling, Mary watched Tim get up from the couch and go upstairs. "Oh, my head," she moaned into her mother's shoulder, snuggling closer.

"I thought it was your stomach that was bothering you before."

"It was. But now my head hurts, too." Mary felt safe and warm cradled in her mother's arm. It would be perfect just to stay there, cozy and content. Even if she never did homework for the rest of her life, even if she failed every course and lost all of her friends, it would be better than losing her mother again.

Tim came downstairs, his arms loaded with Mary's schoolbooks. "Here you go," he said, handing her the textbooks and her spiral pads. "I thought maybe as long as you weren't feeling well, you and your mother could work on your homework together right here on the couch."

Tim smiled kindly, then left the room. "Well," Mary admitted, looking cautiously at her mother, "maybe I *do* have a little homework I could do."

"OK," Mrs. Wallace told Mary, tucking an afghan around Mary's legs. "Why don't I make us some tea, and we'll start working."

Mary sank back into the plump sofa cushions, the fuzzy blanket snug around her. For a sick girl with tons of homework, she felt pretty wonderful!

Seven

"Dear Mr. Houston," Jessica wrote in her huge, loop-filled script. She studied the pink sheet of stationery in front of her and frowned. Then she crumpled the sheet and tossed it into her wastebasket. She took out her fourth sheet and wrote, "Dear Tom—"

"Hi. How'd the Unicorn meeting go?" Elizabeth poked her head out of the bathroom that separated the twins' bedrooms. "Is Mary still in the club?"

"She sure is. Everything's fine. Except for my writer's block. I need help, Lizzie."

Elizabeth frowned. "If you're going to ask me to do your homework for you again, Jess, I'm afraid you're our of luck. I just came from a *Sweet Valley Sixers* meeting and I have a ton of homework of my own to worry about. I just wanted to find out how Mary did."

Jessica glanced back at the letter. The 'T' in Tom looked all wrong. She'd have to start another sheet. "Well, you don't have to worry about Mary. And Lizzie, you'll never guess who came in for some shakes while we were having our meeting. . . ." She paused dramatically. "Mr. and Mrs. Wallace, that's who!"

Elizabeth laughed. "And what's the handsome prince like? Did he ride into the Dairi Burger on a white horse?"

"No, but he's really cute, and Mary told us he's just bought a new boat. It has a crew, and it must be the biggest boat in the marina. We're all going to go for a ride on it!"

"Well, I guess everything's all right then," Elizabeth said, not sounding too convinced. "I'm glad I saw Mary before she went home. Why didn't you catch her after English, Jess?"

"I bumped into Bruce Patman, and by the time I had helped him put up posters for the jewelry class, Mary had already left. Honest, Liz, I really tried. It's just that Bruce needed help. And after all, he's so—"

"Conceited and obnoxious," Elizabeth finished for her. "He thinks he has the right to tell everyone what to do. Next time you've just got to stand up to that bully."

"Oh, I will, Liz, I promise," Jessica said, her eyes wide. "Oh, and speaking of promises," she said, changing the subject. "I told Janet Howell I'd write this letter to Tom Houston. I really could use some help."

"Why are you writing to Tom Houston?" Elizabeth moved a pink mohair sweater and a pair of jeans from the corner of Jessica's bed and sat down.

"Well," Jessica began. "I just thought that if I wrote, I mean if *we* wrote him a really impressive, desperate letter, he might agree to sing at our Unicorn party."

"You must be kidding, Jess!" Elizabeth exclaimed. "What makes you think a famous movie star like Tom Houston has time to come to the Unicorns' party?"

Jessica looked timidly at her sister. "The way you write, Lizzie, I just know you could talk anybody into anything!" She sat down on the bed beside her twin, the pink paper and a pen in her hand.

Jessica's flattery didn't faze Elizabeth one bit. This time Jessica was asking for the impossible. "First of all, Jess," she said, "even William Shakespeare couldn't convince Tom Houston into taking a night off to come to your party! Second of all, I have a ton of homework to do. And last of all, Amy and Sophia are coming over after dinner to do some more work on the newspaper."

But Jessica wasn't about to give up. "That's terrific," she said as Elizabeth got up and started back to her room. "Amy and Sophia are almost as good at writing as you are. Among the three of you we should come up with a great letter to Tom!"

Elizabeth shook her head and closed her door. She sat down at her desk and settled down to work. She had written the first paragraph of her social studies assignment when the bathroom door opened.

"Lizzie, you know that absolutely darling skirt you got at the mall last week?" Jessica said in her sweetest voice.

Elizabeth sighed. She knew she was in for a battle. "You mean the one Mom bought for me, the one I haven't worn yet?" she asked.

"I was just thinking how perfect it would look with my apricot-colored top," Jessica observed. "I was working on that horrible English assignment Mr. Bowman gave us, when I started to think about the awful clothes he wears. You know, how everything he puts on either clashes or is at least ten years out of style?"

Elizabeth laughed. "And Mr. Bowman's wardrobe made you think of mine?" she asked, teasing.

"Well, in a way. I thought about the jewelry classes next week and about how I wanted to look good because Bruce and I are going to work together on a charm for his mother. I thought about how I'd positively die if I had to wear something everyone had already seen. I mean, I'd be as pathetic as Mr. Bowman!"

Elizabeth looked through the bathroom door at the piles of clothes strewn all over her twin's room. Jessica loved clothes—*new* clothes. She tired of something as soon as she'd worn it, and even though her drawers and closets were crammed with sweaters and skirts and dresses, she always complained that she had nothing to wear. "I do not consider Bruce Patman any reason to have you working in my brand-new skirt, Jessica," she scolded. "For your information, jewelry-making isn't a tea party. Ms. Lacey says we're supposed to bring smocks because the solder and glue get all over everything."

"I can't believe it," Jessica wailed. "My own sister wants me to look like a nerd while I'm working right next to Bruce Patman!" She collapsed onto her sister's bed.

"Here," Elizabeth offered, determined to get some homework done before dinner. "Why don't you wear that top with my denim skirt? That way you'll be wearing something you've never worn before, without getting my new outfit spoiled." She strode to her closet and found the skirt.

"Well . . . " Jessica began, getting up. "I guess I *could* wear that, *if* you and your friends help me with the letter to Tom Houston."

Elizabeth picked up the ruffled pillow from her corduroy bedspread, took careful aim, and threw it just as her twin slammed shut the bathroom door. She was still laughing when her mother called up the stairs.

"Dinner, you two! I need some help with the table."

When the twins came downstairs to the dining room, Mrs. Wakefield said, "We'll only be three tonight. Your father and brother went to the basketball game at the University."

"Great! That means we don't have to listen to Steven being a pain," Jessica commented as she helped set the table. "I think his mouth is growing even bigger than he is!"

Mrs. Wakefield laughed. "You know as well as I do, you and your sister thrive on your brother's sarcasm. I don't know what the three of you would do without one another to pick on!"

"We'd probably have a very peaceful dinner." Jessica sat down and peered into the vegetable dish. "Hmmm," she said. "My favorite, mashed potatoes!"

"I'm glad you like it." Mrs. Wakefield smiled. "I made enough food for tomorrow night, too. I have a meeting with a design client, so you'll all be on your own."

Elizabeth was already ladling gravy over her pot roast. "I don't think we'll be suffering, Mom," she said approvingly.

"I don't think a certain friend of yours is, either," said Mrs. Wakefield. "I spoke with Mrs. Wallace about Mary today."

"Maybe I was wrong to worry, Mom. Jessica met Mary's stepfather today, and she said he was terrific."

Her mother nodded. "I got the same report from Andrea. And even though she may be slightly prejudiced, I *do* think the Wallaces are doing everything they can to help Mary adjust. They're even giving her a surprise birthday party on their new boat."

"They are?" Jessica and Elizabeth looked at each other. They both loved parties, especially surprise ones.

"Yes, indeed. I had a long talk with Mary's mother. It seems that she and Tim are really worried about her, too, Elizabeth. But I think they've decided that she just needs time to get used to her new family. And they hope this special birthday will show Mary and her friends how much they care about her."

"Wow!" Jessica was ecstatic. "Wait till I tell the Unicorns!" She leapt from the table but got only a few steps before her mother called her back to her seat.

"I think we should let the Wallaces give out their own invitations, don't you? Andrea wants to call Mary's friends. And, of course, she'll be calling all the Unicorns. It sounds like quite a big party!"

"It sounds like quite a boat," exclaimed Jessica. "Oh, I can hardly wait. I wonder if I should wear my blue blouse or my green boat-neck sweater."

"I wonder if you're going to eat some of my pot roast," added her mother. "You haven't had a bite since I mentioned the party."

"I'm too excited to eat." Jessica stared at her sister's empty plate. "Lizzie, I swear you don't have a romantic bone in your body. How can you eat at a time like this?"

"I can eat *Mom's* pot roast any time!" Elizabeth stood to take her plate into the kitchen. "Come on, Jess, it's time to clean up."

"I can't do dishes now," Jessica complained, following her sister reluctantly to the sink. "I just polished my nails before dinner."

"Fine," said Elizabeth. "I'll rinse, and you load the dishwasher."

"But I have a million calls to make," Jessica protested.

"You heard what Mom said," Elizabeth warned. "Don't breathe a word about the party. Especially to Mary."

"Oh, Lizzie, you never trust me to keep a secret. You should know I won't breathe a single, solitary word of this to anyone except Lila. And Ellen. After all, they're my best friends besides you." With that she rushed off toward the phone.

Elizabeth sighed. "When it comes to secrets," she said softly to herself, "those two are about as good as taking an ad out in the newspaper. Pretty soon everyone will know about Mary's surprise."

Eight

"Personally," announced Lila, who was eating with Jessica and Tamara at the Unicorn table in the cafeteria, "I think a yacht party would be the perfect setting for some dancing. Besides, Mrs. Wallace told Jessica's mom there's going to be music." It had only been a few days since she'd found out about Mary's surprise party, but Jessica had already let nearly everyone at school in on the secret. "I'm just glad Mary's in the seventh grade," Lila continued. "That means Rick Hunter will be at the party. It's going to be just perfect—the waves gently rocking the boat, and me, dancing in Rick's arms!"

"Aren't you rushing things a bit, Lila?" asked Jessica. "None of us has even been invited yet."

"But you said she's calling next week. I wonder if I should wear a sundress or a jumpsuit."

"Wouldn't it be fun if the Unicorns all wore the same thing?" asked Tamara, who loved to start fads. "We could get white pants to go with our purple sweatshirts."

"Yeah!" exclaimed Jessica. "And we could all get

some dangly earrings and wear our club bracelets. After all, we should look our best for such a fabulous party. Besides," she added, glancing across the cafeteria to where a group of seventh-grade boys were joking loudly, "if Mary's whole class is invited, that means Bruce Patman will be there, too."

"Hey!" said Tamara. "I've got a great idea. Why don't we walk over to the mall after school and look for outfits for the party?"

"All right," Lila agreed. "Daddy's off on another trip, and I can't wait to spend some of the money he left me! Let's tell everyone in the club, and we'll all meet outside after school, and we'll—"

All three girls looked up as Mary walked toward them, her lunch tray in hand. They all stopped talking at once.

Mary wondered what was going on. Why had all her friends been whispering behind her back? She decided to pretend she hadn't noticed. "Hi," she said. "Want to go to the Dairi Burger after school?" She slipped into a chair beside Jessica. "Mom and Tim are going out to the harbor this afternoon, and I don't feel like going." In fact, she'd wanted to go with them, but they had rushed off without her.

"Uh . . . gee, Mary," Tamara said, "we sort of had other plans." She shrugged and looked at Lila and Jessica.

"That's OK," Mary said. "We don't have to go to the Dairi Burger. I'll do whatever you want."

Jessica didn't want to hurt Mary's feelings. But even though the party was still two weeks off, she was sure that if the girls didn't get to town that very afternoon, they'd never get to the mall to find earrings for the party. "Well . . . that is, we aren't doing anything special. Nothing nearly as neat as going on your new boat."

Mary couldn't understand why everyone was trying to get rid of her. Earlier that morning her mother and Tim had acted just like Jessica was now. They had gotten very quiet as soon as she came in sight, and refused to tell her why they wanted to race off to the harbor after work. When she had asked to tag along, Tim shook his head. "I think it's time you spent some time with your friends from school, young lady," he'd announced, sounding as if he thought he was her real father.

"Boy," she told Jessica, picking up her hamburger. "If I hear any more about that dumb boat, I'm going to be seasick before I ever get on board. Which I'm beginning to hope is never." She wished everyone would stop talking about the boat. She was afraid they would find out the truth.

Just then a thought occurred to Mary. Maybe they'd already figured out that the "yacht" was nothing more than a battered tugboat. Everywhere Mary went all week long, groups of girls were talking and whispering, but as soon as she tried to join in, they always stopped. Maybe they were all laughing at her behind her back.

"Anyway," she said, "I'd choose you guys over that silly boat any day. So what do you say? Let's do something together."

"Sure. OK," Jessica promised her. "It's just that we were planning, that is, we—"

"Actually, Mary, we were going to work on our designs for the jewelry class after school," Lila interrupted. She knew that Mary hadn't signed up for the workshop.

"Yes!" Tamara and Jessica smiled at each other with relief.

"Don't forget," Tamara reminded Jessica between bites, "classes start at the end of this week, and we want to make sure our club bracelet is the best ever."

"Gee," Jessica said, "Elizabeth loves horses, and she's pretty good at drawing. Maybe I could ask her to sketch a pattern we could trace. Unicorns are just horses with horns, aren't they?"

"Don't let Janet hear you say that!" Mary said, laughing.

"Well, I really need a pattern I can trace. I'm not very artistic," said Jessica. She leaned into the group of girls. "I'm actually going to be working on two jewelry projects," she whispered.

"You are?" Tamara looked curious.

Jessica smiled proudly, but she tried to sound as if she weren't too excited. "Yes. Bruce asked me to help him work on a charm for his mother," she explained casually. "He even fixed it so we're in the same class."

"Wow!" Tamara exclaimed. "Lucky you!"

"I'm kind of sorry I never signed up," Mary admitted. "It's just that Mom and I have started doing my homework together, and I don't want her to feel that I'm letting her down. After that conference she had with my teachers, she's really worried about my grades." Mary didn't have to think about Tim so much anymore. He always made a point of leaving the two of them alone on the couch while Mary reviewed all her assignments with her mom. He'd even started building a desk that would fold out from the living room bookcase so she could work downstairs.

"Well, while you're all making your bracelets, I guess I'd better get busy and try to dream up some way of raising money for our party." She stood up, placing her napkin and empty plate on her tray.

As the other girls got up with their trays and headed for the door, Jessica looked smug. "Well, at least we don't have to worry about entertainment for the dance," she told Mary. "Tom Houston would have to be the biggest jerk in the world to turn down the letter Elizabeth and Amy Sutton helped me write the other night."

The three girls stopped walking and gathered around Jessica. "Is it really good?" asked Mary.

"Good?" Jessica laughed. "I cried while I was writing it down. It's brilliant!"

"You don't really think Tom Houston is going to come to Sweet Valley and sing for us, do you?" Lila looked as if she'd never heard anything so silly in her life!

But Jessica refused to be discouraged. "Just you wait, Lila. I want to see the look on your face when

Tom walks into our dance." Jessica had only mailed the letter that morning, but already she could picture her triumph when Tom Houston appeared. "He'll see me from across the room," she said, her voice soft and dreamy. "Then he'll rush over, take my hand, and say, 'Jessica, I've been dying to meet you.'"

Lila put her hand to her stomach and laughed. "Come on, everyone, let's run to the girls' room before class. I think I'm going to be sick!"

"Tom," cooed Jessica, ignoring her friend's teasing, "I've been waiting to meet you, too. I'm so *glad* you could come." She left the cafeteria with the others, walking down the hall as if she were floating.

"Jessica!" Elizabeth raced up to her twin. "I must have called you three times, Jess. What are you thinking about?"

"It's who, not what," corrected Mary. She laughed, and she and Jessica stopped to talk to Elizabeth while Lila and Tamara waved and hurried off down the hall to class. "Jessica has a lot of faith in your letter to Tom Houston. She's already rehearsing for his visit!"

Elizabeth smiled. "I wouldn't count on anything, Jess," she warned. "Movie stars are pretty busy people."

"No one could be too busy to read *that* letter, Lizzie. You're the greatest writer that ever lived."

"Thanks, Jess. But that's not going to help me get the *Sixers* out on time. We've been writing all week, but now we have so many articles, it looks like it will take another week to type them all." She sighed and readjusted the books in her arms. "I was just on my way to ask Amy and Sophia to stay after school again."

"I'm free after school Elizabeth," Mary put in. "I'd be glad to help."

"That's terrific, Mary," Elizabeth said gratefully. "I didn't even ask you because I figured you'd want to get home quickly."

"Not today. I'll meet you in Mr. Bowman's office after school."

"What a relief! The way *you* type, we'll be done in no time. Thanks a lot."

Mary didn't mind at all. In fact, she was delighted to find someone who didn't want to get rid of her or rush her off somewhere. At the end of school she raced to join Elizabeth and her staff in Mr. Bowman's classroom. She'd been so used to rushing home that she'd forgotten how good it felt to be with friends. "Let's get to work," she suggested eagerly when she found everyone gathered around the old mimeograph machine.

"Too late," Sophia announced happily as she and the others watched Mr. Bowman crank out the first copies of the front page. "Mr. Bowman beat us to it."

Mr. Bowman looked up and smiled. "I took pity on my poor editor here," he said, putting his arm around Elizabeth. "She's been complaining all week, so I went ahead and got Ms. Carey's typing class to work on the articles last period. They're all done, and the presses are rolling."

"Oh." Mary knew she sounded disappointed, but she'd been looking forward to helping Elizabeth. "That's good."

"Hey!" Amy grabbed a copy of the front page as it rolled off into the tray. "Look at our lead article! Doesn't it look great?"

Mary studied the page. Across the top in big, bold letters ran a headline: SIXTH GRADE TO LOSE CLASS PRESIDENT. She didn't understand. "Isn't Linda Lloyd doing a good job?" Linda had been elected their class president in the beginning of the year, and so far everyone Mary knew thought she was doing just fine.

"Oh, she's been a terrific president," Julie Porter explained. "It's just that her family is moving away. Caroline Pearce, our gossip columnist, got the scoop when Linda told her at lunch last week."

"Hey, why don't you run for president, Elizabeth?" Amy suggested. "I think you'd make a really great class officer."

"Me?" Elizabeth was surprised by Amy's idea. But she loved to plan and organize; maybe being the sixth-grade president would be fun. "I don't know," she mused.

"That does it!" announced Mr. Bowman, joining them with a huge stack of papers in his arms. "Who's ready to distribute the latest news?"

Elizabeth, Julie, Sophia, and Amy groaned. The girls loved to write *Sixers,* but none of them enjoyed collating and handing out the paper. Mary volunteered eagerly, though. "Oh, come on. I'll help, and we'll get finished in no time!"

"Now there's the kind of spirit I like to see!" Mr. Bowman laughed and handed her the stack. "Ms. Robinson, I hereby appoint you chairman of our collating committee."

"Thanks again, Mary," Elizabeth told her. "When we're finished here, I think we all deserve a reward at Casey's Place. What do you say to four chocolate shakes?" She paused and smiled back at Mr. Bowman. "Or five," she added, "if you want to come, too."

Mr. Bowman shook his head quickly. "No thanks," he told her. "I tried visiting that hangout one day last year. As soon as I walked in, every boy and girl in the whole place stopped talking at once." He shook his head again. "I don't think a teacher is anyone's idea of after-school fun!"

In half an hour the girls had sorted and stapled all the copies of the newspaper. After distributing them to each homeroom, they were out the door and on their way to Casey's Place.

"Why did you invite Mr. Bowman?" Amy asked Elizabeth. "You know he always turns us down."

"I know," Elizabeth replied, laughing. "I just didn't want him to feel left out."

"Yeah," Mary agreed, falling quickly into place beside the other girls. She remembered how she'd caught the Unicorns whispering behind her back, and how Tim and her mother had rushed off and left her behind. "Being left out is no fun at all."

Nine

"Oh, Lizzie, I wish you and I were in the same jewelry class. I could sure use your help." Jessica, rummaging through her closet, had thrown most of its contents onto her pink shag rug. Dresses, skirts, and blouses lay everywhere.

Watching from the safety of the bathroom doorway, Elizabeth giggled as the tornado of clothes blew across her twin's room. "I don't need to be in your group to tell you what you should wear to work with Bruce Patman. I know for a fact that green is his favorite color—money green."

"Very funny, big sister, very funny." Jessica took several steps back and surveyed the piles of clothes on her floor. Then she scooped up a pink-and-white print blouse and paired it with the blue slacks she found hanging from the doorknob of her closet. Then she carried both to the full-length mirror on the bathroom door. "But I wasn't even going to ask you about clothes. It's about the surprise present I'm making for Mary."

Jessica, concentrating on her image in the mirror, didn't see the look of surprise on her twin's face. "What present?" asked Elizabeth.

"A Unicorn bracelet, of course. Mary didn't sign up for the course, so she's bound to feel awful when everyone shows up at her party wearing their club bracelets." She tossed her blond hair, judging the effect of the pink blouse against her tanned face. "I wanted to make it extra special. Sort of a sign that we all are really glad she's our friend."

"Gee, Jess. That's a great idea."

"Well, what do you think? Does this pink wash out my face?"

"I think it looks terrific," Elizabeth told her truthfully. "It's you."

"I know," Jessica said, frowning, "but I'm afraid it might be Kimberly, too." She threw the blouse back into the pile on the floor. "She wore a blouse almost exactly like it last week. I'd die if anyone thought I bought this after I saw hers!"

Elizabeth groaned. "Well," she said. "I'll leave the wardrobe problem for you to solve by yourself. But I'd love to help with Mary's gift." She watched Jessica make her way through the pile of clothes and sit, Indian-style, on her bed. "What did you have in mind?"

Jessica cleared a space on the bed beside her and patted it, inviting her twin to sit next to her. "I'm going to engrave her name on it and everything. And that's where I need your help, Lizzie."

Elizabeth sat down on the space Jessica had cleared. "But your engraving is much prettier than mine," she insisted. She pushed more clothes out of the way so she could lie down on her side and prop herself up.

"Well, remember the pattern you drew, so we could all have the same unicorn on our bracelets?" In the first class, Jessica had traced her unicorn onto her bracelet and used the engraving tool to cut the picture into the silver band. "I've traced it onto Mary's bracelet, too. But I wanted to do something special with her name. I wanted to put roses around it. You know, like the ones you drew for your bracelet?"

"That *would* be pretty," Elizabeth agreed. "Let's get some paper, and I'll make a sketch." She stood up and started looking in the drawers of Jessica's desk. She pulled out three chocolate bars, a bag of potato chips, and finally a tablet of drawing paper. "Boy," she remarked. "I guess you never have to worry about being sent to your room without dinner!"

"When you hate homework as much as I do, Lizzie, you need all the energy you can get." Jessica turned serious. "Do you really think she'll like it?"

"She'll love it. It's a perfect present!"

"Of course, it'll be from both of us. I mean, since you're doing the drawing and measuring her wrist."

Elizabeth sat back down on the bed. "I'm *what*?"

"Measuring her wrist," Jessica repeated. "I need to know what size to make it." She paused thoughtfully. "Mary's thin, but she's taller than we are. I need to be sure I'm not making her bracelet too small."

"Jessica, don't you remember when Mary gave you her bracelet to wear, before she found out that her real mother had given it to her? We don't have to measure her wrist. We already know," Elizabeth said, excitedly.

The twins worked on drawings until dinner and then, after Elizabeth had finished her homework and Jessica had complained about hers, they did some more sketches. "I think the one with the flowers around the Y is just right," Jessica said as Elizabeth was brushing her teeth in the bathroom. "This is going to be the best surprise ever!" She lay back in bed and flicked off the light on her nightstand. "Mary's mother called everyone in the club today. Our invitations are official!"

"I'll bet she had no idea we've all known about the party for a week." Elizabeth giggled. "For once, Jessica, your gossiping didn't make a bit of difference."

"I know," Jessica answered contentedly. "Mary doesn't suspect a thing!"

Mary had become more and more suspicious as time went on. All week long no one had been able to see her approaching without looking suddenly uncomfortable. Girls who had been talking happily stopped as soon as Mary came into view. "Hi," Mary would say casually, pretending not to feel hurt and lonely. Then she would walk away, wondering what was wrong.

At home things were even worse. Tim and her mother never stayed around when she returned from school. Instead of the homework sessions with her mother she had begun to count on, Mary found herself alone with nothing to do. Her mother suddenly seemed to think the boat was more important than her grades.

"Why can't I come with you?" she asked her mother every day for over a week. "Tim said we were all going to work on the boat together."

"Oh, we will, dear," her mother assured her. "It's just that Tim and I want to get the dirty work out of the way first. We wouldn't want you to get hurt."

But the way she and Tim smiled and whispered each time they set off for the harbor didn't make what they were doing seem dangerous. It was all an excuse, Mary thought angrily. Just a way for them to get away. They didn't want to be with her, after all. Nobody did. Except for Elizabeth.

The next day when Mary got to school, she was greeted by Elizabeth right away. "I have something important to ask you," Elizabeth said eagerly. "Can you meet me for lunch, or do you have to go home?"

Mary was only too glad to eat lunch with someone besides the Unicorns. Lately all they'd done was whisper rudely in front of her. They were always mentioning some kind of secret party, and it was quite clear that Mary wasn't included in their plans. "Sure," she told Elizabeth. "Hey, why don't you come have lunch at my house? Mom won't be home or anything, but it would be fun not to have to eat cafeteria food."

What she really meant was that she'd love to get away from school; where she didn't seem to fit in anymore. She smiled with relief when Elizabeth agreed to walk home with her at lunchtime.

"What a terrific little desk!" Elizabeth said later, when they'd walked into the Wallaces' living room. "It's neat how it folds right into the bookcase."

"Thanks," Mary said. "My stepfather made—uh, designed it for me." They walked through the living room and into the tiny kitchen. "Peanut butter or tuna fish?" she asked, getting two plates from the cupboard above the sink.

"Let's make both," Elizabeth suggested, "and each have half."

They set to work and were soon seated at the table with their sandwiches, pickles, corn chips, and chocolate brownies. "Now, what did you want to talk to me about?" asked Mary.

"Well . . . nothing really. I just thought it would be fun to talk. You know . . . about things like your new stepfather and where you'll be moving to."

Mary was tired of telling lies about her stepfather. She was tired of talking about the wonderful new house. She wanted to tell someone the truth. "Elizabeth," she said, looking a little frightened, "that new house I told you about may not be all that terrific. I mean Jessica sort of got carried away, and I guess I let her. Besides, I don't think Tim has enough money to build a house like that."

"I know," Elizabeth said. "But the point is, it doesn't matter as long as you have two people who really care about you. Not counting all of us at school."

"Are you kidding?" Mary's lips trembled and her eyes filled with tears. "You should see the way the kids at school are treating me. Everyone's whispering and talking behind my back. I feel like I've got the plague or something." She paused, looking anxiously at Elizabeth. "Do you suppose it's because they know I didn't quite tell the truth?"

"Of course not, Mary. You're one of the most respected girls in our class. You've got tons of friends, and you're even a Unicorn."

"They're the worst of all!" Now tears started down Mary's cheeks. "You should see the way the whole club's been acting. I know they're all going to some big party without me. They're always whispering about clothes and presents, and every time I get near them, they change the subject."

Elizabeth was stunned. She and Jessica had been so sure that Mary didn't suspect a thing. Instead she was suspecting something totally wrong. "I'm sure you're just imagining it," she said.

"No. No, I'm not," Mary insisted, now crying hard. Between sobs she told Elizabeth how she'd been left out of things for weeks. How her mother and Tim rushed off after work and left her alone. "No one likes me, Elizabeth," she finished. "Not even my family. Tim's taking my mom away from me. I just know he is."

"How can you say that, Mary?" Elizabeth put her arm around her friend. "Why, your mother loves you a lot. I know she does."

"Then tell me why . . ." Mary asked, the tears still flowing, "why she hasn't even mentioned my birthday? Before Tim came, she promised we'd go to the beach for a birthday clambake. We were going to have a fire and music and everything." She put her head in her hands. "Now that he's here, it's all changed, and Mom's forgotten all about me."

Elizabeth didn't want to spoil the surprise party. But she needed to prove to Mary how much her family and friends cared. She couldn't let her go on thinking she was all alone. "I have to tell you something," Elizabeth said. "It was supposed to be a secret, but I think you should know."

Mary just kept crying. "Are you listening to me?" Elizabeth asked, but didn't wait for Mary to reply. "People *have* been whispering behind your back, Mary."

Mary lifted her head from her hands, her eyes shiny with tears. "I knew it," she said, choking. "Why, Elizabeth? Why would they do that?"

Elizabeth thought of Mary's mother calling all the kids in her class. She thought of Jessica hard at work on the silver bracelet. She thought of all the Unicorns making plans for the party. "Because we love you, Mary," she answered. "Because we all love you."

Ten

"What do you mean, everyone loves me?" Mary declared. "People who care about you don't whisper about you and leave you out of everything. I even heard Jessica talking about a special outfit everyone's wearing for some big Unicorn party I'm not even invited to!"

"That's *your* party, Mary."

Elizabeth saw the look of hope on her friend's face, and knew she'd made the right decision. It was time to set things straight.

"*My* party?" Mary asked.

"Yes. Your very own extra-special surprise birthday party."

Mary's tears stopped at once. She smiled and shook her head. "Oh," she said. "Here I was, mad at the Unicorns, and all along they've been planning this terrific surprise!"

"Well," admitted Elizabeth, "the Unicorns are in on everything, all right. But the people who started it all live right here."

Mary looked shocked. "You mean Mom and Tim?"

"You bet. It was *their* idea to give you a birthday party. That's why they haven't been home after school. They're getting everything ready." Elizabeth watched Mary's smile grow. "They've got a lot to do before your birthday. It's going to be a really big party. They've invited the Unicorns, and the whole class, too!"

"Wow!" Mary exclaimed. "I feel pretty silly. I've been so mad because they told me they were going to the harbor. I thought they were spending time on that awful boat."

"They are, silly," Elizabeth explained. "That's where the party's going to be! Won't it be great?"

Suddenly Mary's smile faded. A giant knot formed in her stomach. She couldn't believe her ears. Her mother and Tim had not only bought the most ridiculous boat in Sweet Valley, but now they'd invited her whole class to a party on it! Wait until her friends saw the lopsided old boat with its peeling paint and silly red smokestack! The day Tim had finally taken Mary to see it, she'd wished she could sink in between the planks on the dock. She was terrified that someone from school would see them.

It *was* good to know that her mother and Tim had meant well and that all their planning and scheming had included her. Still, it didn't change the fact that what was supposed to be a wonderful surprise was going to be the worst, most humiliating day of her life!

Elizabeth was beaming now, and Mary wondered what her friend's face would look like when she saw the ramshackle boat. Would anyone ever speak to her again? How would she ever explain all the ridiculous boasting she'd been doing?

But Elizabeth wasn't a Unicorn. Maybe she would understand how Mary had needed to create a terrific stepfather. Maybe she would like Mary even if her stepfather turned out to be an everyday carpenter instead of a world-famous architect. "Elizabeth, there's something I'd better tell you," Mary began. "You know that desk you liked in the living room? Tim didn't just design it; he *made* it."

Elizabeth grinned. "You don't have to sell me on Tim, Mary. I already think he's great." She popped the last bite of brownie into her mouth and glanced up at the clock. "Look at the time. We'd better hurry if we're going to get back in time."

Mary stood up. Maybe she wouldn't have to tell anyone about Tim after all. Not yet, anyway. Maybe, if the plan that was beginning to form in her mind worked, she wouldn't even have to go to her own birthday party! "OK," she told Elizabeth, leaving her plate in the sink. "Let's go."

On Friday, as she and her classmates were leaving math class, Mary put her plan into action. She saw Jessica and Ellen not far ahead in the hallway. "Ohhhh," she groaned. "My stomach!"

"Mary, what's the matter?" Jessica asked, rushing up to her.

"Ohhh," repeated Mary. She slumped where she stood in the hall. "Maybe I'd better go home." She held her stomach and leaned against the wall near the lockers.

"You—you just *can't* be sick!" Ellen declared. The next day was Mary's party.

"I just want to go home," Mary said feebly. She looked so pale and weak that Jessica and Ellen walked her right to the main office. One look at the thin, miserable Mary, and even the stern old secretary melted.

"Oh, dear," the secretary said softly. "You just sit right down here and I'll write you out an infirmary pass."

"Ohhh," Mary groaned. "Please, I need to go home." She sat in a chair by the secretary's desk and lowered her head. "Ohhh," she murmured quietly, as if she were trying to be very brave.

"But we do have our rules, dear," the secretary said gently. "You can only go home if the nurse gives you permission." She began writing on a form in front of her.

"I—I . . ." began Mary, holding her mouth now instead of her stomach. "I think I'm going to throw up!" She bent lower and rose off her chair, her hand still over her mouth.

"Oh, no!" the secretary exclaimed. "We can't have that. We can't have that. Here, dear, I'm calling your parents right now. Just hold on, for heaven's sake. Hold on!"

When Mary and her mother arrived home from

school, they found Tim getting ready for their regular afternoon trip to the harbor. "What's wrong?" he asked.

"I'm afraid Mary doesn't feel too well," Mrs. Wallace explained, giving Mary a hug.

"She does look a little pale," Tim said, helping Mary over to the couch.

Mary felt really awful by now. She felt guilty for pretending to be sick, but was too scared to stop. She couldn't face that birthday party; she just had to convince her mother to call it off. "Ohhh." She sighed, sitting with relief on the couch beside her mom. "I think I'm going to have to go to bed."

"Darling!" Her mother headed for the bathroom. "I'll get a thermometer and we'll take your temperature."

Mary thought that perhaps by now she really *might* be sick. Her head was throbbing and she felt pretty warm. Maybe she could miss her party without lying. "Ohhh," she repeated, feeling achy and tired.

"I'm glad tomorrow's Saturday," she said just before her mother put the thermometer in her mouth. "At least I can stay in bed without missing school."

Her mother looked worried. "I'm sure it's not all that serious," she said hopefully. "In fact," she announced when she'd waited a couple of minutes and pulled out the thermometer, "I'm sure you won't need to spend tomorrow in bed, young lady. You don't have a fever at all!" She smiled with relief and hugged Mary happily. "Now how about a cup of tea?"

"Maybe," Mary ventured, "I have something that doesn't come with a fever. Maybe we should go see Dr. Costa."

"I think we've bothered Dr. Costa enough with problems that are really our own to solve. Besides," she added happily, "I think after tomorrow a lot of those problems will be history."

But Mary knew that tomorrow wouldn't be the end of her problems. In fact, it would just be the beginning! What would the kids in school say when they saw that dilapidated tugboat? How could she possibly tell her mother and Tim that she was ashamed of their big surprise?

Eleven

"It's just that she thinks we've forgotten her birthday," Tim told his wife after Mary had gone upstairs. "Everything will be fine tomorrow." He sat down beside her and slipped his guitar case from under the couch. "I've even written a song for the party."

He took out his guitar and sang a simple melody about love and trust. Each verse talked about building love like a house, adding room after room until the house had turned into a castle. The chorus was, "There's always room for more love."

"Oh, Tim," Mrs. Wallace said when he stopped singing, "that's lovely. It says just what we want to tell her."

"I hope she gets the message." Tim sighed. He picked up the guitar and strummed the melody quietly while his wife lay her head against his shoulder. A few minutes later, when Mary tiptoed to the top of the stairs, that's how she saw the two of them. Tim was playing, and her mother listening to him with a contented, dreamy expression on her face.

Tears started to form before she knew it. Stumbling back to her bed, Mary felt sorry for herself. Even though she wasn't really sick, she had expected her mother and Tim to be a little worried. Instead there they were, together again without her. *They aren't even thinking about me up here,* she fumed to herself. *Tim couldn't wait to get rid of me, so he could have Mom all to himself. He's playing some dumb love song for her, and he never even came up to see how I was. They just planned the party to keep from feeling guilty. They don't care after all!*

Alone in her room, Mary came to a desperate decision. It was clear her mother and Tim would be happier without her. And it was equally clear that tomorrow's party would make her the laughingstock of Sweet Valley Middle School. There was only one thing to do.

Quietly Mary made her way around her room. She opened some drawers and her closet, pulled out clothes and stuffed them into a little suitcase. Maybe she could spend a few days with the Altmans, the foster family that had wanted to adopt her before she'd found her mother. Then she decided she'd try to find her real father. If he didn't have a new family of his own, maybe he'd want her. Just her and nobody else.

Mary waited until the sky grew dark and she heard two sets of footsteps going up the stairs. As silent as a cat, she tiptoed down the stairs and into the kitchen. She opened the refrigerator as quietly as she could and took out a pear and an orange. Stuffing them into her pockets, she headed for the back door.

It was very dark outside. But anything was better than facing all those laughing kids on the boat tomorrow. They'd never let her forget the way she'd boasted about her "new" life. She closed the door tightly behind her. Then, at the bottom of the back steps, her foot landed on something that suddenly gave way beneath her.

"Ahhh!" The scream didn't even sound like her own voice. As she toppled headfirst onto the ground, Mary felt a sharp pain in her left arm. Then everything was quiet again. She looked up, dazed, to see the reflector on her bike wheel shining in the dark. She had tripped over her own bicycle!

The pain in her arm was terrible, and Mary could barely concentrate on anything else. Finally she pulled herself up onto the last step with her other arm and sat hunched over, wondering what to do. She couldn't think clearly. Her entire arm, from her elbow to her wrist, felt hot and was throbbing.

Her arm hurt too much to consider walking all the way to the Altmans' house. Thank goodness she hadn't woken anyone up. She'd just have to sneak in the way she'd snuck out. Slowly she reached for the door handle and turned it. But nothing happened! She tried again, this time turning it harder. Still the door refused to open. It must have locked when she closed it behind her. Hopelessly, Mary sank back onto the bottom step and started to cry.

She considered calling for her mother. But if she woke her up, there would be a lot of explaining to do. And, of course, her mother would tell Tim. He'd pretend to care, and the two of them would talk it over, without her. No. It would be better to sit here all night long. If only her arm didn't hurt so much. If only she could force herself not to feel the awful pain.

Just when she was sure she couldn't stand it any longer, the door behind her opened. It was Tim. It seemed he'd heard her fall and come to investigate. Silently, he stared first at Mary, then at the suitcase lying beside her. "Night rates *are* cheaper," he said, then started to help her to her feet.

"Ahhh!" Mary cried out in pain before Tim could even touch her arm. Now, looking serious, Tim knelt beside her in the dark and turned on the flashlight he'd brought with him.

"Let's take a look," he said gently, being careful not to touch the arm. The flashlight revealed a long red scrape along Mary's elbow. "It doesn't look bad," Tim said, "but you might have a sprain, too. I'll carry you." As carefully as if he were lifting a baby, he scooped Mary into his arms and carried her back into the kitchen. He walked into the living room and lay her down on the couch. "Now, you wait right here while I get your mom," he said.

"No!" Mary couldn't bear to have her mother find out she'd tried to run away. The whole idea seemed pretty ridiculous now that she was back in her own house. She didn't even *know* her real father. He could be living anywhere. And the way Tim stopped and came to sit down beside her now, made her trust him just the slightest bit. "Please," she begged. "Don't tell Mom."

Tim nodded silently. He went back outside and retrieved the suitcase, stuffing it in the kitchen broom closet. "All right," he told Mary, "it'll be our secret. But I sure would like to know what was so bad you couldn't wait until morning." He leaned over, adjusting an afghan so it covered her. "Can you tell me why you were running away?"

But Mary couldn't tell him. She couldn't explain that she was ashamed of him, of his job, and of his boat. Everything about him was so ordinary. And now as he listened to her so quietly, without telling her how silly she'd been, she was ashamed of herself, too. "I—I just wanted to leave," she told him, not daring to explain.

"Well, I had no idea things were that bad," he replied, shaking his head. "I want you to know, Mary, that if anyone leaves, it's going to be me." He looked very sad, then stood up and walked to the bottom of the stairs. "Andrea," he called. "Honey, come on down here."

True to his word, Tim didn't say a word about Mary's plans to run away. He told her mother that she'd tripped trying to put her bike away. "I guess she couldn't rest until it was safe in the garage," he said convincingly.

Mrs. Wallace bent over to examine her daughter's arm, and winced when she saw the scrape on her elbow. "Maybe we should take her to the hospital, Tim. It could be broken."

"Well, let's clean up that elbow right here first," Tim told her. "Then we'll see how Mary feels."

"All right." Mrs. Wallace left the room and came back a minute later with a moist towel. "Oh, you poor thing!" Mrs. Wallace soothed. "All for a silly old bike." She tried to rub Mary's arm, but Mary squealed in pain.

"Whoa, nurse!" Tim interrupted. "Let me try." Carefully, painstakingly, he cleaned out the scrape while he held Mary's hand. He was so gentle that it hardly hurt at all.

When Tim finished, he stood up. "I don't think it's anything to be worried about, but we should probably go to the hospital just to make sure. Do you feel up to the trip if I carry you?"

Mary nodded, then the three of them went to the car. Tim and Mrs. Wallace sat in the front seat, and Mary stretched out across the back seat. Her mother seemed really worried about her arm, and she kept turning to check on her. It was hard to stay calm when her mother was so nervous. "I *am* going to be all right, aren't I?" Mary asked Tim.

"Of course you are," Tim answered confidently. "You've probably just got a bad bruise." He pulled the car up to the emergency room doors, then stepped out and opened the car door.

Gently as ever, he helped Mary walk through the doorway and up to the nurse at the desk. Mrs. Wallace, teary-eyed, followed. "My daughter's been hurt," she told the nurse in a high-pitched voice that didn't sound at all like the one Mary was used to. "She needs attention right away!"

"It doesn't look like anything too serious," Tim added soothingly. "Probably a sprain, but we'd like to check for a fracture or break."

The nurse nodded and wrote a card up with the information that Tim gave her. Then, when another nurse arrived and called Mary's name, he helped carry her into the emergency room and placed her gently on a bed with a white curtain pulled back beside it. "The doctor will be right with you," the nurse announced, and bustled away.

"I'm not sure I believe that," said Mary's mother. "Look at all the patients they have here. Don't you think we should go and get a doctor before they forget we're here?"

"Mom, please!" Mary's arm was hurting badly now, and she just wanted to wait quietly. "I'm sure he'll be here as soon as he can."

"I think Mary's right, honey. Here, why don't you sit down, and I'll sing you both my hospital song."

"I didn't know you knew a hospital song," said Mary, grinning in spite of herself.

"I don't." Tim grinned back and winked at her. "I'm going to make it up as I go along." Then, in a funny whispery voice, he sang a ridiculous, silly song about being sick and being treated by absent-minded doctors who wrote prescriptions for all sorts of silly ailments. By the last verse Mary was giggling and her mother was smiling.

"Well," observed the doctor, drawing aside the curtain, "I don't usually get such happy patients in here!"

"That's because most of them don't have their own entertainment committee," said Mary, smiling gratefully at her stepfather. For a few minutes she'd forgotten all about the pain in her arm.

"Now we'll take a look at it." The doctor took Mary's hand and began to feel her arm very carefully. She winced in pain, but Tim put his hand on her shoulder, and she felt better.

"There's probably a small fracture here," announced the doctor. "We'll need to take some X rays to be sure. Then we'll put it in a cast for a while."

"Would you like us to leave, Doctor?" Tim asked.

"No!" Mary answered before the doctor did. "Please, don't go. I want you to stay." Suddenly she realized she wanted Tim to stay not only with her there, but at home, too. "I mean stay for good," she added, smiling.

"It won't be easy, you know." Tim looked serious but hopeful. "We've got to trust each other."

Mary knew just what he meant. She remembered what Dr. Costa had said about making room in her heart. She'd been so busy locking Tim out that she hadn't seen how kind and thoughtful he was. Without a word she reached out, and Tim gently took her hand and gave her a smile that told her he understood.

"That's OK," the doctor assured them. "Parents

are allowed to stay. Dad, just sit right down and keep your daughter company."

"But I'm not—"

"Shhh!" Mary commanded, putting a finger over her mouth. "If you don't tell, I won't."

Twelve

"I'm not hungry," Jessica announced, coming into the kitchen with a sigh. "In fact, I don't think I'll ever eat again!" It was Saturday morning, the day of Mary's party, the day she and Elizabeth and almost everyone in school had been waiting for. But Jessica was in a terrible mood.

"I know my French toast is a little burnt on one side," Mr. Wakefield admitted, "but I don't think it's *that* bad!"

"It's not that," Jessica wailed, sinking miserably into a seat beside her twin at the big oak table. "It's the mail!"

"Uh-oh," Steven said, reaching for his sixth slice of French toast, "don't tell me you still haven't heard from Tom Houston."

"Worse!" Jessica glared at her brother. "I *did* hear from him!"

"But that's wonderful dear," Mrs. Wakefield said. "Isn't that just what you were hoping for?"

Jessica waved the single sheet of paper she'd

torn from its envelope. "He says he can't come to our dance!"

"That's too bad, Jess," Elizabeth said. "But you should have known Tom Houston's much too busy and important to take time out to sing at a Unicorn party."

"Some great fan letter you wrote for me, Lizzie!" Jessica handed the paper to her sister. "Just look at the answer it got!"

"'Dear Fan,'" Elizabeth read aloud, "'As I'm sure you know, I would love to have the time to write a personal letter in response to each inquiry I receive. Unfortunately my busy schedule does not permit me to do this.'"

"Hmmph!" interrupted Jessica. "I have a busy schedule, too. But *I* took time out to write my own letter to *him*."

"'I hope,'" Elizabeth continued reading, "'that you will understand that, even though previous commitments will not allow me to attend your function, I wish your organization good luck in achieving its worthwhile aims. Sincerely, Tom Houston, Hollywood, California.'"

"I'll be the laughingstock of the whole club!" Jessica grabbed the letter back and stared at its neatly typed face with fury. "If it's the last thing I do, Tom Houston, I'm going to grow up to be a famous celebrity. And when you ask me to do something with you, I'm going to tell you that I've got too many 'previous commitments'!"

"Well," Mr. Wakefield remarked, "that's a pretty unique reason for wanting a career in entertainment!"

"I mean it," insisted Jessica, tearing up the letter and stuffing it into her empty juice glass. "I trusted Mr. Bigshot Houston, and he let me down. I told the whole club I could get him to sing for us. Now we're stuck with no entertainment and no money."

"I guess that puts an end to your 'worthwhile aims,'" Elizabeth observed sarcastically. One look at the furious expression on her twin's face, however, made her regret her teasing. "I'm sorry, Jess. Really I am. Come on up to my room," she said. "We'll try our outfits on for the party. Maybe that'll take your mind off Tom Houston."

Jessica brightened just the slightest bit. "It *will* be exciting, won't it?" she asked as the two girls headed upstairs. "I mean, this won't be some silly school party held during the daytime. We'll be on a glamorous yacht with *seventh* graders!"

"You have one particular seventh grader in mind, don't you?" Elizabeth took the blue skirt and blouse she'd chosen for the party out of her closet and laid it carefully across her bed.

"Well," Jessica told her, "when I put the finishing touches on his mother's charm, Bruce *did* thank me."

"Coming from Mr. Wonderful, that's quite a lot."

"Oh, Lizzie, you've never given Bruce Patman a chance. He's really very sweet. He even told me he might dance with me tonight if I promised to make another charm for his aunt."

"That's about the most conceited thing I ever heard of, Jessica!"

"Lizzie! I'm talking about Bruce Patman. That's a small price to pay. Besides," Jessica added slyly, "I've got to do something to impress the Unicorns now that I struck out with Tom."

"I wouldn't worry about that, Jess. I think everyone's so excited about Mary's party, they've forgotten all about your club dance."

"It will be *terrific*! The moonlight on the water, the music, the presents . . . Oh, no!" Jessica exclaimed in alarm.

"What is it? What's wrong?"

"I haven't finished Mary's bracelet. I brought some sandpaper home to work on it yesterday, and I forgot all about it." She dropped the earrings she'd been modeling for her twin back into the jewelry box on Elizabeth's dresser and set to work. "I want it to be the smoothest, most beautiful bracelet ever," she said as she polished the pretty silver band.

After the bracelet was finished, the twins went into town to do some last minute errands. When they arrived home it was just about time to get dressed for the party.

"Just think, Lizzie," Jessica said excitedly as she slipped on her purple sweatshirt. "In less than an hour we'll be on board the Wallaces' boat, dancing in the moonlight!"

"I know!" Elizabeth giggled, looking at herself in Jessica's mirror. "I can't wait!"

While Jessica and Elizabeth were dressing, Mary was getting ready to face the worst moment in her life. Alone in her room, she kept telling herself that she owed it to her mother and Tim to go through with the party. She couldn't bear to tell her mother that she was ashamed of the tugboat, especially now that she knew how sweet and kind Tim was.

The night before, as the three of them had driven home from the hospital, Mary had come to a difficult decision. She knew that they were a family now. And she knew that she would have to face up to all the lies she'd told her friends. She'd have to greet her classmates on board the broken-down old boat and put up with their nasty comments.

It's the least I can do for two people who've worked so hard to surprise me, Mary thought as she stared unhappily into her mirror. She knew how much her mother loved her. And after the previous night, she knew Tim really cared, too. She was going to have to return that love the best way she could—even if it meant losing every friend she had. Even if it meant being made fun of by every Unicorn in the whole club!

"Are you ready for your dinner out?" Tim asked, poking his head into the doorway of her bedroom. There was a new, relaxed tone in his voice now.

"Sure." Mary smiled, pretending not to know

about the surprise party. She had chosen a pretty green dress from her closet. It had big, loose sleeves which slipped easily over her cast.

"I have a present for you before we leave," Tim said, handing her the suitcase he'd hidden in the broom closet the night before. "I thought we'd keep it our little secret."

"Thanks." Mary took the bag and put it safely in her own closet.

"I meant what I said last night, you know, Mary." Tim sat down on her bed. "If anybody leaves, it's going to be me. I never want to come between you and your mother."

Mary felt so warm and happy, she almost forgot about the party. She sat beside Tim, looking up at him with an affectionate grin that made him smile right back. "And I meant what I said, too," she said softly. "I want you to stay—for good. I was running away to look for my real father, but last night I realized I already *have* one."

"In that case, why don't we make it official."

"What do you mean?"

"Your mother and I have spoken to the lawyers. They say that since your father has been contacted and has agreed to my adopting you, there's nothing to stop us from proceeding." He put an arm around Mary. "How would you like to be a Wallace?"

"I'd love it!" Mary felt all the pain and confusion of the last few months melt away. Her mother and Tim *did* want her! She was part of an honest-to-goodness family. An important part!

"Hey, you two," Mrs. Wallace announced from outside the door. "I'm hungry. Let's go!"

A few minutes later, when Tim turned the car off toward the harbor instead of continuing on to the restaurant they had told her about, Mary did her best to seem surprised. "Where are we going?" she asked.

"Last pier on the right," Tim announced proudly, pointing to where the tug was moored. There, looming in the twilight, was the big, newly painted boat with its giant smokestack.

But it certainly looked different! Tim and her mother had strung rows of colored lights all around the deck. Now the old boat looked like a wonderful place to have a party. Of course, it wasn't a sleek cabin cruiser or a racing boat, but it did look inviting as it bobbed and twinkled in the water. Then, as they got out of the car, she noticed the neat white lettering painted along the bow. "'S.S. Mary,'" she read out loud. They had named the boat after her!

"We couldn't think of a prettier name," Tim told her, his arms around her and her mother. Mary didn't know whether to laugh or cry. She was dreading the arrival of her friends, but she couldn't help feeling proud and grateful that her two favorite people had worked so hard to please her.

Mary's enthusiasm was short-lived, though. As soon as they all had boarded the tug and begun to look around, Janet Howell and three other eighth-grade Unicorns stepped out of a car beside the pier. Mary watched the girls put their hands above their eyes and survey the boat. "Look, it's a tugboat!" she heard Janet yell.

Bracing herself, Mary took a deep breath and got ready to face the worst. "You're right," she heard another girl squeal. "Isn't it great?"

Mary couldn't believe her ears, but as soon as they'd boarded the ramp and were standing beside her, her guests couldn't stop giggling and chattering. "Mary!" exclaimed Janet. "You never told us your boat was a tug! What a neat surprise! It's just about the cutest antique boat I've ever seen! It must have cost a fortune!"

"Well, actually, Janet," Mary began, determined to set the record straight, "it took a lot of work to fix it up. We're not exactly like lots of the families in Sweet Valley."

"You sure aren't," Bruce Patman observed, climbing on board to join them. "This is just about the greatest thing I've ever seen. I'll bet there's not another one like it for miles!"

"At least not another one as creaky or unreliable," Tim replied, laughing. "Would you like to see how she operates?"

"Would I? Hey, guys, hurry up!" Bruce waved to Rick Hunter and another classmate who was still standing on the dock. "This is going to be the neatest party ever!"

And it was. Everyone who saw the tug was instantly fascinated. Tim was kept busy giving Mary's friends tours of the engine room and showing them the tools he'd used to put the ship in working order.

And Mrs. Wallace got plenty of compliments for the way she had turned the old galley into a beautiful "sea cavern," complete with fish and anemones swimming in nets strung along the walls, and lovely flickering candles on the sailcloth tables.

If Mary had any doubts about how much her family or friends cared, they disappeared when she caught sight of the wonderful whale-shaped cake her mother had made and the heap of presents on the galley table. "Oh, my goodness," she gasped. "I've never seen anything so wonderful!"

With shouts of "Open mine first!" ringing in her ears, Mary began to work her way through the heap of gifts. She got lots of wonderful presents, including a purple T-shirt, an adorable stuffed panda, and a Johnny Buck album she'd been dying to own. But her favorite gift came in a yellow-checked package with a gold bow. She lifted the delicate silver bracelet from its tissue-paper nest. "It fits perfectly!" she exclaimed, modeling the pretty band, then hugging both twins.

The high point of the party came when Tim took out his guitar. "I have a special song I'd like to sing for a special person," he announced. As everyone gathered around him, he sang the song he'd written just for Mary. "Love takes time," he sang. "Love takes work. Brick by brick and stone by stone, we've built a house of love." His voice was deep and rich, and Mary watched the way all the Unicorns' eyes got misty when he smiled at them. "Love takes time," he sang again. "Love takes work, but now my love cas tle is finished, and my princess can move in." He finished his song, smiling right at Mary and making her feel like the most important person in the world!

Mary felt tears forming in her eyes, but she didn't even try to brush them away. Right in front of everyone she hugged her stepfather. "The boat is wonderful," she told him. "And so are my gifts. But you just gave me the best birthday present of all! I'll never forget tonight as long as I live, Tim." Again she felt the heavy, warm tears in her eyes. "I mean, Dad."

Before Tim could answer, he was surrounded by squealing, giggling Unicorns. "Oh, Mr. Wallace, you're as good a singer as Johnny Buck," Ellen Riteman sighed, her eyes shining.

"Don't be ridiculous!" Lila Fowler scolded, pushing her way to the front of the crowd. "You're a thousand times better than Johnny Buck, Mr. Wallace. Would you autograph my napkin?"

Tim laughed, and bent to sign all of the napkins that were instantly held out to him.

Suddenly Jessica knew her problems were over. She pushed her way through the crowd until she was next to Tim. "Do you by any chance know the theme from *Dream Chaser*?" she asked.

"Why, yes I do. I kind of like those songs. Want to hear some?"

Mary's stepfather didn't need to be asked twice. Everyone settled down to listen. After Tim performed the hits from the movie, Mary's friends called out requests.

"He knows all our favorite songs!" Ellen declared. "He's just too dreamy for words."

"I'm afraid my voice is about to give out," Tim finally told them. "What do you say we turn on the stereo and start our dance contest?"

"That's a great idea, Mr. Wallace," Jessica approved. "We've got to take good care of your voice." Her lashes were fluttering furiously, her wind-tossed hair and sweet smile lit by the string of lanterns above her. "That is, if you're going to perform at our Unicorn party next month."

The Unicorns started to jump up and down excitedly. "Oh, would you, Mr. Wallace? Would you? Please?"

Flattered and laughing, Tim Wallace agreed. "Well, I guess I could do one more performance. Would you like to nave your party on the boat?"

The cheers, whistles, and wild applause that followed made the group's answer plain enough. "Now," Tim said, "let's see *you* perform!" He turned on the stereo. Music began to blare from the speakers he had rigged up on the deck. Two hours later, after they'd danced until their feet were sore and eaten six pizzas and the whole giant birthday cake, the tired, happy guests got ready to leave.

"Thanks for coming, everyone." Mary stood at the top of the ramp, saying good-bye. "I'm sorry I told you that Tim was a famous architect," she whispered to a group of Unicorns. "I just wanted you to like him so much, I sort of got carried away."

Janet, who was standing in front of the group, shook her head in amazement. "Mary," she said, "with a dad like that, you didn't have to make up anything. He's terrific just the way he is!"

"Yes," Mary admitted happily, "I guess he is." It felt wonderful not to have to lie and pretend anymore. "Thanks again," she told her friends. "Thanks for everything."

Jessica turned back to stare up at Mary on board the boat. "Boy, she sure looks happy!"

Elizabeth turned around, too. Even from far away she could see the smile on Mary's face as she stood waving from the deck, her arm around Tim. "I have to admit it, Jessica," she said. "You were right. Sometimes fairy tales really *do* come true!"

"Yep! It's just too bad Linda Lloyd missed the party tonight."

"That's right," Elizabeth said, remembering that Linda had to stay home to help her family pack for the movers.

"Linda missed the best party there's ever been, didn't she, Lizzie?"

"She sure did." Just then Elizabeth remembered Amy's suggestion to her about running for class president. "I guess that means it's time to elect a new president," she said. Maybe she would run after all.

"And I hope it'll be me!" Jessica declared. "I've always wanted to run for office. Do you think I could do it?"

Oh, no, thought Elizabeth. If she wanted to be

elected class president, she'd have to run against her own twin sister!